PLEASE PLEASE
TELL ME NOW

PLEASE PLEASE TELL ME NOW

THE DURAN DURAN STORY

STEPHEN DAVIS

hachette
BOOKS
NEW YORK

Hachette Books
Hachette Book Group
1290 Avenue of the Americas
New York, NY 10104
HachetteBooks.com
Twitter.com/HachetteBooks
Instagram.com/HachetteBooks

First Hardcover Edition: June 2021
First Trade Paperback Edition: June 2022

Published by Hachette Books, an imprint of Perseus Books, LLC,
a subsidiary of Hachette Book Group, Inc. The Hachette Books name and
logo is a trademark of the Hachette Book Group.

The Hachette Speakers Bureau provides a wide range of authors for speaking events.
To find out more, go to www.hachettespeakersbureau.com or call (866) 376-6591.

The publisher is not responsible for websites (or their content) that
are not owned by the publisher.

Library of Congress Cataloging-in-Publication Data has been applied for.

ISBNs: 978-0-306-84606-9 (hardcover); 978-0-306-84610-6 (ebook);
978-0-306-84608-3 (trade paperback)

Printed in the United States of America

LSC-C

Printing 1, 2022

Nequiquam, quoniam medio de fonte leporum

surgit amari aliquid quod in ipsis floribus angat.

—Lucretius, *De rerum natura*, IV, 1133–1134

CONTENTS

PART 4

PART 5

PART 6

PART 7

PART 8

PLEASE PLEASE
TELL ME NOW

PART 1

DURAN DURAN

Forty thousand years from now, a beautiful young woman named Barbarella, fleeing a broken romance, will land her rocket on the planet Lythion and launch into a series of battles against galactic injustice. She's a sexy twenty-year-old gamine with long blonde hair, golden skin, and impressive breasts. Over the course of her adventures, Barbarella will often lose her clothes, be ravished by hideous aliens, and take erotic pleasure with the hunky spacemen who assist her and her main ally, a one-eyed gnome called . . . Durand.

Barbarella made her debut as one of the foundational mythic characters in a French comic strip by Jean-Claude Forest, often described as the first comic for grown-ups. After appearing in large-format book form in 1964, she was an immediate sensation, selling thousands of expensive volumes in a matter of weeks to readers (and oglers) who wanted answers to the questions posed by the comic's second frame: "What misadventures, what disappointments in love, have led this girl to wander alone through a solar system far removed from ours?"

Soon French intellectuals began to admire Barbarella beyond just her looks, and they even wrote about her critically. From the literary weekly *Arts* in 1965: "Clothes may cramp Barbarella's style, but nudity doesn't cheapen her. She remains mysterious, fragile but invincible. This crafty, wild creature is the archetype of the modern female, in quest of the Absolute." From the Parisian daily *Le Monde*, the same year: "Barbarella represents the contemporary emancipated and independent young woman in a new era of sexual liberation. She controls her own destiny rather than submit to the dictates of men. The mistress of her own fate, she can pick and choose the men she desires."

It wasn't long before international publishers took notice and Jean-Claude Forest began to sell foreign rights to the Barbarella strip. In America, *Barbarella* was acquired by Grove Press, which specialized in Beat literature and Victorian pornography. In 1965, Barbarella first appeared in Grove's quarterly periodical *Evergreen Review*, making her debut in book form the following year and quickly becoming one of Grove's best-selling titles. The story lines were translated into English by Grove's senior editor, Richard Seaver, who usually worked with Beat and modernist luminaries like William Burroughs, Jean Genet, and Samuel Beckett.

Next, the prominent Italian producer Dino De Laurentiis acquired film rights to Barbarella, and in 1966, the *Hollywood Reporter* announced that America's hottest movie star, Jane Fonda, would play Barbarella. French New Wave auteur Roger Vadim (Fonda's husband) would direct a screenplay written by Terry Southern, notorious coauthor of the comic-porn novel *Candy*.

When *Barbarella* was released in 1968, Terry Southern and seven other writers were credited with a screenplay that made no sense after the first few campy scenes. Roger Vadim's studio sets looked cheap, and the dialogue was pathetic, but even so, Jane Fonda's striptease early in the film seemed to bring highly sexed Barbarella to life. The movie was both hailed as a pop art masterpiece and derided as the worst sci-fi picture ever made. Nevertheless, *Barbarella* was a huge success in Europe, especially in England, where it was the second-highest-grossing film of the year.

Ten years later, two teenage boys were watching *Barbarella* on television in Hollywood. This wasn't in Southern California's glamour capital but in the suburb of Hollywood, located in southern Birmingham, England's second-biggest city. The date was October 20, 1978. The BBC was broadcasting *Barbarella*, and the boys—Nigel John Taylor, eighteen, and his sixteen-year-old friend, Nick Bates—were entranced.

Nigel and Nick had been friends for four years. They were huge music fans who were extremely knowledgeable about rock bands and new trends, and they were currently forming a band with another friend. None of the teens could actually play musical instruments at this point, but this didn't seem important; with their boyish, androgynous looks and lashings of eye shadow and lip gloss, Nigel and Nick already resembled emerging pop stars of the new wave, New Romantic, post-punk era.

Their current preoccupation was finding a name for their new band.

Earlier that day, the boys spent hours in a pub called the Hole in the Wall, trying to think of names. They had been going to concerts and shows together since 1974, and they were very tuned in to David Bowie, T-Rex, and especially Roxy Music. Later on, they were regulars at Barbarella's, a converted warehouse that was Birmingham's main venue for the punk bands coming up from London: Sex Pistols, Slits, the Jam, the Damned, the Clash. Nick strongly suggested that they should call their band RAF, as in the Royal Air Force. Peering at Nick through his thick spectacles, nearsighted Nigel said he thought this sounded a bit "naff," or pretentious. Still thinking about band names, they left the pub and went to Nick's house to tune in to *Barbarella* on the Bates family's big color TV set.

As the movie began on BBC1, the boys tried to make sense of the totally daft plot, in which Barbarella crash-lands on Earth and is taken to meet the president of Earth. Upon her arrival, Barbarella strips off her clothes, and the president explains that an evil scientist, Durand-Durand (played by the veteran comedian Milo O'Shea), has purloined the Excessive Machine, designed to provide women with supersonic sexual pleasure, thus eliminating the need for men. The president then tells Barbarella that only she can save humankind from extinction. "Your mission," the president directs Barbarella, is to "find Durand-Durand, and preserve the security of the stars!"

Nigel jumped up. "That's it! That's our name!"

Nick was confused. "Wait—what's our name?"

"Duran Duran!"

It was fine with Nick. Duran Duran sounded cool and futuristic and unlike any other of the new bands they liked, bands that had names like Human League, Simple Minds, and Tubeway Army. Nick loved *Barbarella* and later said he knew that any connection with this

Euro-kitsch classic had to be a good thing for them. Asked much later why the band's name wasn't "Durand-Durand," Nigel—who later went by the name John Taylor—replied that it was because they couldn't hear the final *D*s in the film, nor the intervening hyphen.

So Duran Duran it was. And still is.

The double-barreled name wasn't the only thing that set Duran Duran apart from most other rock bands.

Most bands are formed around a charismatic lead singer or a virtuosic guitarist. The Rolling Stones were built around Mick Jagger. Led Zeppelin was Jimmy Page's band. The Spiders from Mars were Ziggy Stardust's. No Bono, no U2.

By contrast, Duran Duran was the brainchild of two kids, neither of whom could sing or even owned instruments. When they did "take some time and learn how to play," Nigel found himself playing bass guitar, while Nick stood behind racks of keyboards and synthesizers. In Duran Duran, they would become major rock stars, but they were still seen as sidemen supporting a charismatic lead singer.

Despite these differences, the two Birmingham teenagers had several key traits in common that would propel them to genuine rock stardom. The first was an almost encyclopedic knowledge of pop music, fueled by listening obsessively to the radio, going to shows, and seriously studying English music newspapers. Secondly, they were unusually handsome and naturally good-looking, which they then accented with makeup and hair dye in homage to idols like Bowie, Bolan, Roxy, and other glam icons. The third was a mutual ambition and confidence that enabled Nigel and Nick to predict their new band's trajectory with uncanny precision and then pursue this wild ride with a compelling energy that brought the people they needed into their orbit to help them achieve their goals. This was especially true with Nick, who began having premonitions of stardom when he was ten years old and watched Ziggy Stardust on England's must-see music show, *Top of the Pops*. Even then, Nick was thinking about time-lines: when his band would play at London's main rock venue, the Hammersmith Odeon; when they would sell out Wembley Arena; when they would headline Madison Square Garden in New York City.

Unlike the dreams of many kids who hope to become rock stars one day, Nick's teenage ambitions would all actually come true, almost exactly on schedule.

But it all started in Hollywood, the quiet and leafy middle-class neighborhood south of Birmingham's city center, where Nigel and Nick grew up as only children in quite different families.

Nigel John Taylor was born in Solihull, Birmingham, on June 20, 1960, the only child of Jack and Jean Taylor. The Taylors then lived in Warwickshire before moving to 34 Simon Road in Hollywood, one of the new housing estates built in the fifties for the city's post–World War II population explosion. "I had a pretty happy, normal, suburban childhood," he later recalled. His mother was a devout Catholic and took her young boy to mass with her almost every day. Afterward, they would often go to matinees at the cinema and watch newsreels and cartoons. His father worked in Birmingham's booming motor industry. The only real cloud John later talked about was his father, who could be remote and withdrawn to the extent that John was a lit-tle afraid of him. When he was older, his mother explained that Jack Taylor had been a prisoner of war and had spent some harsh years in a German prison camp. Of course, this was never talked about. John called it "the great unspoken subject."

Nigel was sent to a Catholic school, then later attended Abbey High School in nearby Redditch. He had a collection of lead soldiers and loved the James Bond movies starring Sean Connery. When he was twelve, in 1972, he watched David Bowie perform as Ziggy Star-dust with his sensational band, the Spiders from Mars, on *Top of the Pops*, the BBC's popular weekly national music program, which was watched by almost everyone who had a television. Nigel became an instant convert to glam, the new teen religion inspired by the big-gest rock stars in England performing as feminized men. After his parents retired in the evening, John would sneak downstairs to the family room, keeping the lights off, and tune in Radio Luxembourg, which played rock and roll long after English stations shut down for the night. He'd listen to Marc Bolan's T-Rex and their magical #1 hit single, "Bang a Gong," hooked on what the music press branded "Rextasy." Mott the Hoople's (Bowie-produced) "All the Young Dudes" followed, another #1, and then came Roxy Music with their synthesized rock, space-age costumes, and suave singer Bryan Ferry crooning above it all.

Fifteen-year-old John Taylor was now a lanky, longhaired, near-sighted teen with thick glasses and an obsession with pop music. He couldn't wait to leave school at sixteen, when British students who weren't deemed to be on track for college or university left their education behind, either to pursue an apprenticeship or join the workforce. Despite his age, John hardly ever showed up at Abbey High School to begin with. Instead, he caught the big red Midlands double-decker bus that went the other way, toward central Birmingham, and embarked on adventurous rambles about the city.

On the bus, he always sat upstairs, watching as he sped past the Maypole pub and Bates's Toy Corner, the brightly lit shop owned by his friend Nick's mother. They'd motor through King's Heath on the way "uptown," where he had a weekend job stocking shelves, and then Moseley, a funky neighborhood where you might buy a bit of weed from a local Rastafarian and home to aging hippies, artists, bohemians, and a lot of musicians. Industrial powerhouse Birmingham had been brutally bombed by the Germans from 1940 to 1943. Nearly three decades later, in 1975, he could still see piles of rubble, great swathes of cleared land where the old factories had been, and new construction everywhere.

Birmingham's bus terminal sat next to the Bullring, the city's ancient market; early in the morning, it was teeming with vendors and shoppers, fragrant with the smells of baking bread and fresh flowers. There were Jamaican goat patties to buy and all manner of fresh curries and bacon sandwiches. There was also a tiny record shop in the market where Nigel had first heard the voice of Bob Marley. Just up the elevator was the newish Bullring shopping mall, humming with modernity. After leaving the Bullring, he often had a cup of tea at the bakery by New Street Station before heading over to Threshold

Records, one of a chain of shops owned by the Moody Blues, Birmingham's legendary pop stars of the previous decade. (Everyone's parents loved the Moody Blues.) Next stop was Reddington's Rare Records, which carried Jamaican singles, American imports (New York Dolls, especially the Ramones), and used albums.

John loved these meanderings in the city, hunting for clothes and vinyl, trying new flavors and styles. "I was Birmingham's teenage flâneur," he later wrote, "walking idly along New Street. It wasn't Paris, but it worked for me."

Sometimes he met up with his older friend Marcus, a major Roxy Music and Brian Eno superfan, and his girlfriend, Annette. At lunchtime, they'd check out some of the cooler boutiques like Bus Stop, or maybe Oasis, an indoor emporium of new and vintage clothing. Before he went home, he always went by his favorite stop, Virgin Records. It was a new kind of store, "a hippy enclave," with headphones to listen to records and friendly staff who never rushed you or told you to leave. Nigel was there so frequently that the manager started giving him little odd jobs and let him take home outdated band posters for his bedroom walls.

Then, by midafternoon, it was time to get back on the bus.

"Toward the end of my schooldays," he recalled, "I could time that trip to perfection. I would be walking up to the front door of 34 Simon Road just as the school bus was dropping off my classmates—the suckers!"

Nigel had a best friend his own age named David Twist who was just as into music as Nigel was. They lived near each other, and their mothers were close friends. They talked all the time about forming a band. David was in school with a younger boy in Hollywood named Nick Bates, and he kept insisting Nigel had to meet him. One day, in 1973, Nigel was invited to Nick's house, and they formed a friendship that would change both of their lives. Nick was eleven years old. Nigel was thirteen.

Nigel had never encountered anything as cool as Nick Bates's bedroom. He'd never seen this level of affluent teenage rock fandom. Posters covered the wall: Bowie, Bolan, Lou Reed, Roxy Music, Bryan Ferry. Nick had a good stereo system with a tape deck, big speakers, and all the latest albums, singles, and cassettes. A Roxy Music album was spinning on the turntable. There were neatly stacked piles of the English music papers Nick subscribed to: *Melody Maker, New Musical Express* (NME), *Record Mirror,* and *Sounds.* He had a complete file of *Brum Beat,* a fanzine that covered the Midlands music scene. (*Brum* was local slang for Birmingham.) Nick even got the teenage girl magazines *Jackie* and *My Guy,* explaining to the astonished Nigel that they often had the latest news on cutting-edge bands. He later noted, "I realized in Nick's bedroom that afternoon that I was in the presence of someone unusual, and with almost unlimited resources. He was an even bigger music fan than me or David. I was just kind of in awe."

Nicholas James Bates was born in Moseley on June 8, 1962. His parents, Roger and Sylvia Bates, moved to Hollywood a few years later, where his mother opened Bates's Toy Corner, a popular shop in the neighborhood. (Nick has distant connections to an aristocratic Scottish family through his mother; this rates him a mention in *Burke's Peerage*, the semiofficial register of Britain's landed gentry.) Nick was an adorable baby and his parents' only child; he was doted upon and spoiled by his extended family as he began to grow into an unusually beautiful youth. His androgyny was heightened when he started using light makeup after seeing Ziggy Stardust on television in 1972 when he was just ten years old. Some children in his school were uncomfortable with his androgynous style—he was teased about his short stature and called Master Bates—but when Nigel met him, Nick already had a girlfriend, a slightly taller girl named Jane. At this point, Nigel didn't even have a girlfriend; he was impressed that this younger boy did.

In Ziggy's comet-like wake, Nick became a musical polymath, able to complete the *NME*'s challenging musical crossword puzzle by the age of ten. He was well-informed about all the great rock bands the Midlands had produced, including the Moody Blues, Spencer Davis Group, Traffic, Black Sabbath, Gary Glitter, Judas Priest, the Move, and Electric Light Orchestra, among others. Half of Led Zeppelin and the mighty Slade were from nearby Wolverhampton, in addition to scores of blues groups, metal bands, and glam kids like Nigel Taylor, Nick Bates, and David Twist, eager to form new bands of their own.

Nigel and Nick began going to concerts together. When the Faces announced two Christmas shows at the Birmingham Odeon in late 1973, the boys cut class (Nick was at Woodrush School on Shawhurst Lane) and took an early bus into the city. Nigel was apprehensive because the rip-roaring Faces were the most popular band in England after the Rolling Stones went into tax exile in 1971. Rumors had Rod Stewart going solo and Ron Wood about to join the Stones. These could be some of the Faces' last concerts. Nigel knew from bitter experience that Birmingham ticket lines could get rowdy, with shoving and fistfights. But somehow glam child Nick charmed and insinuated their way to the head of an already formed line, and the boys scored a pair of seats in the front row.

"It was just somehow so smooth, so easy," John later said. "I saw this as evidence of [Nick's] magnetic personal magic. Nick is very creative and blessed with incredible good fortune. How lucky can you get? I knew from the beginning of our relationship that if I stayed close to him, life would be exciting."

The next concert they attended was several months later, in April 1974. They got tenth-row seats to see Mick Ronson, the Spiders from Mars's brilliant lead guitarist, at Birmingham Town Hall. By then David Bowie was exhausted, having played the Ziggy persona around the world while also producing Mott's hit record and Lou Reed's *Transformer*. Bowie had announced Ziggy's retirement the summer before at the second of two concerts at West London's Hammersmith Odeon. (No one was more surprised at this than the poor Spiders from Mars, who hadn't been informed beforehand and now found themselves out of a job.)

Nick and Nigel were excited to see Mick Ronson, whom they rated almost as highly as Bowie himself. Nigel's parents allowed him to go to his first nighttime concert in the city on the condition that the boys were driven to and from the show by Nick's mother. (They'd be beaten up if they tried to take the night bus back to Hollywood.) Like most of the young audience, Nigel and Nick were wearing makeup and silk scarves, somewhat dampened by a pouring spring rain. But the concert proved to be disappointing. Mick Ronson's new songs were mediocre, and he seemed awkward holding the stage alone, while down front a riot was underway with flying chairs, screaming girls, and tidal waves of teen flesh churning like a disturbed sea. This was the first time the boys witnessed a concert riot, but it certainly wouldn't be their last.

Later in 1974, they got tickets to see their favorite band, Roxy Music. Nigel and Nick had both been amazed by Roxy's debut on *Top of the Pops* in the summer of 1972. Roxy's sound was the frontline of rock's avant-garde. They had a pile-driving drummer who wore caveman skins and a platform-heeled guitarist who played lightning bolts. Singer Bryan Ferry was a handsome lounge lizard from Newcastle who crooned over the band's massive attack in vintage-looking suits like a Rat Pack star from Vegas. For Nick, Roxy's main attraction was the exotic, impassive Brian Eno, resplendent in furs, rouge, kohl, and kid gloves. Eno was a keyboardist who didn't play keys but instead manipulated the knobs of his tape recorders and synthesizers. Eno had actually left the band just before this, but Nigel and Nick loved Roxy Music so much they tried to sneak into their afternoon sound check and then joined a boisterous group of fans (mostly girls) that mobbed them when they left the Holiday Inn for that evening's show. (This became their usual pattern when the big bands of the day—Queen, Genesis, Wings—came to Birmingham to play the Odeon or Town Hall. They wanted to see and meet the bands offstage as well as on.)

That night, Nigel and Nick were enchanted by Bryan Ferry's smooth vocal control as his band burned behind him. Roxy's presentation was everything they wanted, a sophisticated mix of art college flair, fashion-forward costumes, and Hollywood clichés set to a driving beat. Ferry performed in suits made by the hot young London designer Antony Price, which appealed to Nick Bates's other obsession: fashion. Nick liked posh magazines like *Vogue* and *Tatler*. He read biographies of Coco Chanel and Christian Dior. He dressed carefully, even shopping for his own clothes, unusual for a twelve-year-old. He liked to quote Bryan Ferry: "Other bands want to wreck hotel rooms. Roxy Music wants to redecorate them."

While the boys in Birmingham were trying to get something going, the world around them was convulsed by social changes and often violent class struggles in a rapidly changing English political landscape. The harsh, gray realities of Britain in the seventies would provide a sharp contrast to the cheery music and vibrant images that Duran Duran would be selling a few years later.

In the midseventies, England was beset with chronic labor unrest, industrial actions, and major strikes by coal miners. The winters were cold, and people shivered in their homes when fuel ran short. Jobs became scarce; unemployment soared. Dole queues—unemployment lines—were long. Taxes were so high that people who could afford it were emigrating. Among the rich fleeing the country were the most well-known rock stars, such as Led Zeppelin, the Rolling Stones, and Elton John. Despite their national popularity, these musicians were now reviled as "boring old farts" by a new generation of radical young musicians who were bursting out of the febrile London club scene, spitting with rage against the nearly bankrupt, demoralized condition of modern England.

The London punk scene was largely inspired by American bands like the New York Dolls, Iggy and the Stooges, and the Ramones: speed-rapping poseurs screaming savage, dumbed-down lyrics over blazing guitars, dressed in ripped clothes held together by safety pins (in a nod to this fashion choice, superfans even wore pins in their cheeks). This was the age of punk rock, spewing phlegm and fury, bursting like a boil out of London. The Sex Pistols led the way in a canny haze of negative media manipulation (insulting the queen, cursing on the BBC) and provocative hit records like "God Save the Queen" and "Anarchy in the UK." The Pistols were followed by the Jam, the Damned, the Clash, the Slits, Generation X, and Sham 69. There hadn't been so many exciting young bands coming up since 1963, the year when the Beatles, the Stones, the Yardbirds, and the Kinks all crashed onto the scene. In England, punk rock elbowed aside the major musical trends of the era—northern soul, pub rock, Euro disco—and was ardently supported by hip media outlets like the crusading *NME* as well as the infamous pirate radio stations broadcasting to the UK from old fishing trawlers in the North Sea.

Music fans across the country were dying to see these new bands, especially in the Midlands, where the Sex Pistols' anguished prophecy of "No future for you" struck a chord for kids growing up in an area rife with unemployment. New clubs sprouted up in Birmingham, and older ones changed their music policy to accommodate both the punk bands and the new local reggae bands following in Bob Marley's footsteps, like Steel Pulse, the Beat, and UB40. Birmingham's main punk venues, Rebecca's and Barbarella's, let younger local bands (Fashion, the Only Ones, TV Eye, the Prefects) open for the big London groups, which introduced even more new music to the ever-expanding fanbase.

Nigel Taylor and Nick Bates went to see almost all of these *NME*-approved bands between 1976 and 1978. Nigel venerated the Clash and was also a huge fan of guitarist Pete Shelley's Buzzcocks, a great London band with more dance-friendly songs. The Buzzcocks were one of the prototypes of the so-called new wave: corporate-sponsored, more professionalized post-punk bands such as Blondie, Elvis Costello and the Attractions, and Talking Heads—groups that would take pop music into a more commercial arena later in the seventies.

Nigel's parents noticed he was spending every shilling that he earned stocking shelves at Sainsbury's on record albums and posters of pop stars, so they bought him a black acoustic guitar for his sixteenth birthday. "It was a copy of something I had seen Bryan Ferry play," he recalled. No lessons came with the guitar, however; he didn't even know how to tune it. Whenever Nigel tried to play it, the strings began to snap, and, frustrated, he decided the instrument was only good for folk music, which didn't appeal to him in the slightest. At the end of his academic term, Nigel decided to leave school. His father, who had just been laid off from his job at a car factory, was particularly unhappy with this. Nigel explained that he and some friends were forming a band, and he begged for a year of support while he learned to play and established his band in Birmingham. Reluctantly, Jack and Jean Taylor agreed.

After following his adored Clash from gig to gig around the UK for a few weeks in 1977, Nigel went ahead and started a band with David Twist. Though Nick wanted to stay involved, he was only fourteen and still in school, and his parents insisted that he remain at Woodrush and keep working weekends at Bates's Toy Corner until he turned sixteen. Desperate for funds, Nigel gathered all his precious albums (except for *Aladdin Sane* and Roxy Music's *Country Life*) and took them uptown to Reddington's Rare Records. He later recalled, "I had to take the pittance he offered me for my record collection in order to be able to buy my first electric guitar and amplifier." The fifteen pounds he got for his albums bought him a cheap Fender Telecaster knockoff in the used guitar section of a Moseley music store.

Now they needed a bass player and a drummer to round out their sound. Nigel knew a boy from school, Roy Highfield, who played a snare drum and a high-hat cymbal. "I convinced him to buy a tom-tom, and then another friend called Gareth emerged with a bass guitar. David was singing. Suddenly we were a band."

Inspired by the Ramones, who sang "Gimme Gimme Shock Treatment," the boys named their band Shock Treatment and started getting down to work. Gareth (Gaz) lived in a big suburban house, and his family didn't mind Nigel and the boys bashing out two-chord rock. Gaz even had two attractive sisters who stopped by to watch them practice, another reason the boys liked to rehearse there. They wrote their first songs—"Freedom of Speech," "I Can't Help It," and "UK Today," which "could have been written by almost any British teenager that week in 1977," according to Nigel. In addition to "Cover Girls" and "Striking Poses" (which seemed to preview later Duran Duran titles), they also played cover versions of the Who's "Substitute" and the Stooges' "I Wanna Be Your Dog."

To get more involved with the Birmingham music scene, Shock Treatment also started following and assisting the local bands: helping them put up their flyers, going to their shows, chatting them up afterward. The guys in Fashion and the Prefects were particularly friendly and helpful, listening to their demo cassettes, offering advice, and warning against predatory agents and club owners who didn't pay after gigs. Slowly but surely, Shock Treatment was coming into its own on Birmingham's competitive junior rock scene.

While Nigel Taylor was launching Shock Treatment, fifteen-year-old Nick Rhodes was trying out new cheap synthesizers in the music stores, falling in love with the machines' buttons, knobs, and sliders. Since he wasn't a trained musician, these simple keyboard synthesizers were something Nick could actually play—and might just be his way into music. Nick's timing and location were also ideal because Birmingham happened to be where almost every synthesizer in England was manufactured.

The word "synthesizer" dates back to patents from 1897, in the wake of Thomas Edison's invention of the gramophone twenty years earlier. These patents were for electronic machines producing audio signals that could be converted to sound waves. As these synthesizers developed, they were later programmed to imitate musical instruments, even entire orchestras, in addition to natural sounds like wind and waves. Early avant-garde musicians (such as Milton Babbitt) used unwieldy, large-frame synthesizers to infuse their work with surreal tones, exotic timbres, and unearthly aural soundscapes.

In the early sixties, American inventor Robert Moog developed a smaller, freestanding modular synthesizer he called the Mellotron. It was an analog-tape protosampler, which was portable but very difficult to play. Still, bands could take them to gigs, and so by mid-decade, the Mellotron's eerie, subterranean tones made psychedelic music available to Friday-night crowds. A company called Mellotronics was even set up in Birmingham to manufacture the Mellotron, and soon, several other factories in the Midlands began making music synthesizers as well.

A young Mellotronics employee named Mike Pinder also played keyboards in the Moody Blues, which began as an R&B band (in blue suits and cravats) from the industrial Birmingham district of Erdington. As part of the midsixties British Invasion of America, the Moody Blues had a huge US hit record in 1965 with "Go Now." However, the money from this American hit single somehow vanished, and now broke, the band was on the verge of breaking up—until Mike bought a preowned Mellotron from the Dunlop Tyre Social Club in Solihull. He realized the symphonic sounds the instrument produced would be perfect for the lush arrangements for his band's new songs. Shortly after he introduced the Mellotron to the band, the Moodies mutated from an English Beat group to caftan-wearing psychedelic gurus. The synthesizer seemed to capture something of the euphoric, hallucinatory spirit that the musicians had felt when they'd taken LSD for the first time in Richmond Park. The band's synth-driven new songs changed the whole trajectory for the Moody Blues.

Mike Pinder then demonstrated the Mellotron to John Lennon and Paul McCartney at EMI's Abbey Road Studios in London, where both the Beatles and Moody Blues were recording. As a result, the Mellotron's cheesy electronic waves were prominently featured on the Beatles' 1967 hit "Strawberry Fields Forever." Later on, Brian Jones of the Rolling Stones played the Mellotron on "2000 Light Years from Home." That November, the Moody Blues released the album *Days of Future Past*, and a string of synthesized smashes followed: "Tuesday Afternoon," "Ride My Seesaw," "Nights in White Satin." Nick Bates and Nigel Taylor, along with the other kids from the Midlands, grew up with the ever-present sound of the Moody Blues's sometimes spacey, sometimes hard-driving songs on the radio.

Though Nick admired the Moody Blues, his main synthesizer role model was, of course, Roxy Music's Brian Eno. Eno had been studying at Winchester College of Art in the late sixties when he first began experimenting with reel-to-reel tape recorders. He started working with Roxy Music as a sort of ad-hoc sound engineer, recording their concerts and playing the tapes back to the band after the gigs. Then Eno suggested feeding the band's instruments and microphones through Andy Mackay's EMS VCS3 synthesizer, basically a primitive sound generator and processing tool. Eno added a tape echo deck and a customized delay unit that enabled him to bend and filter Roxy's live output, giving the band inter-frequencies that seemed to transfer sound between actual dimensions. This addition was very ahead of its time and years before the development and standardization of the MIDI, or Musical Instrument Digital Interface, which would allow a producer to integrate and synchronize synthesizers and other instruments and which indeed would change the way music was recorded.

For his sixteenth birthday, in 1978, Nick's mother drove him to a music shop and bought him an inexpensive, locally manufactured Wasp synthesizer and an amplifier. Equipped with the tools he needed to become a real musician, he asked Nigel to come over and help him set up his new synthesizer. Black and yellow like its namesake, the EDP Wasp was a small and compact machine manufactured by a new Midlands firm, Electronic Dream Plant. The Wasp didn't have a mechanical keyboard but instead used touch-sensitive copper plates covered by a silkscreened vinyl sticker. The little machine had a small internal speaker with a distinctive sound. The Wasp was also ahead of its time largely because it was one of the first synths to use digital technology. (1978 Wasps are eagerly sought after by early-synth collectors today.)

Nick spent the next months experimenting with the Wasp, learning the sounds it could produce. As soon as he turned sixteen, he was ready to get his school days behind him, join forces with Nigel, and start the new band they'd always dreamed of. All they needed were songs, a drummer, and a cool name.

In February 1978, Nigel and Nick found themselves pacing outside of Barbarella's, worried they wouldn't be able to get in to see Blondie because they were too young. Blondie, one of the best and hottest of American new wave bands, was on its first headlining tour of England. Nick and Nigel met outside Nick's home in Mill Close and walked down the hill from Hollywood to the Maypole bus station. It was a freezing Saturday night, just beginning to rain ice. They calculated their chances of getting into Barbarella's, which had an eighteen-plus age limit. Nick was only fifteen and John seventeen. But they'd already gotten in to see Generation X and the Clash. "Be cool and don't attract attention when the bouncers give us the eyeball," Nigel counseled younger Nick, "like that scene in *Saturday Night Fever.*"

Despite the advice, the lads were practically asking to be noticed. Both were paradigms of Anglo-Celtic teenage young male beauty, tonight enhanced by generous swipes of eye shadow and pale lip gloss. Nick wore a plain white dress shirt and a skinny black tie, the sigil of the new wave. Like Nick, the much taller Nigel wore his hair long, with thick clear plastic glasses and a black shirt with the year "1977" stenciled across it to proclaim fealty to the Clash.

From Birmingham city center, it was a twenty-minute walk to Barbarella's, self-proclaimed "the biggest nightclub in Europe." A shivering, smoking crowd of punks and new wavers waited outside the big double doors in the sleet, anxious to get inside. The boys gladly handed over the £1.30 entrance fee, earned from Nigel's supermarket job and Nick's at the toy store. They were almost overwhelmed by the smell of cigarettes and beer as they managed to nimbly glide past the club's bouncers and dodge down the dimly red-lit, tunnel-like carpeted hallway. The lights grew redder and dimmer as they narrowly avoided the club's toilets, where younger fans like them were vulnerable to attack from beer-sodden older customers.

Once inside the club's main room, loud reggae boomed from the walls. DJ Wayne ("the Plastic Poser") blasted Jamaican toaster Dillinger's "Cocaine in My Brain" at ear-bleeding volume. Barbarella's had the best sound system in Birmingham, and it was the most faithful reproduction of recorded music either boy had ever heard. The dance floor was packed with fans aged from eighteen to midtwenties. Eager to avoid the crowds, Nick and Nigel made their way over to the tables and chairs toward the right, which afforded clear sightlines to the stage. Next to them, steps led up to a brightly lit bar, where dozens of customers were yelling at the bartenders to make them drinks.

The stage, about three feet tall, was across the dance floor, the front already crowded with kids who didn't want to dance but wanted to see the live band. At eleven o'clock, the boys grew nervous. It was a school night for Nick, and the last bus back to Hollywood left at one in the morning. They made their way up to the bar and ordered two Cokes, and Nigel lit up a Player's No. 6. The opening band finished their set, and the crowd in front of the stage started to chant, "Blondie! Blondie! Blondie!"

Hearts beating harder, Nigel and Nick smiled at each other, whispering, "We made it."

Blondie hit the stage at eleven fifteen in an arc of white light, playing "Call Me." Looking almost unreal under the hot lights, Debbie Harry was a sexy bleached bombshell in a chic white stage dress and heels; she worked the heaving young crowd as the skillful band vamped behind her. The band played all their hits for a little over an hour that night. Elated, Nigel and Nick ran back to the bus terminal in the freezing rain and barely caught the last coach to Hollywood.

The next day in London, Blondie would lip-synch their new single "Denis" for *Top of the Pops*, and Debbie Harry would become the hottest rock star in the UK.

By this time, Nigel's band, Shock Treatment, had already played a few gigs themselves. Their first performance was in front of Nigel's high school class in June 1977. The Hockley Heath Rugby Club had been rented by the sixth form (senior class) for the end-of-term dance. Shock Treatment set up their gear on the floor across from the bar because there was no stage. From their friends the Prefects, they'd borrowed a highly coveted Carlsbro Stingray amplifier whose one-hundred-watt output would give them a little more power. Nigel felt a spiritual charge just from plugging his guitar into the amp. The rugby club had high windows, and it was June, so the room never really got dark. But Shock Treatment gave it their all, playing their own new songs, plus "I Wanna Be Your Dog" and "Substitute," which even the Sex Pistols had covered.

As he strummed the three chords he knew on his cheap electric guitar, Nigel could see astonishment on some of the faces of his class-mates, especially the girls. Suddenly he was no longer "Nerdy Nigel" who didn't do well in school, didn't have a girlfriend, and didn't play sports. The guitar sounded huge, thanks to a Big Muff distortion box he was running it through. Some kids danced (or pogoed), and Nigel even earned some applause at the end of the set, not to mention some admiring pats on the back.

"At the end of that night," John Taylor later remembered, "there were two new facts I knew for certain. One was that Shock Treat-ment was awful. Two was that I couldn't wait to do it again."

Though not sharing the stage, Nick was supportive of his friend's musical endeavors and saw every gig Shock Treatment played, as well as Nigel's later gigs with his subsequent bands: Dada and then the Assas-sins. In July, Shock Treatment opened for local band TV Eye in a pub. On August 22, they supported the Prefects at Rebecca's. Singer David Twist recalled, "We couldn't play a fucking note! John, as he later became, thrashed away on guitar until his hands were bleeding. Gaz the bassist couldn't play, so he kind of did a Stuart Sutcliff [the Beatles' first bassist, who couldn't play either] with his back to the audience. I was incompe-tent. We finished our set and walked off to stunned silence." After a cou-ple more gigs with the Prefects, Shock Treatment even got a friendly notice in *Brum Beat*. Nigel's parents, happily surprised, began to think their lovely boy might actually be on to something with his music.

John Taylor would later dub 1978 as Year Zero for Duran Duran. It was the year he and Nick changed their names, changed their style, and finally formed the band they'd been talking about, nonstop, for five years.

"I started playing guitar when I was seventeen, in the summer of 1977, the Punk Year; that was the year when everyone who could play was forming a band. I bought a cheap guitar for fifteen pounds and played my first gig with a school band called Shock Treatment, after the Ramones song. It was a party for our class at Redditch County High School near where we lived in Hollywood. I must have spent the next year living at home and playing in that band, along with being in another band called Two Six Two, and then another band called the Assassins. I was also in another band called Dada. As true as possible to the surrealist name, there was an avant-garde, art school dimension to Dada, with projections and definitely being into multi-media ideas. I stayed on guitar, and David Twist moved to drums. An older guy we knew called John Brocklesby, who owned a boutique, sang his own songs and various covers while playing a pink Vox bass guitar. My old friend (and Roxy fan) Marcus played the Stylophone, which he perched on an old ironing board. (Some thought this the most Dada thing about the band.) Our sets would open with 'Toy-room' about idyllic childhoods; the chord sequence was DA/DA, and it lasted seven minutes over a steady, four-on-the-floor disco rhythm. (We wanted Dada to sound different.) We all liked the chic clothes John sold in his store, so his wife, Heather, put our kit together: short white stage jackets with leather collars, expertly sewn and fitted. This gave Dada an elegant look that sort of made us stand apart from other bands. We had no place to rehearse so John spoke to the landlord of the Crown, the pub on Hill Street, and he said we could use the big upstairs room on Tuesdays. This turned into a residency for Dada that lasted a few weeks in May 1968.

"We were also close to the best Birmingham band of that era, the Prefects. [BBC disc jockey] John Peel really liked them and played their record—'Birmingham Is a Shit Hole'—which lasted about five seconds—on his popular show. Another Prefects song called 'Going Through the Motions' could last half an hour. The singer used to shave himself during the long, long instrumental parts of their show. The Prefects were *très* cool and even loaned us their amplifiers. Me and David Twist loved them.

"Meanwhile, my parents watched me staying up all night and sleeping until noon and were urging me to either get a real job or return to school. I was spending most of my time at David's house, because at that age—seventeen, eighteen—it's like, anywhere but your own house. Know what I mean?

"I was more attracted to the side guys in the band, rather than the singer: guitar players like Phil Manzanera with Roxy, Ronnie Wood with the Stones. I never wanted to be seen to like the obvious. I used to love showing up at school with records by bands nobody knew—Be-Bop Deluxe! I fucking held a flame for them for a long time. And I was definitely—and this counted for something then—the first one in the school, really, that knew what the Sex Pistols were. At the same time, I realized that all the girls at school were into Bolan and Bowie and Rod Stewart. (Or Sir Rod, as he now is.) They all read the teen girl magazines and would tape the pinups in their lockers, and I was kind of into that too. So was Nick. It was really the only connection I had with the girls; the only way I would even have a conversation with a girl was about music.

"The late seventies was an amazing time for us, really, with Bowie blazing the trail with each new album: something different every time. Queen was huge for us. *Top of the Pops* was like a religion. Every week, you could not miss it because for every Mud or Sweet there'd be a Queen or a Roxy Music. The Buzzcocks—incredible! *I loved them!* I'd watch this and be like, *What the fuck is this?* I didn't even realize it at the time, but all this was changing the direction of one's life. The sheer allure of this world was my siren song. I know it's a cliché, but I was just a teenage moth drawn to pop music's glamorous flame. Where this came from I don't really know; not because there was music in my family; not because there were instruments lying about the house. But my mum did love popular music, and the radio was always on. I heard a *lot* of Moody Blues growing up.

"As I told you, I was useless at school and failed all my A-levels, but my parents said I needed to get more education while I was being in local bands. Somehow I managed to get a place at a sort of experimental art college that was part of Birmingham Polytechnic. This was the summer of 1977. On the first day there, I met Stephen Duffy, a fellow student. He was this intense little spikey-haired punk with a camera, wanting to study photography. That first day, talking to Stephen, I knew we were going to form a band together: Stephen, me, and Nick.

"That was around the time I first got Nick into playing. He wanted me to teach him how to play guitar, which was kind of like the blind leading the deaf. What completely changed our lives was the Wasp synthesizer, an affordable, user-friendly keyboard. It was to the synth what punk had been to the guitar. You didn't need to be fucking Tony Banks [Genesis keyboardist] anymore. The Wasp made a lot of things possible for young musicians. Sylvia Bates bought the new Wasp for Nick at Woodroffe's Music Store. It cost her two hundred pounds, and later she said it was her best investment ever.

"Nick and I went through the whole punk cycle together. We loved the Faces, would never miss their gigs, but by '76 we were starting to see the new bands. We knew immediately that you could not top the Clash. You could not top the Heartbreakers. Human League came along [from nearby Sheffield] and was instantly important. We saw them opening for Siouxsie and the Banshees at Mayfair Ballroom in the Bullring. Human League had no drummer or guitars. They had three synthesizers, a drum machine, some amazing songs, and were incredible. It was the same thing with Kraftwerk—who we never actually got to see. Of course, disco was massive where we lived, especially [German producer] Giorgio Moroder. He was huge, especially in the clubs.

"But my classic moment was sitting in a pub with a friend, ruminating about my dubious future as a musician, and hearing the Sex Pistols' 'Anarchy in the UK' on the pub jukebox, followed by 'Good Times' by Chic. And there was the sheer naivete of me blurting to this friend of mine, 'I like *both* of those records!' This was naive because Chic was disco, and disco was verboten to anyone that was into punk. But that was when we got the idea of developing a rhythm section that actually played together, that actually could do four-on-the-floor dance music. It would be cool music that people could dance to. True to the punk ethic, we didn't go away and practice and take music degrees to be serious, the punk ethic being the attitude: If we want to do it, why can't we do it?

"But different, of course. Changing up the music a little bit. And doing something new that would still be a work of art. Then we looked around and saw that there was now quite a lot of that kind of music happening. Major rock stars were turning to disco. The Rolling Stones' 'Miss You' was on the radio every minute. Rod Stewart's 'Do Ya Think I'm Sexy?' was massive. It was like, for them, at the end of the day, you could not out-punk punk. Even Bowie was on the dance floor with 'Young Americans.'

"Plus, the whole punk / new wave scene was getting nasty. You'd show up to a gig—Nick and I went to see the B-52's at Barbarella's—and the show kept stopping because of violence in the crowd. It was getting hairy, going to shows. Plus, we'd be hassled by hooligans on the bus home. So yeah, late seventies, things were changing. Punk was being subversively supplanted by something new sprouting in England: the two-tone movement. These were integrated bands: Madness, UB40, the Beat, the Selecter; Black and White musicians playing speedy ska for skinheads and punks alike. And of course we realized the eighties were coming and would bring in new styles, new worlds even. We couldn't wait to meet them!"

When Nigel first met with the careers officer at his high school in summer 1978, he seemed dubious after the skinny, nearsighted boy told him he wanted to be a pop star. Instead, Nigel was referred to a "foundational art course" run by Birmingham Polytechnic College of Art and Design, a decrepit and gloomy Victorian building under a flyover bridge on Fazeley Street. He'd been accepted after presenting the hand-drawn posters and collaged flyers he'd made for his bands and then playing a cassette of Shock Treatment for the admissions committee. Jack and Jean Taylor were quite content their son would continue his education—free of charge—for at least another year.

At Birmingham Poly, Nigel would take courses in drawing and graphics, textiles and fashion, photography and design, in hopes that by the end of the term, he would be well prepared for starting a career in the arts. On the first day of class, Nigel met a fellow student who had also dreamed and fiddled his way through grammar school and then been shuffled off to art college. This was Stephen Duffy, age sixteen, a dark-eyed punk with spikey black hair and an intense gaze, dressed in dark clothes and makeup, chain-smoking Gitanes. Stephen's admission into the college was thanks to his bleak, black-and-white portfolio of photographs set across Birmingham (New Street Station, the Bullring, the rag market, the Crescent Theatre) as it was being rebuilt from wartime devastation. One stark series, titled "My Birmingham," depicted the music venues Stephen frequented: Barbarella's in Cumberland Street, the Red Star club, Rebecca's, Goddard at the Arts Lab, the Crown and Golden Eagle pubs, the Cannon Hill Arts Centre.

Looking back, Stephen Duffy recalled, "It was my first day at Birmingham Poly. I didn't even *do* art at school, but I'd taken some photographs, and maybe they thought I'd liven the place up a bit. I was wearing a pair of dress trousers and this crazy woman's jacket and some winkle-picker boots, and I realized I was walking behind the guitarist from Dada and the drummer from TV Eye and the Prefects [David Twist]. I couldn't believe it—people from actual bands! People I would have been *far* too scared to talk to at the Crown or the Golden Eagle. I didn't talk to them the first day or the second day. But then Nigel was alone, and I went up and said, 'Hi, I saw you in Dada. What are you doing at the moment?' And he said he wasn't doing anything. So we decided to start a band. That was literally our first conversation."

Nigel took to Stephen right away and couldn't help noticing his obvious creative talent. "In drawing class, while we tried to reproduce the model or whatever in detail, Stephen would scratch the paper with a few harsh strokes of his charcoal stick. He'd insolently show the crude results to the teacher, who would always say something like, 'You see, everybody? Stephen *gets it*.'"

As the summer days passed into September, the pair's friendship extended beyond the school walls. Nigel wasn't surprised to find that Stephen was a songwriter, and he played a fretless bass guitar. Stephen could speak eloquently about his heroes: Bob Dylan, the Band, Jack Kerouac, F. Scott Fitzgerald. Stephen played Nigel a song demo he'd written called "Newhaven to Dieppe (And No Wonder)." Nigel was impressed by his classmate's talent and wanted to team up with him on a new endeavor: "By then, our band Dada had hit a wall and would go no further. Now I wanted to be in a band with Steve, but I was going to need reinforcements. I suggested Steve meet Nick Bates."

As it turned out, Stephen had already met Nick. Early in 1978, just after the turn of the year, someone had brought Stephen round to Nick's house. Stephen and Nick were both sixteen, but Stephen was in awe of Nick's obsessive material fandom collections: the records, the posters, the pinups, the newspapers, the magazines. Then there was Nick's dedication to carefully curating his glam look: the makeup, the hair dye, mascara, kohl, chiffon and silk scarves, glittery boutique fashions. Over the course of their first meeting, they listened to Kraftwerk's *Autobahn* and new waver Elvis Costello's *Armed Forces*, which Nick had just purchased. Later they watched a rebroadcast of Elvis Presley's epic 1968 TV comeback, with the King of Rock and Roll reasserting his mastery of the form after years of making cheesy Hollywood movies.

When Nigel and Stephen connected later on that fall at Birmingham Poly, Nick already had his Wasp, and former bandmate David Twist left Dada to rejoin the (very good) Moseley band TV Eye. So Nick, Nigel, and Stephen began to pull their new band together based on Stephen Duffy's funny, effete songs and the self-confidence and charisma they shared as a trio. After class, they would gather in the cafeteria of Rackhams department store and talk about what they wanted to sound like: "What if the Velvet Underground was produced by Giorgio Moroder? Could we sound something like that?"

According to Stephen, "We were so hungry to consume everything there was out there. Nick and John knew a lot more than I did. They seemed to know everything. I had to try hard to catch up! John could sit there and complete the *NME* crossword. And Nick had more records than anyone else I knew. . . . He was sixteen, a bit younger, but he'd already actually written to Morrissey about the New York Dolls [prefame Stephen Morrisey ran the Dolls' UK fan club], and he had a Wasp synthesizer. . . . It was exciting because we started the band at a point before music began repeating itself. Right after that, we had two-tone and ska, *very* repetitive, more or less derivative. *We* were more into Kraftwerk and the Bowie albums—*Low* and *Heroes*. You just thought [music] was going to go more and more futuristic."

Stephen's moody, melodic songs gradually came together in rehearsals in the back room of Bates's Toy Corner that autumn, inspired by his literary heroes. "Lost Decade" was inspired by F. Scott Fitzgerald's 1925 novel *The Great Gatsby*. Other titles included "Dust and Dawn," "Dark Circles," and "Kiss Me." "Aztec Moon" was inspired by Jack Kerouac's book of song lyrics, *Mexico City Blues*. "Hawks Don't Share" came out of Stephen's reading of Ernest Hemingway. This nameless trio—now a typical art college band—was

Stephen Duffy singing and playing bass, Nick Bates on keyboards and rhythm machine, and Nigel Taylor on guitar. They made some cassettes of completed songs and began playing them for friends in other local bands, including a hard-charging teenage punk band, the Scent Organs.

For the first few weeks, they obsessed over what to call their band. Two early candidates were Jazz and RAF, as in the Royal Air Force. Then on October 20, the BBC broadcast *Barbarella*.

"That's it!" Nigel said.

Stephen liked the name too. "Taylor and I stood in the stairway outside the college kitchen, Victorian and untouched since the war. He said that we should call ourselves Duran Duran. It was an exciting moment. To hear the space-age name in such a dark old Dickensian sort of place—to hear the future christened in the past. For some time, it was by far the best thing about the band. . . . Maybe I misheard him, but I printed up the name at art school the next day— DURAN DURAN—in red ink. But even if I had heard him correctly, I don't think there would have been enough Ds. I think I used them all up."

The members of newly born Duran Duran started changing their own names as well. After appearing as "Dior" on the band's earliest flyers, Nick dropped his last name "for aesthetic reasons" and became "Nick Rhodes." Nigel dropped his first name and became "John Taylor." He also got contact lenses and bumped up a hundred degrees of boy band cool. Stephen Duffy became "Stephen Dufait," a louche teen flâneur on the streets of Birmingham. It was also decided that the glam look was over, save, of course, for the makeup, hair dye, and scarves. The look Nick had in mind was now definitely more pirates in space.

Much later, Stephen recalled, "Duran Duran was a real art student band. We spent hours at the college photocopying [Andy] Warhol's books, cutting up fashion magazines, producing collage for our posters. Duran Duran's roots were post-punk: a dark, provincial, Red Brick [middle-class] type of thing. We felt closer to what was happening in Liverpool and Manchester, with bands like Echo and the Bunnymen and Teardrop Explodes. One of the reasons we liked Warhol so much was that he was this working-class guy from Pittsburgh who drew shoes and then completely redefined art, invented a whole new school of thought."

Pop artist Andy Warhol was a huge inspiration for Duran Duran, as he had been for Bowie, Lou Reed, and all tomorrow's parties. Little did the band know, but in a few then-unimaginable years, Warhol would be Duran Duran's friend and ardent admirer as well.

"John Taylor and I are from Hollywood, a nice middle-class suburb of Birmingham. We lived only a few streets apart. We met when I was thirteen and John was fifteen through a mutual friend named David Twist. John and I met, and it was a big sort of standoff, trying to impress each other. I think we might have swapped David Bowie and T-Rex trading cards. I took John to his first-ever concert—Mick Ronson at Birmingham Town Hall. We were going to Barbarella's, all the time, to see bands. There was someone great on almost every night: Generation X, Blondie, Television, Talking Heads. Plus all the punk bands who were just extraordinary live on stage. It was awe-inspiring. Suicide was one of my favorites. I watched them get bottled offstage when they were supporting the Clash.

"That—people throwing beer bottles at you—really made me want to be in a band even more, actually.

"John and I both decided we wanted to play guitar when we were in our early teens. I wasn't good, and fortunately neither was John. He swapped to bass, and I swapped to keyboards, which seemed like the answer to me because I wanted to play synths, not classical piano. Also, the synths had all just come down in price, and I bought a thing called a Wasp, which looked rather more like a toy in my mother's shop than a serious instrument.

"John was in a couple of punk bands, which I went to see. He was playing guitar at the time, and I was very impressed, mostly because he was so striking as a young human being. I saw him in sort of an art-punk band called Dada. They had a guy who played Stylophone, and at the gig he had set it up on an ironing board—which I was deeply jealous of.

"When I left school at sixteen, fortunately, John got free and we formed the first version of Duran Duran. I was on keyboards and tapes, recording things on a reel-to-reel machine and fading them in and out of songs. And also I had the Wasp and a Stylophone and a rhythm unit. John was playing guitar, and Stephen Duffy played bass and sang. We rehearsed during the fall of 1978 and into the winter of 1979. Then a chap called Simon Colley, who John and Stephen knew from Birmingham Polytechnic, came in to play bass and sometimes clarinet. Stephen was writing interesting songs for Duran Duran, like 'Kiss Me' (which would be a big hit for him as a solo artist in 1985). Also 'Memory Palaces,' 'World Exclusive,' and 'Come Alive.'

"The truth is that this first Duran Duran was an extraordinarily bizarre art school lineup. We covered the amps in white plastic sheeting we'd found somewhere. We projected Stephen's color slides of depressing buildings on the walls while we played. At least John, Stephen, and Simon were all at art college. I probably should have been too, or at least I wanted to give the impression that I went to art school. But I was ambitious and had the strong feeling that I didn't have the time for it. I was sixteen and knew what I wanted to do, which was getting this band off the ground.

"Finally, in April [1979] we began playing in front of their fellow students at Birmingham Polytechnic. I think we did four gigs together there as Duran Duran. The first one was booked very late, and we didn't have a name. We only had a couple of days to come up with something because we had to put it on a poster to advertise our first show. We remembered we'd watched *Barbarella*, and when the character Durand-Durand came on, John had said, 'What about that? That's a really fucking unusual name!'

"And I just said, 'Yep. OK. Let's go.'

"So we had that lineup with Stephen and Simon. I think our first gig was in early April in the lecture hall at Birmingham Polytechnic in front of about a dozen people, including Andy Wickett (the singer in TV Eye), members of the Prefects, a couple guys from a record store we liked, and a girl who was waiting for her photographic prints to dry in the college darkroom.

"Our earliest sort of success was a gig at Barbarella's where we were supporting Fashion, local heroes we admired at the time, who we thought were really on to something. They sounded a little like the Police and were the band that most people thought would break out of Birmingham. They were electro-punk, really, with a bit of reggae thrown in. At Barbarella's, we came on with our rhythm unit— really, really slow, countering Fashion's more speedy punk ethos. Our singer, 'Stephen Dufait,' in his most camp/fey voice, a sort of strangled Franglais, introduced our first song, 'Lost Decade,' as having been inspired by the writer F. Scott Fitzgerald.

"The crowd groaned, audibly, and I thought we're going to get bottled off. 'Oh no,' I thought. 'Here they come. This is the moment we've all been waiting for!' But the audience just stood and watched, were respectful, and by the end of the set I think we actually got an encore. We were like—dead chuffed! We were thrilled. We thought we were on our way. We played again [on May 8] in the tiny puppet theater of Cannon Hill Arts Centre, again with projections and my tapes of Gregorian chant and tolling gongs. Stephen taped a cassette of the show, about a dozen songs, and we thought we did pretty well and were pleased with ourselves."

PART 2

Duran Duran kept playing and rehearsing, but Nick and John sensed that something wasn't quite right with Stephen Duffy. They were mostly playing his glacial, breathy songs: "Signals in Smoke," "Big Store," "So Cold in El Dorado," and "Hold Me Pose Me" (the last title inspired by the copy on a doll box in Bates's Toy Corner). With Simon Colley now on bass, Stephen concentrated on his fey, breathy stage persona, "Stephen Dufait," as John strummed the few guitar chords that he knew and Nick produced electronic signals and pulsing beats from his simple rhythm machine. Nick thought Stephen was maybe overdoing the makeup, the beret, and the campy, faux Parisian moves onstage, but that wasn't the only issue. Their sets only lasted half an hour, but that posed a problem for the projections because they didn't have enough slides to last that long without repeating them over and over. But at least they were on their way.

The most important thing going for them was that Duran Duran got the kids dancing. The drum machine's various disco settings were propulsive, and Nick's buzzing drones gave the rhythms a dark, Eno-like aura of mystique and control. John's guitar tapped out Morse code over it all, like a telegram from an asteroid. Their sound was definitely unique, especially for Birmingham.

On May 8, 1979, Duran Duran played at the Cannon Hill Art Centre. They gigged again at the Hosteria on May 22, and then at the Hexagon Theatre on May 29. They played at Barbarella's for the first time on June 1. As Stephen remembered, "We did four gigs. First one at the art college, April '79, and the last gig was supporting Fashion at Barbarella's. I wore silk jodhpurs that I'd found in a sales bin in

Wallis. Nick made this amazing noise on his Wasp synth. For the first song, I danced around but didn't sing. When we came offstage, I remember thinking that it had been an absolute triumph. But then John started bugging me about this album he wanted me to play—*Life in Tokyo* by [the band] Japan—saying *this* was what we needed to do. I thought, why would we want to sound like Japan when we can dance around to buzzing? No one was doing dancing to buzzing."

Then, suddenly, Stephen Duffy ghosted Duran Duran. He disappeared. Nick and Nigel couldn't get ahold of him, or Simon Colley, for days. Then they heard that Stephen and Simon had hooked up with TV Eye and were rehearsing in TV Eye's illegal squat in a semi-derelict old house in Cheapside.

Stephen and Simon had officially quit Duran Duran.

"John and I were absolutely shattered," Nick recalled. "When we finally made contact, Stephen and Simon told us they were quitting to pursue a career in 'rock and roll,' which wasn't something we were dreadfully interested in. So we had to set about reshaping Duran Duran and rethinking the whole approach to what we were about."

In its early days, Duran Duran couldn't shy away from some of the harsh realities of daily life. Many of Stephen Duffy's slides projected on the walls during their earliest concerts depicted the shabby degradation of the English Midlands in 1977–1978. Britain had declined into economic depression and political chaos not seen since World War II. All over the country, but especially in the Midlands, factories shut down, people lost jobs, and inner cities rioted. The powerful trade unions were fighting for their lives as whole industries collapsed, working-class communities crumbled, and the ruling Labor Party self-destructed. The press described England as the Sick Man of Europe—when it printed at all. The *Times* of London—published daily since 1788—shut down for months in 1978–1979 when management and the printers unions could not even agree on a place to negotiate. John Taylor's father was out of work as the Midlands car factories foundered, were dismantled, and were sold for scrap. Birmingham reggae band UB40 reproduced the UK's unemployment relief application (Unemployment Benefit Form 40) on the cover of their first album. Many saw England as a wounded, unhappy, no-future land, just as the Sex Pistols had predicted.

Stephen Duffy later said he felt as though Nick and John were oblivious to all this. They seemed like spoiled children, still living with their parents, whose only concern was fame. "John and Nick were the first people I'd met who actually admitted that they wanted to be famous. I didn't think people actually said things like that. I was still at that wanting-to-be-a-poet stage."

Stephen would take his music in a more socially aware direction. His new band, with Simon Colley and David Twist (defecting from TV Eye), was first called Obviously Five Believers and then the Sub-terranean Hawks; they were aiming for the rocking rebel energy of Bob Dylan and the Band, tempered with the moody grace of Nick Drake.

"Duran Duran wanted to make electro-pop records like *Life in Tokyo* by Japan," Stephen recalled, "and I didn't. I wanted to make electro-pop records that were even worse than *Life in Tokyo*. In fact, my first album was so dreadful that I should have been forced to return to Birmingham and work in B&Q [home furnishing store] for the rest of my life."

And so, the Subterranean Hawks began rehearsing in this new direction, while Nick and John figured out how to keep Duran Duran alive.

Without Simon and Stephen, Duran Duran now needed a bass player and a singer. Nick and John were forced to cancel a major gig at Birmingham University, a big disappointment, but they also needed new songs, since Stephen Duffy had taken his with him when he left. Prefects bassist Eamon Duffy (no relation) joined Duran Duran briefly around this time, but they still needed a vocalist.

As Nick remembered, "At first, we went with a couple of differ-ent ones [singers], Andy Wickett being one of them, who used to be in a band called FBI in Birmingham. He worked in the Cadbury [chocolate] factory. He had an amazing voice but also an unfortunate propensity to knock beer all over my keyboards. He was really some-thing, though, an amazing talent that could have made it big if he'd been luckier. He was with us for a while, and he even came up with an idea for a song called 'Girls on Film'; but then one day he went and had all his hair chopped off, and that just wasn't working for us at all. We felt there was a different attitude prevailing between what Andy wanted and what we wanted. So Andy was persuaded to drop out of Duran Duran.

"We also had a guitarist in there somewhere called Alan Curtis, who didn't actually leave the band until just before Simon [Le Bon] came in. Then we had another singer, who was in the Scent Organs, called Jeff Thomas. He was good, a bit more artsy, and sort of fitted in quite well, but somehow there was something that wasn't right. He did write one song with one of my favorite titles ever, called 'Enigmatic Swimmer.'"

At this point—May 1979—Duran Duran realized that if they were going to get on the dance floor, they had to find a drummer.

Nick recalled "[hearing] about a drummer called Roger, who lived in Birmingham and played in a band called the Scent Organs, and before that in a band I hadn't heard of called Crucified Toad. But we heard he was absolutely the best drummer in town. So we got hold of Roger, met with him, liked him. He seemed to be one of us and was the same age as John. He was quiet, self-contained. He only spoke when he had something to say, and you listened. Then John decided to swap to bass. So we got Roger in, and he started playing with John, and then the three of us started to jam together, and it was really starting to sound very different and . . . unusual.

"So this was the point where we emerged from 'art rock' and into more of a hybrid of glam rock, disco, and electronic music. The records we were listening to were mostly Chic albums and other acts produced by [Chic principals] Nile Rodgers and Bernard Edwards. We were listening to Kraftwerk. We were listening to Human League. We were listening to Bowie obviously, and to Giorgio Moroder a lot because he was played in the clubs all the time. There was the band Japan we liked and Simple Minds too. All of it influenced what we were trying to do with Duran Duran. And then getting Roger to play drums changed everything about the way we sounded."

Aston Villa Football Club is one of the oldest and most venerable professional soccer teams in England. It was founded in Handsworth, now part of greater Birmingham, in 1874 and became an original member of the Football League (now called the Premier League) in 1888. Aston Villa, known as the Villans, or the Lions, began playing in its own stadium, Villa Park, in Aston, just northeast of central Birmingham, in 1897. The team's uniform still features colors officially termed claret and sky blue. In the late seventies, around the time Duran Duran was forming, Villa was surging forward after years in the lesser divisions of English football. Mighty Aston Villa, accompanying the national success of Duran Duran, would go on to win the league title in the 1980–1981 season.

Two of Aston Villa's biggest fans were the young drummer Roger Taylor and his father, who attended as many matches "down the Villa" as possible, especially the Second City Derby, the ancient rivalry between Aston Villa and the Blues—Birmingham City F.C. Roger Taylor (born April 26, 1960) was also a star keeper, or goalie, on his various school soccer teams. One of his earliest ambitions was to play in the goal for Aston Villa when he grew up.

"I lived in a part of Birmingham called Castle Bromwich, a suburb on the other side of town from Hollywood, where Nick and John are from. But it's a small city, really, and there was a very small nucleus of people our age who were into music, went to the same clubs, and were starting bands. It was natural that we'd meet up eventually.

"My older brother Stephen was a big influence on me. He liked old reggae from the sixties—Jimmy Cliff, Desmond Dekker, and the old rocksteady artists. I was brought up on his collection of Motown and Tamla records—those great musicians. It's probably still present in the way I actually play.

"Then I started getting into the music I liked when I was about thirteen, fourteen; no music lessons, completely self-taught. I started on bass actually, but I wasn't very good at it. A bunch of guys at school were forming a band and told me they needed a bass player. So I went down to the secondhand music shop and bought like a twenty-quid bass. But I couldn't get my fingers—or even my hands—around the neck. So they said, 'OK, try drums.' I thought that sounds like an idea, so I saved up and bought a set of drums for a hundred pounds or so. I actually found them in an advert in a newspaper somewhere—an old drum kit. I'd saved up my pocket money for weeks and weeks to get them. My dad came with me to help me pick it up. I set the drum kit up in my bedroom. We lived in an attached house, in a terrace, and years later our next-door neighbor told me that during my allocated practice hour, between when I got home from school, at five o'clock, and six, when my dad got home from the factory, they would take the pictures down from our common wall so they wouldn't fall off when I started hitting the drums. It was very tolerant of them. They were so nice.

"Like I said, I had no formal training. I used to play along to records. Then I got very into heavy rock, our local heroes Black Sabbath and Led Zeppelin. You know, Birmingham was an industrial town, a hard city during the era I'm talking about. Maybe 1968 to 1978. We had hard times then; business was bad for almost everyone. Brum was a pretty gloomy place, and coming out of a hard, industrial city, I suppose that's the sound that you'd associate with it—heavy rock.

"Then I got into the big bands like Rush. And I also liked most of what the DJs were playing on BRMB, our big local radio station. The kids in my school, Park Hall, were either into playing sports or forming bands. My first band was called Crucified Toad: electric violin, female bass player, me on drums, and a guitarist. We didn't do any gigs, just played and practiced. But this was when I realized for certain that drums were the instrument for me. Then I drifted through several bands and played some small shows. One band I was in played Saturday-morning matinee shows in a movie theater before the film came on. There we were, and all these kids in the audience started chucking things at us while we tried to pump out cover versions: 'Brown Sugar,' 'All Right Now' by Free, Fleetwood Mac's 'Albatross'—all those kinds of songs. I was like this fake hippie, with the long hair and the red Afghan sheepskin coat, sort of a junior Ginger Baker.

"Then punk came along and changed everything. I morphed into a total fucking punk. Spit, snot—the whole fucking thing. Ah, God! The hair came off, and what was left I dyed raven black. Bought a black leather biker's jacket and stuck safety pins in it. My playing went into the bog because I was more into seeing these sensational new bands and being part of the extremely sexy punk scene that was going on. We—everyone, girls and boys—were screwing each other blue! The sexual tension was stupendous when the Clash would come to Birmingham; then the Damned, Sham 69, and then the Slits. This was mind-blowing for myself at seventeen years old.

"But after a while I started playing again and got involved in a band called the Scent Organs, a punk band that played at punk shows. The singer was Jeff Thomas, who would sing with Duran Duran a bit later on. The Scent Organs were a good band. We actually won an award in 1978—Midlands Young Band of the Year. I've still got the tapes of the Organs, a true punk band—one hundred fucking miles an hour!

"I'd been to see a couple bands John Taylor was in, although he was still called Nigel then—a skinny kid with thick glasses. His band Dada was interesting and different, with back projections and clips, very Warhol type mixed media, circa sometime in 1965, much different than a stripped-down punk presentation. But anyone could see the whole thing had to go the other way now. John was playing the guitar in a rudimentary but swinging sort of way. He was untrained, like me, but he had great feel! I only saw them because the Scent Organs were dissolving, and Dada played at a pub I used to go to regularly. There was always a gig upstairs every Friday night.

"Then I was out of a job because the bass player went off to art college and the guitarist got a real job, so I was left with nothing to do since I'd already left school when I was sixteen. Suddenly I got a call from the guitarist in Dexys Midnight Runners, who were forming around that time in Birmingham: 'D'you wanna be our drummer then?'

"I turned them down.

"Within a few weeks, they had a smash hit record and were on *Top of the Pops*. I thought, 'Maybe that was my chance in life. Maybe I've missed it.' After all, I was almost eighteen years old. But then around that time, I went along to see the original Duran Duran. They were supporting a band called Fashion, red hot in Brum at the moment, fronted by a sharp character called Bob Reynolds. Duran came on with their riveting sequencer thing and an already astonishing stage presence, and just—well, I knew and thought they were great. Incredible. It was the kind of band that really does something for you, lifts you higher. And I remember thinking, 'This is really interesting. Duran is going to be the next big band out of Birmingham.'

"I also remember thinking, 'Hmmm—they don't have a drummer.'

"A couple of weeks later, I got a call from Andy Wickett, who had replaced Stephen Duffy in Duran Duran. We all knew each other from the Birmingham punk scene. He said, 'How do you fancy trying to play drums in this band? They use a rhythm unit, but they want to try a rhythm section.'

"And I said, 'Yeah, yeah, I saw them a few weeks ago and really thought they were ace. Yeah, I'll come along.'

"I was glad I wasn't a Midnight Runner. Glad I turned Dexy down.

"I found Duran Duran rehearsing in a little squat deep in the back streets of Birmingham, a broken-down decrepit house in a wasteland in a remote part of the city, no other houses around, just factories and warehouses. It was a Sunday morning, and nobody was around. But John Taylor, looking like some Renaissance prince, came out and helped me get my drums into this little brick house in an industrial estate. I just set up my kit and started to play. John picked up his bass guitar and started playing, and Nick fell in on keyboards, and the singer started to sing, and within minutes it began to jell. Me and John—we seemed right away to have something that locked in together. John told me straight out, 'We want to be like Chic. We want the rhythm section to be like Chic, like a disco-rhythm feel. We want you to play your high-hats [cymbals] like [Chic drummer] Tony Thompson does.' I think they'd never had a drummer who could do that. They all could play, but they had no feel on the high-hats.

"But I could do it. No problem. Like I said, I'd grown up with those Motown drummers in my brother's record collection. So there's what I call a subconscious influence there—like I knew that you had to *do* all that, to get that truly funky drumming. And I believe at the end of the session, it was like, 'Yeah, great—we'll see you at the next rehearsal. Shall we say Wednesday night?'

"That's how I got into Duran Duran."

Later on, Nick recalled that "one night, John and I were talking, and we realized to our horror that we didn't know our new drummer's last name. Eventually we asked him, 'Erm, Roger, what's your surname?'

"'Taylor,' he said. 'What's yours?'

"And we couldn't believe our 'luck'! Two unrelated Taylors!"

With Roger Taylor now in the band, Duran Duran was too loud for the back room of Bates's Toy Corner. Since singer Andy Wickett was living in the TV Eye squat in Cheapside, Duran Duran set up on the house's second floor—an awkward situation since the Subterranean Hawks (John: "The bastards!") were rehearsing their roots-oriented, Dylan-influenced new songs on the third floor. According to John, "Invariably the parties would meet in the dilapidated ground-floor kitchen where the dishes never got done, and sneers and cigarette papers would be traded." After Roger started playing with Duran Duran, and the rehearsals sounded more four-on-the-floor, someone scrawled "Disco Sucks" on Andy Wickett's door.

John later admitted, "Nick and I like rock, but we're not rockers. There's a distinction. We've always drifted toward the arty side of music: synthetics, costumes, Euro disco, whatever. So those two guys left Duran Duran to form a more straight-ahead rock band, which left Nick and I sort of scratching our heads, wondering where we should go with it. We ended up hooking up with members of another Birmingham band called TV Eye, named for the Iggy Pop song—a great band, amazing! When Duffy and Colley left to form a band with three members of TV Eye, it left their singer in the cold. So that's how Andy Wickett hooked up with Nick and me."

Around this time in 1979, John and Nick were starting to hang out in the newish wine bars that were sprouting up on Corporation Street as an alternative to Brum's gritty pubs. The girls were more attractive in the wine bars and the music more au courant. This was where

John first heard Chic's "Everybody Dance," with funk, rock, and disco sounds all blended together in the same song. He recalled, "The impact of that song was huge, because the bass guitar came across as the lead instrument. I had never heard bass played that way. . . . Later I picked up a bass guitar that Andy Wickett had in his bedroom and started playing around on it. I found I could quite easily imitate the style of the Chic bassist, whose name I didn't then know, as well as the bass lines of other disco hits like Sylvester's 'You Make Me Feel (Mighty Real).' So just on pure instinct, I decided to switch to bass. I told Nick we'd find a guitar player later. So I took what little savings I had and bought a bass of my own, a cheap Hondo knockoff, but it sounded good when I started jamming with Roger.

"Duran Duran's recording career began around that time with four demos we cut with a great local guy named Bob Lamb. He was the drummer with the Steve Gibbons Band. Steve Gibbons was a famous face around Birmingham, a guy with a lot of style. Everyone liked him. His band got signed to the Who's label, Track Records, and then made it to *Top of the Pops* with 'Tupelo Mississippi Flash' and then actually toured America with the Who. They were the kings of the Birmingham pub scene, which of course didn't mean that they were particularly interesting, but they *were* one of the great pub-rock bands.

"Then the drummer, Bob Lamb, got out of the band and set up a four-track studio in his bed-sit [studio apartment] in King's Heath. He'd put the bed up on a loft and the gear underneath. A corner of the room was turned into a drum booth. He did the first UB40 album in there on a rough, simple eight-track machine—this huge-selling album! He did the first few Duran Duran demos, he did the Fashion demos, TV Eye, and Lilac Time, which was Stephen Duffy's band after the Hawks were unable to get off the ground. Bob was a really important guy, because he showed all these local, younger musicians what they could really do. Bob took that extra little bit of care with his recordings, and he had a nice and gentle touch with the kids he was working with.

"Now, thinking back, I realize that the whole Bob Lamb thing— that tiny studio—was *so* Birmingham, in that era. It's a great city; there's a certain humbleness and humility there, not like fucking

Manchester, where you've really got to shout to be heard. Birmingham is kind of low key. It's multiracial. There was a lot of interesting music going on, most of it drawing on Black music in a way. We
had Dexys Midnight Runners doing their soul-rebel thing. We had
UB40, with Black and White musicians. Fashion was following the
Police into playing White reggae. And there was the whole two-tone
movement; they were mostly from Coventry, but it was very close
to us. These were Black and White ska bands: Madness, the Selecter.
Birmingham's two-tone band was the English Beat, real good, Dave
Wakeling and Ranking Roger. They shot their video for 'Mirror in
the Bathroom' in the city's biggest nightclub, the Rum Runner on
Broad Street.

"So we recorded four songs with Bob Lamb. One of them was
an early version of Andy Wickett's song called—yes—'Girls on Film.'
[The others were 'See Me Repeat Me,' 'Reincarnation,' and 'Working
the Steel.'] We'd never had any experience with multitrack recording.
Bob took great care with the microphones on Roger's drum kit. The
little studio was a jungle of cables and amps and mic stands. I played
bass and then overdubbed the guitars because we hadn't found anyone by then, although we were starting to get serious about looking
for one."

The members of Duran Duran were astonished when they listened to the playback of Bob's rough mixes, surprised to hear what he
had done with their sound. He totally nailed the dance-floor groove
they wanted. He'd recorded Roger's high-hat cymbal by itself, which
made Duran Duran actually sound a little like an American disco
band. Smiles all around! John recalled, "We sounded tight and funky.
We were like, 'That's us?' With Bob's help, we had suddenly moved
on from our brittle art school atmospheres to create a danceable, via-
ble, pop group sound."

The band's confidence, somewhat eroded by betrayals and defec-
tions, was restored by how massive Bob Lamb had made them sound.
They began discussing their next step: even before finding a guitar
player, they would be taking their demo tapes to record companies
and trying to land a deal.

Autumn 1979 was unusually rainy in the West Midlands, and a cold winter was predicted. England's politics had entered a period of substantial turmoil as new prime minister Margaret Thatcher began her program of disrupting a failing status quo and realigning the country's political economy to the right. For Duran Duran, it also was a time of upheaval, with difficult personnel shuffles. They hired a London guitarist named Alan Curtis, attracted by an ad in *Melody Maker*, and added their cool Black friend Fozzi (from the band Vision Collision) to sing harmonies with Andy Wickett. This lineup of Duran Duran played shows at the Golden Eagle pub, the Cellar Bar, and the Red Star on Essex Street. But they weren't always well received. In November, Duran Duran was booted off the stage in the student cafeteria of Birmingham University. The scholars threw anything they could find at the band, who walked off after a few songs, soaked in beer, ketchup, and HP Sauce.

Duran Duran then eased out Andy Wickett, who'd been a less-than-dynamic front man. They replaced him with Jeff Thomas, the singer in Roger's former band the Scent Organs. Fortunately, Andy Wickett departed on relatively good terms; he left Duran Duran with "Girls on Film" (very much a work in progress) as well as his own girlfriend Jane, who began dating Nick and helped manage Duran Duran's fledgling career. Meanwhile, John Taylor hooked up with the former girlfriend of the Subterranean Hawks' guitarist. "She was the first girl I slept with," he later wrote. "We went to church together the following morning, good Catholic girl that she was. That settled the battle of the bands."

Later that November, Duran Duran booked time in Bob Lamb's tiny studio and recorded another demo tape, including the nascent "Girls on Film," "Enigmatic Swimmers," "See Me Repeat Me," and "Breaking Away." Again, Bob Lamb had worked his magic, and John and Nick decided it was time to try to land a recording contract. Jeff Thomas drove the group, including Jane, down the M6 motorway to London, where they tried to storm the big record companies— without appointments. At EMI—the Beatles' label on Manchester Square—they couldn't even get into the building. It was the same at Phonogram, just off Oxford Street. They had better luck at Island Records' headquarters in a white Edwardian mansion on St. Peter's Square in Hammersmith. This was great because Duran Duran really wanted to be on ultracool independent label Island Records, home of Bob Marley, Grace Jones, Robert Palmer, and the B-52's.

The little group from Birmingham was received by Island's press officer, Rob Partridge, who took note of the boys' eyeliner and lip gloss. The glam look was considered passé in London. John handed him the band's demo. "Birmingham," Rob joshed. "North of the border, eh?" He explained that Island owner Chris Blackwell was in Jamaica and that the company's A&R (artists and repertoire) people weren't around. But Rob let them play their demo cassette over studio speakers, told them it sounded promising, and said he would give the tape to Chris when he returned to London. Had they heard of Island's new signing, U2? Rob thanked them for coming in and wished them luck. Duran Duran headed back to Birmingham. At least they had tried.

And that wasn't the only loss of the year. According to John, "By Christmas, Jane had drifted away. Shame. She had legs for days. They just weren't enough to get us a record deal."

Upon their return, Bob Lamb explained to Duran Duran that big record companies never signed new bands unless they had management whom the label could trust. No one was going to give a substantial recording budget to a bunch of teenagers with a couple of catchy little tunes. But then, in the early days of 1980, as the much-anticipated new decade began, Duran Duran caught its first big break—in the form of a gig at Birmingham's biggest nightclub. This was the Rum Runner, at 273 Broad Street in central Birmingham.

John and Nick knew about the Rum Runner but thought it out of their league. The club was an old warehouse that had once been a casino and was patronized by an older, more affluent crowd: playboys, characters, reputed gangsters, professional athletes and the girls that loved them, plus older local musicians from bands like Black Sabbath and the Move, who came in late after gigs. The club was the most happening adult venue in the Midlands and was crowded almost every night.

Meanwhile, John and Nick had been looking for new places to play, desperate to avoid the upstairs rooms of depressing pubs. They were thinking of wine bars and art galleries instead. One cold Friday afternoon, they were in the Ikon Gallery near the Bullring, playing their most recent demo for the owner. While walking up Hill Street afterward, they noticed a poster touting a Bowie night at the Rum Runner, advertising "New Sounds / New Styles."

This looked promising, so they walked up to Broad Street and knocked on the club's front door. John recalled, "The only thing I knew about the Rum Runner was that it was very old-school. Nick and I had never been in there. It wasn't on our radar. We knew it drew an older clientele, more sophisticated. It had been used as a location for a BBC TV series called *Gangsters*, which gave the Rum Runner a somewhat shady reputation, the kind that didn't hurt the business after dark."

The club's doorman let them in and led them up an outside fire escape to the club's office, where they met Paul Berrow, one of the owners. He was older, taller, about thirty. John described him as "a tall, rather debonair guy, suavely dressed in very un-Birmingham clothes: silk scarves, cravats, handmade shirts." Paul explained that he and his brother Michael owned the club, having gotten it from their father, who operated many of the city's casinos, clubs, and venues for jazz. The Berrow brothers had recently been in New York and had gotten into Studio 54, the legendarily decadent hub of Manhattan nightlife, which had opened two years earlier, in 1977. Now they were back in Birmingham, determined to turn the Rum Runner into a Midlands replica of Studio 54, with a thunderous sound system, glamorous decor, lots of mirrored walls and green glass, bars on three different levels, and a velvet rope with a long line outside, filled with eager clubbers desperate to get inside.

Nick handed Paul Berrow their demo cassette and murmured something about playing it when he had a chance, but Paul Berrow was keen to hear it right then. "Follow me, chaps," he beckoned. "Let's have a listen to this downstairs."

Nick and John exchanged glances on the fire escape. This guy seemed to really get them. Paul Berrow threw a switch in the club, and the room lit up in fairy lights, which sparkled and reflected off the Perspex mirrors lining the walls. Another switch turned on the amplifiers, and four giant speakers began to hum in each corner of the club. He ran through the whole tape, listening intently. "Girls on Film" and "Aztec Moon" had never sounded better. When the tape was finished, Paul Berrow smiled and gave Duran Duran the news they were longing to hear.

John recalled him saying, "Well, chaps, this is bloody very interesting. My brother and I have been thinking about getting into management. Why don't you come 'round to the club tonight and bring the rest of the boys with you?"

Later that night, Nick and John returned to the Rum Runner with Roger Taylor, Alan Curtis, and singer Jeff Thomas. Paul Berrow greeted them effusively and introduced his younger brother Michael, who seemed quieter, less eager, "more circumspect," as John put it. Colored lights twinkled and strobes flashed as the club's DJ blasted Studio 54's disco-heavy playlist through the six-foot-tall speakers: Chic, Grace Jones, Sylvester, Chaka Khan, Rod Stewart belting "Do Ya Think I'm Sexy?" The Rum Runner seemed to be full of characters: tough guys, well-dressed women, people who looked as though they knew their way around a line of cocaine. The only young people in the Rum Runner were the service staff. Roger Taylor was immediately taken with a beautiful, dark-haired teenage dance student named Giovanna Cantone, who worked in the coatroom. John and Nick proceeded to convince Paul Berrow to book a Duran Duran show in March, opening for Fashion. Several days later, the boys excitedly moved their equipment into one of the unused upstairs rooms at the Rum Runner and set up their gear after Paul said they could rehearse there in the daytime.

Nick remembered, "They [the Berrows] were young, hip, quite smart. They were also ambitious. When they mentioned a management deal, we said, 'Sure, let's keep talking.' We were thrilled someone was interested in us."

John added, "Having a connection with the Rum Runner was crucial. Paul and Michael became our patrons, and now we had this establishment behind us. . . . The deal was clear. Our job was to write the songs and develop a sound, and it was the Berrows' responsibility to find us places to play, buy us whatever gear we needed, and ultimately find us a record deal."

Duran Duran's daily rehearsals at the Rum Runner soon turned them into a tight five-piece band. They played the Rum Runner for the first time on March 12, 1980, working on a low stage in the club's main room. The club's clientele seemed to like them. People were pounding Paul Berrow on the back and saying congratulations, predicting that these kids could be massive. John Taylor thought it was the band's best performance to date. But it wasn't all aces. Early the next morning, the phone rang. It was their guitarist, Alan Curtis, calling from a pay phone on the M1 motorway. Alan told John that the "heavy" scene and rough clientele at the Rum Runner scared him. He was just a hippie, Alan explained, and he was quitting Duran Duran and going back to London.

But that wasn't all. Jeff Thomas and Paul Berrow began to have "artistic differences" because Jeff seemed to be in the band as a lark. What's more, Paul also told Nick and John that Jeff couldn't sing. Jeff told Duran Duran that it was him or Paul. *Someone* had to go. Michael Berrow got the job of telling Jeff Thomas he was out of Duran Duran. And with that, as John later noted, they "were now looking for a guitarist *and* a singer."

By April 1980, Duran Duran had become part of the Rum Runner inner circle. Paul and Michael Berrow, excited about this development in their lives, invested in equipment for their new mascots, which included notably better and bigger amplifiers and speakers. Nick, John, and Roger were given jobs in the club to offset their expenses: Nick took on DJ shifts, expertly spinning records that gave the club a much hipper ambience; Roger collected glasses and bused tables; John worked the front door and did odd jobs. As he later recalled, "Every night at the Rum Runner, we were exposed to the best of contemporary music—European dance music, electro, funk, disco, and jazz funk—all accompanied by a steady stream of vintage wine, champagne, a little smoke now and again, and even a little toot."

Auditions for a new singer and guitarist carried on, with the Berrows taking out ads in *Brum Beat* and the national music papers, trolling for young musicians looking for work. Guitar players arrived from all over the Midlands and further afield, but no one had the look that Nick and John wanted. The ones who played great had the wrong look. The ones that looked perfect—hair, makeup, wardrobe—couldn't play. The boys were also taken up by young local fashion designers Patti Bell and Jane Kahn, *très* chic boutique owners who began working on Duran Duran's crucial style—New Romantic for the new decade.

Duran Duran working at the Rum Runner also gave the big club a new cachet, especially with the girls. They were tired of having beer spilled all over them every night at Barbarella's. The boys followed the girls, and on weeknights Nick sharpened his DJ skills as the young crowd danced to the newest music and vintage Bowie, Roxy, and Ultravox. Nick remembered his club gig fondly: "I had two turntables, stacks of twelve-inch vinyl records, and I worked hard on figuring out what worked with an audience, rhythm-wise, what the crowd would respond to. In fact, sometimes I'd deliberately try to empty the floor to see what didn't work. I'd have to say that DJ-ing was a very important element of my career. I used to be quite good at mixing. Like Bowie's 'John, I'm Only Dancing' [blended] quite well into Roxy Music's 'Both Ends Burning.' I'd fill the dance floor with three popular songs and then play something that none of them knew. And it was so crowded they couldn't move, so they had to dance to it. And that's the way you break new music in clubs.

"So, we were lucky; we never starved like some bands. But I was grossly underpaid as the DJ because after a bit, I was able to take the club, on a stone-cold Tuesday night—the night from fucking hell when no one came—to being absolutely packed. On my Bowie nights, all of Birmingham's gays began showing up, in costume. For many of them, it was the first time they 'came out,' and it ballooned into a big thing, drawing people from Coventry and suburbs like Kidderminster. In the end, they had to give me Friday night as well, which was so mobbed by glam humanity that words cannot describe the scene.

"I got fifteen pounds a night for this.

"Truth is, this was a great learning curve for me, being the DJ at the Rum Runner. I was sixteen years old; it was the biggest club in the second-biggest town in the country. I was learning how to entertain a big crowd that wanted nothing more than to dance, get high, have fun. Our early fans—these mad people at the Rum Runner—were some of the best people I've ever met—*in my life*. I still love them all."

Nick's DJ sets usually included Duran Duran's contemporaries like the Human League, Ultravox, and Simple Minds (everyone liked singer Jim Kerr's Glaswegian vocals). Inspirations and influences also featured David Bowie's "Always Crashing the Same Car," Mick Ronson's "Only After Dark," Bryan Ferry crooning "The 'In' Crowd," and Iggy Pop's "Passenger." Pushing danceable electronica, Nick programmed Japanese electro-pop band Yellow Magic Orchestra, Kraftwerk's "Robots," Tubeway Army (Gary Numan's first band), post-punk band Magazine, the Normal playing "Warm Leatherette," and Brian Eno's "The True Wheel." To fill the dance floor, Nick deployed disco warhorses like "I Feel Love" by Donna Summer and Grace Jones belting out "Private Life." Local heroes UB40 were on all the time. Every once in a while, he would sneak in surprises like art-punk band Wire's "I Am the Fly," with its minimalist synth and guitar effects, or the Psychedelic Furs' "Sister Europe." When OMD (Orchestral Maneuvers in the Dark) came out with hypnotic "Enola Gay" (named for the airplane that dropped an A-bomb on Japan in 1945), Nick had to play it almost every night.

When Nick suggested to Paul Berrow that he get a bit more money for packing the Rum Runner's dance floor, Paul raised Nick's DJ fee to twenty-five pounds per shift.

In May 1980, something happened that, to some, seemed to foreshadow Britain beginning to pull itself out of its long, post-imperial downward spiral.

For years, England had been living through very hard times. A year earlier, Margaret Thatcher had been elected Britain's first female prime minister, inheriting an economy with 22 percent inflation and almost two million unemployed. The Irish Republican Army was setting off bombs all across the United Kingdom, blowing up pubs and buses, murdering and maiming hundreds, including members of Parliament in Westminster and Lord Mountbatten, a member of the royal family. Entire streets were blown up in Belfast, Northern Ireland. This was war. Brixton, in South London, was still smoldering after a violent race riot. Soccer fans—hooligan "firms"—battled each other in the streets at matches all over the kingdom. An entire generation of school-leavers, like Nick Bates and the Taylors, was contemplating how they'd make a living in the nation's decimated economy.

Then, on May 5, six terrorists seized the Iranian embassy in London's South Kensington. When negotiations broke down, they began shooting hostages and dumping bodies out the front door. Finally, Mrs. Thatcher ordered in teams from the elite SAS, the Special Air Services. As the nation watched a live broadcast on the BBC, the SAS broke into the embassy, killed five of the six terrorists, and freed the nineteen remaining hostages. The whole operation lasted just seventeen minutes.

The rescue inspired nationalism that had long been dormant in the UK. The SAS motto—"Who Dares Wins"—was on everyone's lips. Finally, England had gotten something right. Congratulations poured in. The flag, the Union Jack, which had been hauled down all over the world as bands played and an empire collapsed, was now flying in the springtime breeze with renewed pride. Margaret Thatcher, a grocer's daughter with an Oxford degree in chemistry, who had come to power as an economic reformer determined to balance the national household budget, was now seen as a formidable woman warrior. The Russians called her the Iron Lady—a nickname that foreshadowed events still to come in the faraway Falkland Islands.

In the early eighties, "Who Dares Wins" would become emblematic of a new national narrative, liberating Britain from its battered reputation of the seventies. And when Duran Duran and the other young New Romantic bands broke through into America and the rest of the world, they became—through their music and especially videos—colorful cultural symbols of Mrs. Thatcher's new spirit of reform, renewal, and enterprise. To young aspirant rock stars like John Taylor, Nick Rhodes, and Roger Taylor, "Who Dares Wins" prophesized a more vibrant and confident era into which they were coming of age and an exciting sense of the present rushing to meet the future.

Meanwhile, Duran Duran kept rehearsing upstairs at the Rum Runner almost every day, hammering out the basics of what would become the bedrock style of the band—a chic rhythm unit with the glacial icing of Nick's synths. Still, there was this nagging absence of a lead guitar. John remembered, "I wanted someone like Gary Moore, the Belfast guitarist, who we'd seen on [the TV show] *Old Grey Whistle Test* around that time. What I liked about Gary was that he had this really rowdy, rock side to him, but he could also slip into this cool, clean Steve Cropper kind of rhythm. I knew for certain that we didn't want a guitar player that could just blaze away like Steve Jones [of Sex Pistols]. It had to have a funky side as well."

Searching for a new guitarist, Paul Berrow took out a larger ad in *Melody Maker*, hoping to attract more attention and find the guitarist that his band now desperately needed.

Between April and September, on the northeast coast of England, the warmer air of the summer months tends to condense as it sails toward the North Sea, creating a heavy layer of fog, known locally as a sea fret. A bright, sunshiny day can turn gray and damp in a moment. And yet the charged ocean atmosphere also produces beautiful red dawns and flaming sunsets over St. Mary's Lighthouse, Whitley Bay, near where Andy Taylor grew up.

One hundred seventy-five miles northeast of Birmingham, near the great brooding city of Newcastle upon Tyne, nineteen-year-old rock-and-roll guitarist Andy Taylor (born February 16, 1961) unpacked his gear in his father's house, tired after weeks of playing "Shotgun" and "Green Onions" for officers and soldiers at American military bases in Germany. The Cold War was still on, full scale.

Andy's mother was nowhere to be found. She had abandoned the family for another man when Andy was just five; he came home from his first day of school to find all traces of his mother—including her clothes and possessions—had disappeared, and it would be years before he even saw her again. So Andy and his brothers were raised by their father and, especially, by their grandmother.

"I'm actually from a small northern fishing village called Cullercoats . . . about a mile north of the [River] Tyne. My whole extended family all still live there. My brothers, my cousins, all surviving aunts and uncles: everybody still lives in Newcastle, almost without exception. They're basically in Cullercoats or in the next village up, Tynemouth. No one's moved anywhere.

"When it's northern, it's real working class. You have to get a trade or go and do what your dad did. There's this social pressure to stay and keep it going. I go up there now and see all the guys I grew up with, and it seems to me like everyone's just stuck in a tunnel. At the other end, you come up middle-aged and what's happened? One of my cousins was a top-level civil servant, almost cabinet level, but she still lived in Newcastle because there's a lot of government offices up there. Another cousin was a top lawyer—'Young Lawyer of the Year'—but he still practices in Newcastle.

"It's like the pub names never change. The families just stay there. Scotland is like that [too]: Glasgow, Edinburgh. The further north you get, the more people tend to stay, or the less easy it is for them to escape. It depends which way you want to look at it.

"But my grandmother, see, she wasn't from the village. She moved to the village to marry my grandfather. She was a country girl, and all my family were inshore fishermen. My father was too, until the midsixties. The corbel was a small inshore boat, flat bottom, single mast, they use in the northern English fishery. Every male Taylor was a fisherman. But my grandmother wasn't from fishing folk, and I don't think she ever really settled into our life.

"But it was really she who brought me up. Elizabeth Jean Taylor—she was the one. Because my mother split when I was very young. In the north of England in the seventies, to have a one-parent family was strange. To have that parent be a father was even stranger. I was the only kid in the village to have a one-parent father. There was no divorce up there at all. But my parents eventually divorced, yeah, and my father won custody. But his mother, my grandmother, was in the house and brought us up.

"And she was probably more sympathetic to us than two parents might have been, you know? Sometimes it's that gap in life that allows you to manage these things. When you have two parents, you're watched by them. But when you only got one, it's easier to fall through the cracks, socially, and become a little more experimental, explore, do other things.

"My grandmother was from a rural area, further south about forty miles but completely different. Fishing areas are very hard: docks, boats; all the families are very tough. *Very* tough. A lot of poaching went on, tax fiddles, how much you declared when you weighed in. I mean, we all grew up on lobster—fresh lobster—just what they didn't declare, we used to eat. We used to get fresh sole, almost given away around the houses, an amazingly healthy diet. Everyone is physically fit, and most live to old age. Fish oil, salmon, cod, the northern sort of fish stock. My grandmother lived to ninety.

"Because she didn't come from there, from Cullercoats, when I started exploring music and I was in my teens, and actually thinking about going away and trying to start a band, she was like, 'Leave. Leave. Go on—take your chance!' And also she was spiritual; she used to go to séances and all of that, and that she had *seen* it—that one of the grandchildren was going to travel afar, and it was me.'"

Andy had been playing the electric guitar professionally since he left school at sixteen, though he was more focused on having fun and learning his trade than making money. By June 1980, he was itching to move up and out—away from Newcastle and into some bigger city where he could make better money and maybe have a place of his own. With this in mind, he walked to the newsstand around the corner from his house and bought the latest issue of *Melody Maker*. He checked out the paper's classified ads for musicians, and a large black-bordered ad caught his eye. It was the biggest ad on the page. These people meant business. A few days later, Andy and his guitar were on a train to Birmingham.

Andy had a good feeling about Birmingham right from the start. "You know, I used to love that UB40 album before I ever went to Birmingham—such a great record. You had the whole punk thing, and then the new wave thing, and then—this freakin' reggae band from Birmingham? You know? And he—[singer] Ali Campbell—sounded a bit like Stevie Wonder to me. So there was a lot happening around the Midlands area at the time I moved down there. And from where I come from—Newcastle—down to there, it was just like, *fuckin' hell!* There were so many bands, so many weirdoes, and so many chicks.

"I walked into the Duran Duran rehearsal at this big club called the Rum Runner. The first thing I noticed was they all had these weird shoes on. How can you *wear* shoes like that? I'm in like, some sort of pumps or something. The whole Brum thing really did have a sort of different feel about it."

"The guitar? See, the errant ways of my mother actually led me into a lot of this, which is a frightening thing for me. I didn't talk to her. I had no relationship with her. It's very weird, but it is what it is. You know—you have to let sleeping dogs lie. But, *because of this family situation*, my father had to get a babysitter for him to have any freedom to go out because my mother was always 'working.' (But she wasn't working, as we found out later. She was out partying—a lot.) So he'd go out, the babysitter would come, who was like a young apprentice who worked with him. The babysitter played guitar—a bashed-up old acoustic—and later he gave it to me. I repainted it and just sat down and started up. No, I don't have it anymore. I traded it for something like two quid when I bought my first electric guitar.

"Back then, BBC2 had a guitar program called *Hold Down a Chord*, and there was a book that went with the videos. I had to get that book! And this book basically had the chords and country-style finger-picking lessons, which I loved. That's the first thing I learned, to play finger-picking acoustic and all the chord shapes that go with it. That's what became my technique.

"I've always been really lucky. I've always fallen into techniques or working with older people when I was younger. So I learned all this sort of bar seven and eight. We had these old fishing houses, terraces [row houses], we used to live in. We lived downstairs, my grandparents lived in the middle, and upstairs at the top was where they used to keep old stock and things for making lobster pots and twine and fishing stuff. It was now an empty loft because they had another workshop down the road, so I used to go up there and practice and learn, where nobody could hear me. I'm ten years old—this is 1971. So you had the whole family living in the house, and to get out of the way I used to have to go to the top. I just sat there for months and months, and this TV program was on, and then eventually the chords make sense when you're listening to records. And then you can start playing the chords—to music.

"There was nothing else to do when you were a kid in Cullercoats, apart from going to the beach. That little old terrace where we lived is gone now. It's a car park. Color television started in England around then. And people used to buy a lot of records, stack them all up, and play them. Then the cassette came in, and you could sit and practice your guitar with your little cassette machine, see what you sound like. And Radio Luxembourg—that was the other thing, especially further up north. Radio Luxembourg came in loud and clear, so I used to listen to it every night when I was a kid because it had a much more diverse selection of music, long before [BBC] Radio One.

"My father was a big music lover, a brilliant harmonica player. And then—this was the freakiest thing—when I was about nine or ten, and we moved after he split up with my mother, and the fishing cottages we lived in were slated to be pulled down, I found a fucking guitar in his wardrobe! His guitar! And I'm like, 'Why didn't you tell me?'

"And he's like, 'I never had the balls to do what you were doing, especially at only ten years old.'

"I'd always wondered how he learned to play the harmonica so good. He'd dabbled with the guitar but couldn't really play and had kept the guitar hidden. Really weird. It was his skeleton in the closet, so there's this funny thing I've always shared with my father. And also in the wardrobe I found his old teddy boy suits: pegged jacks, drainpipe trousers, the full Elvis. It was switchblades and tire irons on Saturday nights. Violence and style. My dad! Who knew? He was an absolutely beautiful man. His name was Ronnie Taylor.

"So you start discovering these things about your family. It turned out my grandmother was a part-time singer, but only when she'd had the one or two. Of course, no one actually did music; it was just a pastime for them. You wonder why your family is so supportive, and then you find these things out.

"Because all of our family lived in close proximity, we got together a lot, played music and sang—just little things like that. It was [the] Beatles, Amen Corner, and all those old sixties things like Herman's Hermits and the Kinks and the Who, of course, and all the old Hendrix stuff—my father had absolutely everything. We loved the Animals, from Newcastle, of course. I was six when *Sgt. Pepper* came out, and I've still got the copy my cousin gave me when I was seven. My cousin Marjorie was my other big musical influence. She had all the Faces and the Stones and Rod Stewart. She was a massive music fan. Between her and my father, they used to buy every record that came out.

"So, you learn the music, and you can relate it to the record, and you begin to figure out little things, like the guitar's got to be in the same pitch to be able to play. You have to tune it properly. And then there's E: you hear it on the record, a place to start. You say to yourself, 'There's the C chord.' Then what's the fuckin' next one? D? *Ooooo.* There's only three—is that all they need for a song? Ha ha ha! That process—I mean, it's so fundamental. These days, there's too many ways to hear yourself doing music without going through that fundamental process. But—sitting on your own as a kid, learning to play in time—I didn't know how valuable that was to me.

"But I did have some lessons when I was older—half a dozen lessons from a guy called Dave Black, who—incredibly—took Mick Ronson's place in the Spiders from Mars. When Bowie left the Spiders from Mars, it was Mick Ronson, Woody Woodmansey on drums, Trevor Bolder on bass, and a guy called Pete MacDonald singing—he was from Newcastle! Then Mick Ronson quit, and this guy called Dave Black got Ronson's job.

"He lived across the road from us. So I—a *massive* Bowie fan—used to see Woody and Trevor Bolder come up to Dave Black's house in their platform shoes, just walking in across the road, and I'm thinking—'Wow!'

"Anyway, one day—I was about twelve or thirteen—I plucked up the courage to ask Dave Black if he could teach me some of the tricks on lead guitar. Bless his heart, he showed me like, from the chords, the scales that go in major and minor, et cetera. He charged me one pound per lesson, for about six weeks. And then he said, 'Look, there's nothing more I can teach you. You just gotta learn it.' But it was really like leapfrogging, because it would have taken forever to figure out scales and stuff by myself. So—lead guitar: most of the lead guitar [technique] I learned was a combination of [AC/DC's] Angus Young and Dave Black, who was more of a bluesy, Clapton, traditional sort of English player—*really sweet!*"

Still working on his skills, Andy joined his first band as a teenager. "So I was about thirteen when I got all that together, and then I started playing in bands. And Dave Black helped me again by introducing me to some older guys. He was such a really good, helpful fellow, and he just kind of thought I could do it. The first professional gig that I got, he introduced me to that band as well. They were called the Gigolos—when I was fifteen. Ha ha ha ha! But it was school-leaving time, and I got a job in a band instead of on a building site or a fishing boat. The Gigolos played in workingmen's clubs. That was it. The pay was thirty-five quid per week, about double what you'd get 'on the buildings.' We played all over the northeast in 1978, up and down the motorway, playing covers of other people's songs. The clubs put on strippers on Sunday afternoons, and we'd have to play 'Devil Woman' by Cliff Richard. The punters were all wearing cloth caps, were all reading the racing papers, and were all pretending not to notice the girls. One Sunday in Sunderland, I watched a fire-breathing stripper called Singed Minge put on her show.

"Then in mid-1978, I signed a contract with a cover band to play gigs at American military bases in Germany and Italy. The Cold War was still happening, there were a few hundred thousand GIs in Europe, and they needed entertainment. My dad came to the ferry to see me off to Ostend and a different life. This band played everything from Stevie Wonder to Aerosmith in massive fortresses like Ramstein Air Base, near Frankfurt. I worked up a fifteen-minute guitar solo for 'Free Bird' that drove the soldiers crazy. They would chant between songs, stuff like 'Let's nuke Iran!' They really went nuts when we played too much AC/DC. The soldiers went bonkers; the colonels who ran the shows told us to cool it down. In the officers' clubs, we played jazzy stuff and the Eagles. Then I started sharing lead vocals, singing harmonies, and I had to learn the words to all the great American songs we were covering.

"It was great to hang out with the Americans, most of them not much older than me. They turned me on to American weed, and they'd throw big parties on the weekends. I remember thinking, 'Shit—if the Russians attack now—we'll be partying.' They'd have talent shows, and we were the band. Some dude would get up and do 'Gimme Some Loving,' and then six huge Black sergeants would get up and sing 'Papa Was a Rolling Stone.'

"Our contract called for us to play six hours per night. Exhausting, but it made my voice much stronger when I was very young. So those years. . . . Now I've done the whole northern circuit and most of the American bases in Germany and Italy. I hung out with GIs from the age of sixteen, and that's sort of how I got into weed. Eventually our contract expired and I had to return home, but the experience exposed me to a world beyond Cullercoats and Newcastle.

"By then, I estimate I'd played something like six hundred gigs, and I was only eighteen years old. The Americans had shown me what self-confidence was all about, and I knew it was time to join a bigger band. I started checking out the ads in *Melody Maker* every week; it used to feature adverts seeking musicians for bands. Even Led Zeppelin started out that way. Then one day [in April 1980] I spotted one that said something like, 'Live Wire Guitarist / Ronson, Jones, Gilmour / Powerful, Bluesy, Melodic.'

"And I thought, powerful, bluesy, melodic. Of the three criteria, I was all three. And then, when I got down there [to Birmingham], it turned out that they [Duran Duran] were very much into Chic—John Taylor, particularly. Now, when you do all those air force bases we used to do, you have to learn every different technique—you've got to—and you can't fuck up because they knew their music and they'll send you packing. Or you'll get stuck with the officers' mess gig, and you have to play—I can hardly bring myself to say it—'Midnight at the Oasis' all night. So you learn all these Stevie Wonder chords and structures you get from doing hours and hours of cover versions for drunken soldiers and airmen, backing big-titted German strippers, working shit hours in grimy clubs in the north of England where they couldn't fucking care if you were there or not. All that experience gets you to a point where something significant happens to you as an artist. It's actually a brilliant grounding for any artist, but especially a musician.

"So I cut out the advert, which was not one of the usual puny three-liners. It was in a box! I thought, 'Oh, that's cost them at least ten pounds.' So I walked down to the call box by the news agent and made the call that would change my life forever.

"Margaret, who was the secretary at the Rum Runner at the time, answered the phone, and I'm like, 'What's the band like?'

"She replies, in this thick Brummie accent, 'Wull, their name is Jirn Jirn.'

"'What? What's their name?'

"'Oooo, they're culled Juu-run Juu-run.'

"I couldn't understand what she was saying, but I did learn that they had management, and I would have to go down to this club in Birmingham. So I sold some stuff, got a train ticket with the money, and I'm on British Rail with my guitar and a fifty-watt Marshall combo amp that you could carry around. Four hours later, I walked into the Rum Runner on Broad Street, not far from New Street Station. The first person I bumped into was Mulligan, the keyboard player in Fashion. And he was right *out there*, fucking dressed up and all that, in the middle of the day: silks, scarves, blond dreadlocks, sharp suit. The shoes alone would have gotten him stabbed in Newcastle.

"The band was actually called Duran Duran. They did have management, but they did not have a singer, or any lyrics, or a record deal. But it didn't take me long to suss that the band rehearsed in the club—not bad! That was a great breeding ground for a band, because you'd rehearse in the club, hang out in the club, get drunk for free. Half the girls we married, we met in the Rum Runner. Tracey [Andy's future wife, from Wolverhampton]—I met her there. Her and her brother used to do our hair; we'd go down to the salon, and they'd put dye in our hair that no one else would do, and that's how I met her. Giovanna, who married Roger, worked in the cloakroom.

"The first one I met was John. He came up to me, held out his hand, and said, 'Hello, my name is Nigel.' He was a tall skinny kid with thick round glasses. He looked a little like Harry Potter. Roger Taylor was also there, and we had a good larf that we all had the same last name. They had long, floppy hair and wore eye makeup and were into the whole look that later would be called New Romantic. I'd arrived wearing jeans and a scruffy pair of sneakers, obviously coming from a different background, maybe a different world.

"Nick Bates arrived next: naturally androgynous, even without the eyeliner and lip gloss. He was the youngest, not quite eighteen. He was late, but then Nick was always late. His voice was nasal, his accent flat, like he wasn't trying to sound local. I thought he sounded a bit like a robot, the way he talked. (They thought I sounded like I was from Scotland. We could hardly understand each other at first.) When we got to playing, I saw that Nick couldn't sing, or dance, but also that he produced fascinating keyboard textures that he built into layers of sound, something that I'd never heard before. They didn't have any songs, except for the chorus to 'Girls on Film,' written by Andy Wickett, the singer they'd just fired. Nick told me, 'This is one of the songs we've got, and we really think it's going to be a hit.'

"We jammed that afternoon, and I think I helped them come up with more of the arrangement for 'Girls on Film.' They were interested that I could do all these different styles—rock, blues, R&B, funky stuff. I knew I was doing well because gradually all the secretaries and staff came downstairs to hear us and watch us play together. There were a lot of smiles, and they invited me to stay on for the evening. The Rum Runner was about to open for the night, and I could see from the people lining up to get in that the place was going to be full. I got the last train back to Newcastle, having been driven to the station by the Berrow brothers, and I was very excited by what had happened that day at the Rum Runner. They told me they had a few other guitarists to audition, but I could tell I'd impressed everybody. My hopes were high, and I needed this job. England, especially the north, was in a bad way financially, and my band money from the German contract was running out. Three or four days went by, and then I got the phone call inviting me back down to Birmingham. I borrowed thirty quid from my dad, packed up my gear, and my new life began. I was now in Duran Duran."

John Taylor recalled, "So when Andy came back to Birmingham and joined the band, I felt we moved up another level. I don't know how Gary Moore came up in conversation, but it turned out he was one of Andy's favorite guitar players. There were some good guitarists around Birmingham at that time, but Andy—he *really* knew how to play well. The thing that impressed me, when we met him, was that he seemed to be living the guitar rather than just being an ordinary musician. He was just what we needed."

Though Nick was skeptical at first, he warmed to Andy as well. "We put the advert in *Melody Maker*. . . . Within about a week, we had seventeen responses. One of them was from Andy Taylor. And I just pointed to his name—another Taylor—on a list on a piece of paper, and I said, 'There's *no fucking way* we're having this guy.'

"So of course they all came, did their auditions, and were a very mixed bunch: people with wah-wah pedals, one guy looked like a fisherman in his parka, older chaps—Andy Summers wannabes. But there was one of them—absolutely dynamite—and that was Andy Taylor.

"He came down on the train from Newcastle with his amp under his arm and his guitar. He was wearing brown dungarees and a T-shirt with a slogan that was a spoof on the Kit Kat candy ad: It said, 'Have a Kwip Kwap.'

"This was not something that impressed Roger and John and I. We were future New Romantics with cool hair, tailored clothes—we had a certain look.

"We thought, 'Oh no.' Also we could barely understand a word he was saying because Andy spoke with a profound Newcastle accent, a thorough and impenetrable Geordie [someone from the Tyneside area]. John and I just looked at each other and tried to stifle the giggles.

"But, my God, Andy Taylor was just so good, a seasoned player, six hundred gigs in two years, he told us. He could play the guitar. He was the only one we liked. So we said, 'Yeah.'

"We also told him that, yes, of course, we have this singer, a good one, but it was just that he wasn't there that day. 'You'll meet him next time we get together to rehearse.' So Andy moved down to Birmingham from Newcastle, knowing he'd got the job."

The third and last Taylor in Duran Duran had an immediate effect on the band. Andy Taylor, teenaged veteran rocker, gave the band the jolt of adrenalized power and swing. Andy's musical experience and expertise were immediately obvious, and even control freak Nick deferred to him when it came to arranging and rearranging songs, verses, choruses, and bridges. Andy taught them songwriting rules like "Don't bore us; get to the chorus." Andy's tasty, minimalist arsenal of guitar riffs, licks, and fills sharpened the band and gave them renewed confidence. Much later, Andy would say, "I was the balls in Duran Duran," and nobody could really object.

Now all they needed was a singer, someone who could write his own lyrics and front Duran Duran. In the meantime, Andy joined the rest of the band with backstage gigs at the Rum Runner: "To earn a little money, I worked as a chef in the kitchen, cooking hamburgers. I'd steal a little filet steak and feed myself every day. Sometimes John and I did the glass collection and the bar work, polishing the mirrors, but we tried to get the better jobs. Nick was the DJ. Blondie was at number one with 'Call Me,' which he had to play every night. All this was happening while we were getting on our feet. In the beginning, I was sleeping on people's sofas or crashing in the club.

"The Rum Runner had a big jazz/funk night that was quite influential, especially to tracks like 'Rio.' We used to go to that night, mostly because there was fuck-all else to do, and we had our own room there anyway. I mean, it ended up that we had our own rehearsal room where we had all those weird clothes that the girls were making for us and our hairspray and makeup and all that. And then we had what we called 'the Sex Offenders Room' further up the back because it was this massive building; only the lower levels were used. The rest of it used to be an old gangsters' boxing club, and there'd been a casino in there too. We found out that Jimi Hendrix had played there, and even fucking Little Richard. Bill Haley and the Comets had played there in '56!

"But the heritage of the Rum Runner was a bit off. The club had been in the same family—the Berrows—for decades. It was infamous to some people. One of the main men of the Krays' [London] gang got arrested walking out of there when the gang was busted up. Illegal boxing matches. The casino was dodgy. World War II ration coupon scams. It was right next to the canal where untaxed liquor came in, hence the name. Eventually it became a cocaine den in the eighties, when all that stuff took off. It was the most salacious of venues in Birmingham but also the most exotic as well. It was great, and it was terrible. In the bars, after midnight, the guys in the Glasgow Rangers shirts started demanding kisses from your girlfriend. If you didn't let them, they stabbed you. If she didn't let them, they stabbed you."

It was around this time that the club's beautiful cloakroom girl, Giovanna Cantone, shaved her head.

"All the great-looking girls used to go to the Rum Runner. We had 'Page 3' girls, who posed topless for the *Sun* and other newspapers. The Rum Runner was *the* scene. The first two Duran Duran albums are both products of that time. Without being overly sentimental about it, we were a happy, fun-loving bunch—the whole cast of characters, not just the band but all the people that were involved with us at that time, that sort of six to twelve months there in 1980 and '81.

"I should mention there was a huge gay scene involved. It was very gay and very open and very cool in that respect. Gay John and all his crew were big fans of the band. In the 'Planet Earth' video, you see our gays dancing. They were prepared to drop everything and come with us wherever we played and wear every outrageous thing they could possibly wiggle into, like rubber and PVC way before bondage and all that shit became semirespectable. None of them had a straight dress sense. We took two busloads to Paris for a gig once, and the customs guys nearly didn't let them into France because they were so off their heads, and none of them looked like their passports.

It was, 'Which is ze man, and which is ze woman?' At the gig, the French kids could not believe what had come over with us.

"Ahhh . . . it was just so colorful, and so exotic, to me at least. So there was this huge androgyny factor in Duran Duran. That whole cast of characters, the whole thing that happened to us around then. I can't describe the craziness and insanity that went on. I mean, my old lady used to say, 'I didn't even want to *know* you then.'"

As for the Rum Runner? "It's gone now. They pulled it down a few years later, and now it's the Hyatt Hotel Birmingham."

PART 3

Fiona Kemp was a smart, attractive student who started working as a barmaid at the Rum Runner in May 1980. Like everyone at the club, from the secretaries to the hard men who worked the door, she enjoyed listening to the house band, Duran Duran, developing songs as they rehearsed upstairs, especially after Andy Taylor joined and sharpened the group's focus into solid, rocking arrangements. She really liked their song "Girls on Film," which at that point only existed as a chorus. When she started at the Rum Runner, Duran was trying out a new singer, Oliver Watts, but he only lasted a couple of weeks before he wasn't invited to rehearsals anymore. They badly needed a singer who could write.

Seeing how involved her boss was with the band, she mentioned to Paul Berrow that she had this ex-boyfriend called Simon who might be right for Duran Duran. He wasn't exactly a singer, she explained. This Simon was studying acting at the university, but he was also writing poems and lyrics in this ledger book that he always carried around. Simon was a big guy who liked to dance. Fiona told Paul that she'd always thought Simon to be a sexy, "lead singer" type of bloke.

Paul told Fiona to bring Simon around the club as soon as possible because Duran Duran was getting increasingly desperate for someone to front the band.

Simon John Charles Le Bon was born in the small town of Bushey, Hertfordshire, on October 27, 1958. His father, John, worked in the

British civil service; his mother, Ann, had two more boys after Simon: his brothers, David and Jonathan. The Le Bon family, of Huguenot ancestry, then moved to Pinner, Middlesex, a comfortable suburb northwest of London, when Simon was about to start school. (Pinner was also the boyhood home of Reg Dwight, later to become Elton John.) Simon attended Pinner County Grammar School, which Elton had attended ten years earlier.

"My mother was very ambitious for me," Simon remembered. "She saw something in me, and I think an astrologer or someone like that had predicted a bright future for me. So when I was about five, she started taking me to auditions for adverts and child actors. We'd take the train from Pinner and go to these places in Soho and the West End [London's theater district] and audition for parts. The first television advert I appeared in was for Persil [soap powder]. This is 1963. My TV mother was dropping me off at school, and she was ashamed to see the other boys' shirts were much whiter than mine. So began my career. Later, when I was thirteen, I was on stage in the West End, appearing as one of a gang of boys in *Tom Brown's School Days*. It didn't hurt that from an early age, I loved to dress up. I had the usual cowboy outfit but also the police uniform, a jockey suit, and kit from Manchester United. In fact, I'm a bit surprised I didn't turn out gay.

"Aside from her hopes for me, I learned a lot from my mother. She was only eighteen when she had me. She wanted us to be positive about life, free from petty jealousies and holding grudges. There was classical music playing on the radio in our house all the time. She was a great singer and a wonderful cook and knew a lot about many things. She was probably the most important person in my life.

"So I kept up the drama lessons and also joined the choir of St. John's church in Pinner High Street when I was about eleven. This is where I learned to sing for the first time. The organist and choirmaster, Mr. Tervey, thought enough of my voice that he arranged for a recording to be made of me singing four Anglican hymns with him playing along. We did 'Taste and See,' 'O, For the Wings of a Dove,' and two others. They were pressed onto a record, and so my recording career began in 1971, when I was thirteen. And my voice didn't break until I was seventeen!

"Then I went to Nower Hill High School, where my mother had gone. I was pretty useless with the girls at school. I didn't have a proper girlfriend until I was sixteen. But I played soccer and rugby and began to grow toward my father's height, which was six foot two. But I still lived in fear of the teds [teddy boys] and hooligans who seemed to be everywhere, especially on the train from Pinner to Baker Street, where I might have an audition. I'd have to lie flat on the seats after Harrow station so they wouldn't harass me. There was the whole class thing in England. When I was sixteen and into the punk thing, I went to a Sham 69 gig at the Roxy in London, and the singer pointedly looked down at me in the front row and sneered, 'This next one's for rich kids—*like you!*'

"But we weren't rich. I had a job on a milk float, running the glass bottles from the lorry to the doorsteps.

"I think I had premonitions of being in a big band one day. My first concert was seeing Genesis at Earl's Court, a big seventies megaproduction that made a huge impression on me. Then I was in a punk band called Dog Days. I think we played exactly one gig, fourth of the bill in the school cafeteria, playing on the floor, as there was no stage. I had a little Phillips cassette player and lived under the headphones, trying to take in everything but obsessed with the Doors, especially Jim Morrison's poetry. I spent hours mesmerized by Bowie's *Aladdin Sane* and Lou Reed's *Transformer*. I had this feeling inside me that this was the right general direction to be heading.

"When I was seventeen, I left school without quite knowing what came next. I had a job as a porter in the hospital in Pinner. Then I went to Israel with a girlfriend to volunteer at a kibbutz, but we broke up early on, and I found myself rather alone in the Negev desert. The kibbutz still had bullet holes in the walls [from the Six-Day War]. The only tape I had was Patti Smith's *Horses* album. She obviously liked the Doors as much as I did. I didn't speak any Arabic, but I still managed to make friends with some of the local guys who worked on the farm, sitting with them playing flutes under the desert stars at night. I'd never been out of England before, except for a school visit to Amsterdam, so this Israel journey really opened my eyes to a lot of things. I wrote the lyrics to 'The Chauffeur' in the desert, which became an early Duran Duran fan favorite.

"When I got home, my parents wanted me back in school, but I wasn't ready."

⁓

At just twenty years old, Simon Le Bon was a big, strapping blue-eyed kid, extremely intelligent and something of a bruiser. He played rugby in school, coached to tackle opposing players head-on, lift them up and onto their arses. Around this time, he had a friend named David Miles who was a little older, a little taller, and even better looking. David was something of a model for Simon, who looked up to him and was often seen in his company. David liked the Clash and the Damned but also Miles Davis and Charles Mingus. He could also talk with quiet authority about Jean Genet, William Burroughs, Francis Bacon, and the Sex Pistols.

David Miles was charismatic, talented, and ironic, and he had vague pop-star dreams of his own—if only he could harness his obsessions and fantasies into something real. He would take Simon on the train to seaside Brighton, where their skintight trousers and athletic bodies attracted the attention of gay men cruising the city's famous pier at night. In those days, the London Underground shut down at midnight, and the boys often found themselves running to catch the last train; anyone arriving on the last train from Brighton without taxi fare to the suburbs had to spend the night under Paddington's huge vaulted arch or else under a bush in nearby Hyde Park.

In 1978, Simon was accepted into the drama department at the University of Birmingham, but he wasn't sure which direction he wanted to take. He thought he might be more writer than actor. Contemplating his options, he went over to David's house, where he found his friend "chasing the dragon"—smoking heated lines of heroin off a sheet of aluminum foil. Simon was shocked by this, but he thought it might be a good idea to try it.

"No, no, man," David said. "You don't want to get into this. It's not for you."

Simon would later tell interviewers that David's refusal to give him a taste might have saved his life. A few weeks later, he enrolled in drama school and never saw David again. But years later, Simon Le Bon would write one of his best songs about his wayward friend.

"So I was then a drama and theater arts student at the University of Birmingham . . . learning to be an actor," Simon recalled later. "The classrooms were in Edgbaston, a part of Birmingham where there'd never been factories or warehouses, so it was the nice part of town. I was working on a student production scheduled to play at the Edinburgh Fringe Festival when I first heard about these kids at the Rum Runner.

"I had this girlfriend. We were flatmates for a while, but then we broke up. There were other people involved as I recall. She said she was leaving town and maybe going to London. Two weeks later, I got a phone call from her. I thought it was a booty call, but it wasn't. She said she was working at the Rum Runner, the big club on Broad Street. I'd never been there.

"She explained [that] the house band [was] looking for a singer and said, 'I think you really need to go meet these guys because they're good and they're looking for someone.' She gave me the phone number of the Rum Runner office. I think she told me to wear some makeup when I went to see them.

"I called, and Mike Berrow answered the phone. He set up an audition with them, and I showed up in a white dinner jacket over a pair of maroon leopard-skin jeans, faded pink because they'd been washed so many times. Outside the Rum Runner, a young guy was on a ladder, painting a wall. This turned out to be the drummer, Roger. Nick, the youngest one, looked a bit askance at the trousers, but I knew it was going to be good. It was so natural. I was right for them, and they were right for me. We dressed the same, had the same kind of outlook—positive, happy people, not given to complaining. We all wanted to do something about our situation. It was a magical day."

Nick remembered the first time he heard about Simon. "So one night, one of the barmaids at the Rum Runner came up to us and said, 'You really need a singer, don't you? Well, I know someone who would be perfect for you. He even dresses the same way you do, and he likes all the same things you like. And he really wants to be in a band.' Oh yeah? 'Yes, and he's been in bands before. His name's Simon.'

"'Don't tell us—Simon *Taylor*, right?'

"'No, silly. His name is Simon Le Bon.'

"So anyway, we said, 'Bring him on down.'

"Simon came over to the Rum Runner, and the famous story that he showed up wearing tight purplish-pink leopard-skin trousers is absolutely the truth. The thing I noticed, though, was that he had a large ledger-type notebook with him. It had the word 'ROSOVTROV' inked in large capital letters on its cover. And inside the book were simply loads of lyrics. There was one called 'The Chauffeur,' which I was very impressed with. And we thought, 'Wow. He looks great. He's called Simon Le Bon, his real name. He can't really be Simon Le Bon, can he? Pink leopard-skin pants!' He almost got the job on that alone. 'And he's got a book filled with words!'

"And when he opened his mouth, and when we heard that he really could sing—and that it was a unique, unusual, and communicative voice as well; it wasn't like any of the other singers we'd auditioned. Simon had a style of his own, which was the final selling point. Then, after, we said to him, 'Brilliant. Thank you. Jolly good.'"

Andy remembered Simon's entrance too. "So there we all were, in the Rum Runner, when in walked this tall, good-looking guy with long legs and lots of confidence. 'Hello, I'm Simon Le Bon,' he said in a southern accent. The first thing I thought was, 'Fuck me—he looks just like Elvis!'

"We liked him. Then we discovered he could write lyrics. He'd brought along a book with a paisley pattern on the cover, which was packed with his own handwritten poems. The book turned out to be a real Aladdin's lamp because it contained all the lyrics we could ever wish for. This was our Ground Zero. For me, the defining moment of Duran Duran was when Simon pulled out that little book of lyrics."

It worked from day one. The band was impressed that Simon could sing into a live microphone and move with ease. Simon asked the band to play one of their vamps again, listened intently, and then instantly matched it to a lyric from his book called "Sound of Thunder." The tune was Andy's, and he was amazed that the words fit the song so well. Simon obviously had a keen ear for commercial pop. They played him their "Girls on Film" hook, and he immediately began to rework it. As an added bonus, Simon also mentioned in passing that he liked Simple Minds, a band that John and Nick admired as well.

John felt a strong musical connection with Simon: "The music— it came quick. He had cool lyrics already written, stuff he wanted to sing with a band. We had this song that the four of us had whipped into shape. We'd been working with the sequencer—*ddit, ddit, ddit*— that whole Giorgio Moroder thing, and putting that energy together with big rock power chords and over a Chic rhythm groove. What could go wrong?

"Simon just came in with his book, got out a page, and started singing 'Sound of Thunder.' That was it. That was *it!* I clearly remember saying, 'I don't care what the guy's wearing—*he's got the job!*' 'Sound of Thunder'—that was our manifesto. It had all the elements of what we were about.

"Because the truth was, I now felt—*we had to get on with this*. We'd been in turnaround for four or five months. This seemed like a long time to us."

And with that, John told Simon, "Good, you're in. We've got a gig in four weeks." In bed that night, John wrote in his diary, "Finally the front man! The star is here!"

Nick told Simon, "'We're going to do a gig July fourth, so you've got to write a bunch of material.' In fact, I say that now to everybody that wants to start a band. Book a gig—then you're forced to write a set. So, we had some songs in the early gigs with Simon Le Bon that made it onto the first Duran Duran album: definitely 'Sound of Thunder'; 'Girls on Film'—probably. But when the lights went down, we put on the song 'Tomorrow Belongs to Me' from the movie *Cabaret*. I hadn't connected it to the Hitler fucking Youth anthem that it was. Afterwards this guy in another band started bawling us out. 'You fucking wankers! What are you—Nazis?' And so on. We didn't know about that stuff. *Cabaret* was just a big movie of the time. Anyway, that first gig we also played 'Night Boat' and even 'I Feel Love,' the Donna Summer song. Andy played the whole gig with five strings because the top E string snapped and there was no road crew to change it."

Simon Le Bon joined Duran Duran by late June 1980. Initially, the Berrows told Simon that he was only in the band for that summer, and then they would see. He was also still enrolled in drama school and may have appeared in a student production in Edinburgh that summer. Upstairs at the Rum Runner, he was something of a mystery; the Berrows were still unsure about him. Was he a talented singer with a bulging songbook or a camp actor playing the part of a rock star?

Simon himself soon hated the tacky, provincial scene at the Rum Runner, which he later described as "stale smoke, stale beer, stale people." One of his earliest songs for Duran Duran, "Friends of Mine," was about his ambivalence about the club and some of its shady denizens.

Simon later said he was impressed by John and Nick's ambitions for the band: Duran Duran, they explained, would play London's Hammersmith Odeon by 1982, Wembley Arena by '83, and Madison Square Garden in New York by 1984. It was as if this were preordained (indeed, Duran Duran would duly meet all these self-imposed dead-lines). Simon was a little intimidated at first because Nick and John were so intense; they made it clear to him that they wanted Duran Duran to be the biggest band in the world. They didn't care about street credibility or any of the old punk ethos.

"At first I thought it was like a hobby kind of thing," Simon said later. "Then I realized they meant business, *real* business." Simon was also worried because he was, in his own words, "a god-awful singer." But he was also confident he could grow into the front man the band needed.

After Simon joined, things started speeding up for Duran Duran. The Berrow brothers bought new synths for Nick, a Roland guitar synth for Andy, and a better Japanese bass for John. They started to rehearse new material, like "Tel Aviv" and "The Chauffeur." By June, they signed a formal management contract with the Berrows, who then formed a production company called Tritec Music, reputedly named for the three levels of bars in the Rum Runner.

Accounts vary, but most fans believe the first official Duran Duran gig with the classic lineup took place at the Rum Runner on July 16, 1980. They had ten songs ready ahead of their big debut. "We were nervous," John later wrote, "and there was even less acknowl-edgment of one another than there had been in the rehearsal room. But cool detachment was so 1980." John was also concerned because he'd exchanged his thick spectacles for contact lenses. Everyone said he looked incredible now, but he was still worried that he might miss a note. On top of that, there was no stage at the club. Andy was annoyed that he and Roger had to build one out of some big wooden boxes from the warehouse.

In matching clothes and newly dyed hair, the band walked onstage, plugged in, and Simon said, "We're Duran Duran, and we want to be the band to dance to when the bomb drops. . . . This is 'Late Bar.' We wrote it for you to dance to."

After Roger yelled, "One, two, three, four!" Duran Duran was off and running. They played all their original songs. "Planet Earth" had the house literally shaking. So did the Euro-techno storm of Donna Summer's "I Feel Love." Mike Berrow had insisted on joining the band onstage for their early gigs and played his saxophone badly in front of an unplugged microphone. Afterward, they told Mike he had to stick to his management role. Duran Duran was paid fifty pounds for the show.

Duran Duran played around various venues in the Midlands during that summer: the Cedar Ballroom, the Holy City Zoo, Hosteria One, and Aston University in Birmingham. They started really baring down on new songs like "Careless Memories," "Anyone Out There," and John Taylor's "Secret Success."

At the end of July, Duran Duran drove to London and recorded two songs—"Girls on Film" and "Tel Aviv," with its original lyric that was later dropped—at AIR (Associated Independent Recording) Studios. Ever insistent, Mike Berrow played his sax on these demos as well. Simon had never sung to instrumental tracks under headphones before; his vocals were shaky, and he couldn't quite get it right. This made the Berrows even more nervous. What if Simon was great as a front man but couldn't hack the recording studio?

John and Nick were impressed that Japan was also recording tracks at AIR. They'd always liked Japan; Nick admired their blond, impossibly post-glam photogenic singer David Sylvian. Nick and John made sure to give Sylvian a copy of their demo tape, and Nick even wanted to ask him to produce their first album once they got a record deal.

At the same time, Paul and Linda McCartney were also recording at AIR, which was partly owned by Beatles producer George Martin. At the end of their session, Paul and Linda came in to say good night to Duran Duran. For a group of young boys from the Midlands, it was surreal.

Word about Duran Duran's sexy boy band energy was radiating out of Birmingham, helped along by friendly bands like UB40 and Dexys Midnight Runners. In June, BBC disc jockey Peter Powell taped Duran Duran at venerable Broadcasting House in London. Their radio debut was on August 11. When their white-hot electro music was on the radio that summer, it caused a sexy stir. The Berrows immediately found their cold calls returned faster.

By September, the Berrow brothers were desperate to land a record deal for Duran Duran. John, Nick, and Roger were living with their parents; Simon was still at the university; Andy spent nights in Michael Berrow's spare room, sometimes with the beautiful Rum Runner regular Janine Andrews. Andy and Simon were also experiencing relative poverty without the support of nearby families. There was often zero money for groceries after the rent had been paid. Soon Andy moved into Simon's student house in bohemian Moseley. Andy made a connection with a Rastafarian ganja dealer and began making hashish cakes in the Rum Runner's kitchen after hours for extra cash.

Though word of mouth was in their favor, they were far from the only exciting new group on the scene; the music weeklies were reporting other young groups—Spandau Ballet and Boy George's Culture Club—signing with major labels like EMI, Phonogram, and Virgin. Paul Berrow organized a showcase for the band at the Hosteria wine bar in Birmingham; Duran Duran shook the house, but no offers came forth. The main English record labels were still all in London, and it was hard to get their A&R guys to come two hours north for a listen. What they needed was visibility. Duran Duran had to go on the road, opening for a bigger act, so the whole country could see their look, energy, and style.

The perfect opportunity soon appeared. Everyone in England had seen *Breaking Glass*, the year's best music movie, about a post-punk rock star named Kate, played by actress and singer Hazel O'Connor (from Coventry). The film follows the upward path of Kate's band until the story descends into a miasma of drugs and burn-out. In the end, a recovering Kate is visited in the hospital by her best friend (who gives her a synthesizer). *Breaking Glass* was a big hit in England, and the movie's soundtrack album went to #5 and then double platinum. When it was announced that Hazel O'Connor and her band Megahype would tour England, Ireland, and Scotland later that fall, Paul Berrow knew he had to get Duran Duran on that tour. Everyone—new fans and record execs—would finally be able to see his band.

The Berrows had to buy their way in. Michael Berrow obtained a reported £8,000 by mortgaging his house. Duran Duran played an auditioning gig at the Marquee in London on November 9. They opened with "Night Boat," and the basement club began to rock to Roger's pounding beat and Nick's spectral, pulsing drone. By the end of the evening, Duran Duran was booked as the opening act on the Hazel O'Connor tour, thirty dates, and celebrations ensued. Simon left the university to sing on Duran Duran's first tour, calling it "the best decision I ever made."

The Berrow brothers wanted to have a record to sell during the tour. Tritec Music planned to release an indie Duran Duran single with "Planet Earth" and "Anyone Out There," recorded during the AIR Studios sessions in July. A promo clip was filmed at the Cedar Club (only released years later), and five thousand labels were printed with a new band logo, but then the real record companies came call-ing before the single was ever pressed.

The tour began at Ulster Hall, Belfast, Northern Ireland, on November 14, then moved down to Dublin before returning to England. Duran Duran's short opening sets went well—fast-rocking "Careless Memories" was a big crowd-pleaser—but the band all caught colds traveling from Cardiff, Wales, to the Manchester Apollo in their Bedford van. Duran Duran could only afford one hotel room per night, so they took turns sleeping in the bed while the rest bunked in the van with the gear. In the morning, they all took turns in the room's shower. Then it was on the road again, to Sheffield, Bristol, and Brighton. Simon, unused to belting songs every night, developed a sore throat. He saw a doctor in Brighton, and Duran Duran was forced to cancel that night's performance. But Simon was a trouper. Hazel O'Connor's audiences were hard-core punk fans who mocked Simon's frilly blouson shirts and eye shadow. Hazel later recalled Simon's bravery and dedication: "He faced abuse, and people spitting at him every night, and he just took it."

Simon rallied for the sold-out Birmingham Odeon show, crowded with friends, family, and other bands (like Fashion) that Duran Duran was about to leave behind. Then it was back in the van and on to Liverpool, Edinburgh, and City Hall, Newcastle, on December 1, where Andy's entire extended clan crowded the band's pitiful dressing room and teased them about their ten-pound-a-week stipend.

Back in the Midlands early in December, there were rumors of a bidding war among record companies wanting to sign Duran Duran. EMI executive Dave Ambrose joined the tour for the concerts in Leicester and Leeds and kindly let the band shower in his hotel room. They played him their demo cassettes, and Ambrose was sure that "Girls on Film" could be a hit record, but the singer didn't sound right. They explained that the singer on the demo was actually Andy Wickett, who wrote the song as it was then, but he'd since been replaced by Simon. Phonogram, based in Holland, also wanted Duran Duran, convinced the band could be massive with European kids. But the band was leaning toward mighty EMI—the Beatles' label. They all liked Dave Ambrose, an amiable former musician who'd been in one of Mick Fleetwood's early blues bands, before Fleetwood Mac. Ambrose was similarly enthusiastic about Duran Duran, even after he got caught in the middle of a sloppy porkpie fight between Nick and Andy in the back of the van. He told A&R colleagues in London that Simon could be in movies, could be another young Elvis.

Dave Ambrose reflected back on Duran Duran's early days, noting, "It was amazing because even though they were still rough, you could see their audience beginning to form around them. They already had lots of pretty girls and lots of people dressing up. It was a big splash of color with a cool sense of style. I knew when I saw them at the Holy City Zoo, with all these girls, that they could be very, very big."

The tour played at the University of East Anglia in Norwich before concluding at the Dominion Theatre in London on December 6, by which time there was an all-out bidding war for Duran Duran between EMI and Phonogram. The encore of the last show saw a recovered Simon singing Bowie's "Suffragette City" with Hazel O'Connor and finished with hugs and popping corks all around.

~⌒~

The tour was over, but Duran Duran stayed in London, camping at a cheap hotel in Fulham, near Chelsea's Stamford Bridge soccer stadium. John's cold turned into the flu, and he got very sick. Paul Berrow was in intense negotiations with the record companies, trying to get a better deal than the exploitive contracts usually offered to young bands. Andy recalled that when the bidding started for the band, Phonogram offered them more money. "We decided to go with EMI," he said, "because we knew they had a global network and they could launch bands across America [on their Capitol Records label]." It didn't hurt that EMI was still run by the famous executive Bhaskar Menon, who had been there since EMI took a flutter on a northern rock-and-roll band called the Beatles. Nick also hinted they signed with EMI out of patriotic feelings, preferring to be with an English company.

On December 7, Paul Berrow shook hands with Dave Ambrose, and Duran Duran was signed up as EMI artistes. Technically, however, it was the Berrows' company, Tritec Music, who signed with EMI, with an advance of £42,000 to produce an album, a tour, and some videos. Tritec and Duran Duran kept control of the creative side—music, album art, video content. The five members of the band—some still underage—found themselves contractually described as salaried employees of Tritec Music Ltd., earning fifty pounds a week each. Decades later, Nick—only eighteen when the contract was signed—summed up the contract as follows: "We got appallingly ripped off."

At the same time, the young men of Duran Duran instinctively developed an honorable band cohesion. They agreed that everything—songwriting, tickets, merchandise—would be divided among the five of them. Duran Duran had been formed by "sidemen"— John and Nick—and so had no "leader," unlike most bands. No one told anyone what to play. Compliments and approval were signaled with winks, nods, body language. Everyone had his strength. There was Nick's aristocratic cool and John's beauty and hard-won mastery of the bass guitar. Roger was the quiet, stolid one, the dependable engine of the band. Andy brought a saw-toothed edge to the group. Simon was older than the others and had seen more of the world. His lyrics impressed the others with their Beat outlook and abstruse storytelling. Only child John Taylor later wrote that he looked up to Simon Le Bon as the older brother he never had.

On December 8, almost immediately after signing their deal, Duran Duran recorded demos of four songs with Dave Ambrose at EMI's Manchester Square studio: "Planet Earth," "Anyone Out There," "Late Bar," and "Friends of Mine." The next morning, after Duran Duran played a headlining gig at the Marquee in Soho, they learned that John Lennon had been shot and killed in New York as he was returning home from a recording session for Yoko Ono. Later that day, the members of Duran Duran were at EMI's offices in Manchester Square to sign some papers and found the label's staff in shock; some of them had known John Lennon for nearly twenty years.

Duran Duran remained in London until almost Christmas, gearing up for eventual chart domination. They weren't the only ones so inclined, and they soon found themselves part of a much-hyped artistic movement being called the New Romantics by a brash London media eager for an insurgent energy to liven up the eighties.

The term "New Romantics" was generally credited to London publicist Perry Haines, who was then hired by the Berrows to manage Duran Duran's public image. Pop writer Betty Page included Duran Duran among the New Romantics in the December 13 edition of *Sounds*, and it was the first article about the band in the national press. The idea of the New Romantics conjured up the Old Romantics—the English bards Lord Byron, Percy Shelley, and John Keats, with their wild spurning of Regency-era norms and conformity—and such acts included Duran Duran, Spandau Ballet, Depeche Mode, Adam and the Ants, Heaven 17, Visage, and others. Then there was Siouxsie and the Banshees. For the bands, the New Romantic style meant frilly shirts, floppy hair, designer suits (preferably by Antony Price, who dressed Bowie and Roxy Music), cosmetics, and silken cravats or ascots. The fans who jammed into hot London venues like Billy's, Hell, and Blitz were there to dress up and be seen, to dance, to get high, to have fun, and to not be spat on or assaulted.

Snobby, fashion-forward Nick Rhodes and John Taylor weren't that happy about being compared with the other New Romantic bands, especially kilt-wearing Spandau Ballet, who the newer fan magazines like *Smash Hits* tried to position as Duran Duran's bitter rivals. Andy thought Spandau pitiful, but then Spandau released a single that went Top 5 in December. John later remembered, "We rushed out and bought a copy, brought it back to the Rum Runner, put it on. We thought, 'This won't be a problem. We've got them licked.'"

Nor were Duran Duran much impressed by the London crowd packed into Blitz, the hot club of the moment. Just getting into Blitz could be a problem, as impresario Steve Strange (later of Visage) presided over the door, ruthlessly rejecting anyone who didn't have "the look," which encompassed everything from Japanese kabuki to tribal and ethnic clothing, to Victoriana, proto-Gothic, and fetish wear. Even fame couldn't guarantee entry; Mick Jagger was famously turned away from Blitz, while David Bowie was almost a regular. The Blitz kids were mainly art students from nearby Central Saint Martin's College of Art, so the vibe was elitist, exclusive, and much less friendly than the Rum Runner.

Nick recalled, "We loved hanging out at the Rum Runner with our designer friends Jane Kahn and Patti Bell, who made some of our clothes. That club was wild, but in a beautiful way. It was local people at the end of the week, going out and dressing up and doing what they wanted to do."

When Duran Duran slithered past condescending Steve Strange and into Blitz, they were unimpressed by the scene. "The Blitz Club was what was going on in London, and we thought that theirs would be trumping ours [the Rum Runner] somehow. So we all went to the Blitz one night, and I have to say it was really pretty dull, because everything was much more uptight. It didn't feel that real and didn't have that incredible spirit of fun that we had in Birmingham."

Even so, Duran Duran did enjoy their time in London. The Berrows took them to the King's Road in Chelsea and bought them new clothes. They set up studio sessions with famous photographers like Gered Mankowitz, who had shot the Rolling Stones almost two decades before. They also bought a cool car for the band—a late-model Citroën CS estate wagon, painted French blue—to shuttle them between gigs. The driver (and the band's new minder), Simon Cook, caused some initial confusion about having two Simons in the group. Andy Taylor found this annoying and asked Simon Le Bon if he had a middle name. "It's Charles," he replied.

"Right," said Andy. "From now on, you're Charlie, and Simon Cook can keep his fucking name." To this day, Simon Le Bon is generally referred to as Charlie within the Duran Duran family.

Duran Duran also bonded with their new London booking agent, Rob Hallett, who got them the Marquee gig and then a slot opening for Pauline Murray and the Invisible Girls at London's Lyceum Theatre. This was intimidating, the largest stage anyone in the band had ever been on, but Duran Duran pulled it off, and the London crowd, usually disdainful of a new band from the north, called them back for an encore.

As the December days ticked off, Duran Duran was looking forward to getting home for Christmas, but first they had to finish their album. As it turned out, EMI's Dave Ambrose had found the perfect producer to realize Duran's ambitions and sonic dreams.

Colin Thurston's qualifications were impeccable; he had coengineered David Bowie's midseventies Berlin albums *Low* and *Heroes*. As Nick explained later, this was a crucial factor in going with Thurston. "David Bowie was responsible for British music in the first half of the eighties. There was a decadence about him, something dark, something very German but something very exciting." Thurston had also worked on Iggy Pop's Berlin albums and, more locally, with the Human League and Magazine. He was also eager to work with Duran Duran because the minute he heard their demo recording of "Girls on Film," he knew that his charges were on to something unique. It was his job to help the band inject remix and nightlife culture into mainstream pop. Colin was impressed when Simon told him that Duran Duran's music was going to be what you heard when newly elected American president Ronald Reagan started lobbing rockets to Russia. With that in mind, Colin booked Duran Duran into EMI's Abbey Road Studios for a month of recording sessions.

It didn't go well at first. As Colin recalled, "The first thing we did at Abbey Road was to go in with Roger [Taylor] and try to get a drum sound. We spent nine hours trying . . . and basically couldn't. Their technology was difficult to work with, and honestly, I was in awe because it was the Beatles' studio! *Everything* they'd done was recorded there. I couldn't get *anything* to work. I was just standing there with my mouth open. They [the engineers] were looking at me funny. So I canceled the month I'd booked there.

"Then we went to Red Bus studio [in West London] and got the drum sound in fifteen minutes! In two weeks, we had the whole album done, apart from the vocals, which proved to be something of a problem while we had to teach Simon to sing over the instrumental tracks."

Andy says that Colin was the most influential producer that Duran Duran worked with because he was so crucial in shaping the young band's sound. "This is where Duran Duran came to life. Colin was the filter that allowed us to come together as a whole." Colin was older, straighter, easygoing. Nick was fascinated just by watching him work the knobs and faders of the studio's sound console, and Colin in turn appreciated Nick's intense interest in record production, answering questions, explaining the tricks of the trade. He was also patient about the way the band composed: music first, then lyrics. "We worked well with him. With his help, we recorded all our own beats on the first album, all our own chords, all our own melodies, and all our own lyrics."

The lyrics were the only problem Colin Thurston was having with Duran Duran. He admired Simon Le Bon's witty and clever wordplay, but getting him to sing the lyrics properly was difficult. After the instrumental tracks were done at Red Bus, the project relocated to Chipping Norton Studios in quiet Oxfordshire to cut the guitars, keyboards, and vocals. All went well until it was time to record the lyrics. Simon, usually cheery and optimistic "Charlie," seemed tentative and uneasy about singing into a microphone with headphones on. It was even worse when EMI guys drove up from London to listen in.

"Colin Thurston was a nice man," Andy observed, "but he could be a bit pedantic. He was very rough on Simon and kept asking him to redo things." This seemed to fluster Simon even more. EMI was putting the group under a bit of pressure to speed things up and get the album out, as momentum was building for the band. A couple of the A&R people were muttering about Simon in the studio lounge as Colin prodded him into doing multiple takes. Andy recalled there was a brief moment when Simon's future was even in doubt. The Berrows thought his singing sounded flat, and they were worried. Colin agreed that, yes, he was singing out of tune sometimes, but it was because it took time for an inexperienced singer to work under headphones. Sure, he sounded a bit off sometimes. They just had to be patient and wait for Simon to relax and learn the technique.

But then avuncular Dave Ambrose arrived in Chipping Norton and put things right. "Dave had worked with Queen and AC/DC," Andy said. "He'd seen it all before and knew there was nothing to worry about." He told Simon to chill. "If you've never done it before, you just have to take your time. Anyway, it's all about the songs."

Paul Berrow blamed drinking for Simon's problems. At a band meeting at the Rum Runner, he rebuked Simon. "I told him, 'If you don't get your act together, there is an inevitability that you won't make it.'" He told Simon to stop smoking, take care of his voice, stop partying every night; otherwise he could ruin the goodwill of the band and EMI. "I thought he was letting everybody down," Paul recalled. "Simon was read the riot act and took it like a man. He got on with the job, and we didn't have another problem with him."

Duran Duran returned to Birmingham for Christmas. They played a wild gig at the Cedar Club, packed with gorgeous girls, flamboyant gays, and straight guys in makeup, trying to look New Romantic. Everyone ended up onstage, singing every Bowie song they could think of.

The next day, Andy and Nick traveled back to London by train. They'd written "Planet Earth" at the Rum Runner just after the tour, and they started mixing it on Boxing Day with Colin Thurston at Utopia Studio. The track was rollicking, powered by Andy's hard-riffing, metallic lead guitar and John's lively Chic-style bass playing. Nick mentioned the track was inspired by Rod Stewart's hit "Do Ya Think I'm Sexy?" Colin told him that Rod had actually stolen the melody from Brazilian superstar Jorge Ben. Nick laughed and said, "It's going to be a hit."

Duran Duran was back at the Rum Runner on New Year's Eve. It had been exactly one year since Nick and John had shown up at the club with their demo tape, impressing the brothers Berrow, who offered them a place to rehearse and maybe a few gigs. In just one year, Duran Duran had shed some members and found Simon and Andy. It had been a wild 1980. A foreshadowing of the future came at midnight, when the band stopped and clinked glasses and the PA played the Rum Runner's house anthem: Frank Sinatra's "New York, New York."

PART 4

For Duran Duran fans, "the eighties" really began in January 1981, as the band put the finishing touches on their first album and prepared to release the first of its three singles. Nick carefully monitored Colin Thurston's techniques at Unique Sound, watching and learning as the producer tweaked and blended the thirteen tracks the band had recorded with him.

"Girls on Film" was the first track on the album, introduced by the mechanical sound of the motor drive from Paul Berrow's Nikon camera. (Andy Wickett's composer's rights to "Girls on Film" had been bought out for £600, and he was not credited on the album.) Duran Duran's sonic signifiers blasted into action with Nick's sci-fi washes and John's popping bass. Simon's Beat-poetic blank verse called forth models and fashion, water and bridges, but an undertow of sexual exploitation was also woven deep into the lyrics. "Planet Earth" came next—a spacecraft touching down amid a clipped bass line and sirens. The lyrics acknowledge the new wave, "like some New Romantic looking for the TV sound." There's no sign of life on the planet, and some fans felt the song was about the arrival of aliens, but Simon also said (much later) that the song could be about the moment of a child's birth. Andy's fuzz-tone guitar lick almost guaranteed that "Planet Earth" would be explosive on the radio. "Anyone Out There" followed with another guitar stutter and Simon crying over lost love and unreturned calls—"just left me ringing on the line." Then came "To the Shore," a tidal pool of a power ballad with lyrical neologisms ("gorging your sanhedralites") and an oceanic electric guitar solo. Band favorite "Careless Memories" would end the album's first side—a great rock song with menacing sequencer repetitions and shouted, crazy-sounding imprecations to "Look out! Look out! Look out!" The fear of whispers and unwanted thoughts gives depth to the anxious lyrics, and Simon Le Bon sounds harsh and bitter notes that wouldn't be heard from this band again for a long time.

Classic forties film noir informs "Night Boat," which opens side two: foghorns, whirring motors, and buoy bells surround the existential angst of Simon's lyrics while Nick's restless, brooding synths make a dark impression. There's a subterranean vibration of something being not right. Roger Taylor plays steady warpath drums that give the song a Doors-ish feel. "Sound of Thunder" was the first song Duran played together with Simon. Now the story of a man who starts World War III (in Simon's early poem) had a hard dance-floor groove. "Friends of Mine" is another gangster movie with juddering rhythms, gunfire rim shots, and beatnik verse celebrating the release from jail of one Georgie Davis, an actual armed robber wrongfully convicted in a notorious Midlands case of the time. Andy's chopping guitar fills could have been played by Chic's Nile Rodgers (and would be, one day in the future). The album ends with Simon's "Tel Aviv," minus its original lyric, called "On My Own in Tel Aviv." In Nick's hands, it became an orientalist synth-phonette, with an orchestral string section conducted by Richard Myhill at AIR Studios.

Extra tracks would be used in various formats over the next few months. "Night Bus," a song Simon had originally written while waiting for the late bus back to Pinner, became "Late Bar," an all-night dance party in room 7609. Churning "Late Bar" would be the flip side of the "Planet Earth" single release. A cover of David Bowie and John Lennon's "Fame" and the droning ballad "Khanada" were the B-sides of "Careless Memories," Duran's second single release. "Faster Than Light" was thumping disco-rock used as the flip side of "Girls on Film." That single's twelve-inch, 45-rpm UK release also featured "Girls on Film (Night Version)," a sparkly extended remix that subbed synths for the guitars. A similar "Planet Earth (Night Version)" would also be issued in Japan a bit later in 1981.

In those days, 1981, the word "video" was on the lips of everyone in pop music. Dave Ambrose explained to the band that the Americans were preparing a cable television channel that would broadcast music video clips twenty-four hours a day to the wealthiest audience in the country—cable TV customers—beginning in the summer of 1981. Warner Cable was calling their new music video channel, currently being developed in New York, MTV (short for "Music Television").

But putting together the new channel wasn't going to be easy; one problem the young Warner execs were having was programming. No one was sure that there were even enough video clips around without playing the same clips repeatedly. Until 1981, bands and their labels had only produced clips for screening in nightclubs, video juke-boxes, and occasionally on network and syndicated television. With MTV looming in the immediate future, the entire music industry was pivoting toward music videos being as crucial a marketing tool for a band as their appearance and the music itself, and Duran Duran would be in the vanguard of this artistic movement.

Earlier, the band had been introduced to the young Australian video director Russell Mulcahy. He was very in demand as someone who could produce flashy-looking videos with the limited budgets that record companies made available for this new technology. Late in 1980, Russell showed Duran Duran his clips for Ultravox's "Vienna" and the Buggles' "Video Killed the Radio Star" (which ended up being the first video played on MTV when the channel went live). Mulcahy's simple storyboards for Duran Duran's first video (stage scenes, kids dancing, sci-fi studio set) appealed to both the band and its management, who agreed that likeable, funny (and gay) Russell Mulcahy absolutely "got" Duran Duran; he was going to be the key player in their parallel career as video artistes.

Much later, Nick would tell an interviewer, "Video is to us like stereo was to Pink Floyd."

In January 1981, the media really began to take notice of Duran Duran, and their popularity soared after they recorded some songs for broadcast on BBC Radio 1. BBC television also ran a profile of

Duran Duran just prior to the release of the first single, "Planet Earth"/"Late Bar," early in February. But it wasn't all rave reviews. The *NME* ran a condescending article about the band with the headline, "Just Fine and Dandy."

Six thousand miles away in Los Angeles, the executives at Capitol Records were talking about Duran Duran in their round tower at Sunset and Vine. Capitol was EMI's American subsidiary that had enjoyed huge success with Frank Sinatra, the Kingston Trio, the Beach Boys, and the Beatles. Now the Capitol execs were looking at pictures of Duran Duran and wondering what to do with them. No one there really liked the album. The A&R guys regarded the New Romantic clothes and the flossy hair with disdain. No new English band had broken through in America for years. Still, Capitol badly needed a big hit in the wake of a disastrous campaign for the Knack, an LA band with a hit single ("My Sharona"). Capitol had tried to promote the Knack as nothing less than the new Beatles, including reviving the orange and yellow seven-inch single label familiar to Beatles fans and booking them into Carnegie Hall. This crass promotion was mocked in the American music business and basically killed the Knack. Capitol staff were now more interested in a recent signing, a new local act called Missing Persons, which consisted of some guys from Frank Zappa's touring band and a coquettish blonde singer the label thought could be the next Blondie. London EMI was insisting Capitol release "Planet Earth" to coincide with the UK single, but Capitol decided to issue "Planet Earth" on its Harvest Records subsidiary label instead, with "To the Shore" on the flip side in place of "Late Bar." No one was happy about this, especially Paul Berrow, who wanted an aggressive marketing push for Duran Duran in North America. He wasn't going to get it—yet.

Still, Duran Duran was all over TV and the radio in England now, building a seemingly unstoppable momentum by February. Russell Mulcahy's "Planet Earth" video (taped in a North London studio with a budget of £10,000) depicted the teenage band in full New Romantic drag, especially Simon's Cossack-style pantaloons, which served to emphasize his clunky dance moves. They brought Gay John and Patrick down from the Rum Runner to do the finger-snapping sideways New Romantic dance on camera. Godard-inspired computer code and planetary birth stats flashed onscreen. The video was unabashed boy band candy, with half-nude Simon consumed by flames and the band shown playing atop a crystalline column that looked like an unused set from *Barbarella*. Nick would explain years later that "Russell laid in all these effects, supposed to represent the four elements. He was shooting through glass with mattes on the glass. We didn't know what it was going to look like. But that was the beginning for us. We built on it with each video we made after that."

Then, hard-charging "Planet Earth" (released in both single and twelve-inch vinyl formats) rose in the UK sales charts against daunting competition. The week it hit #20, the memory of murdered John Lennon still hung heavy, with Roxy Music's cover of "Jealous Guy" at #1. Kim Wilde's "Kids in America" was #2. Adam and the Ants were surging. Also high in the charts were the Teardrop Explodes, Visage, Ultravox, and Linx.

The next week, "Planet Earth" reached #12. This was great for a new band, but there was still some disappointment that the single hadn't reached the Top 10. With no airplay and minimum promotion, the US release of "Planet Earth" would fail to crack either the *Billboard* or *Cash Box* magazine charts. But the single did hit #1 in Australia after important DJs started playing the record and the kids Down Under got a load of the band's sexy "promotional video."

Around this time, when asked about the inspiration behind the lyrics for "Planet Earth," Simon explained, "I just had this idea of what it would be like if you were coming in and seeing this planet for the first time. In my head was also the idea of being born, but at an age and with a mentality where you can actually see what's going on. It's all about waking up, really."

Meanwhile, disagreement and conflict—even shouting—ensued at EMI's Manchester Square offices over the band's second single. Duran Duran wanted "Girls on Film" released next and even taped a short set for the BBC featuring that song and "Friends of Mine." But EMI execs Dave Ambrose and Ken East were insisting that "Careless Memories" was more radio friendly and had to come next. Nick worried that this would hurt Duran Duran's forward momentum.

Russell Mulcahy was busy churning out videos for other clients, so the band turned to Perry Haines, their PR guy, to make a quickie clip for "Careless Memories" at the Rum Runner. This video is infused with New Romantic fantasy/cliché: Simon is wearing Jim Morrison's castoff leather trousers, and the band dons vaguely Byronic costumes. Andy's blond hair is in spikes, styled by his new love interest, Tracey Wilson, whose family salon in Wolverhampton was now dressing Duran Duran's floppy coiffeurs. Impassive behind his Roland synth, Nick maintains a frozen coolness as Roger bashes away. A white room, red tulips, and champagne completed the enigmatic image the director was reaching for. Duran Duran hated the video, but the EMI marketing execs had the final say.

Duran Duran was booked for a live TV performance on February 24, but this was delayed due to the national furor following the unexpected announcement that Queen Elizabeth's son Charles, Prince of Wales and heir to the throne, had become engaged to an aristocratic teenage London nanny: Diana Spencer. Within a year or so, Her Royal Highness Diana, Princess of Wales, would be Duran Duran's biggest fan.

John Taylor was excited to start Duran Duran's first tour on top of the bill, which started in Birmingham on February 27 and then moved across the Midlands, Liverpool, and Manchester before touching down for a London showcase at the Sundown Club on March 4. Dave Ambrose and EMI execs invited London's most important music men to see the band, including the BBC's John Peel and legendary Andrew Loog Oldham, who had discovered the Rolling Stones playing in an Ealing pub twenty years before. "It was a career-breaking moment" for Duran Duran, Oldham recalled. "The group were on that exciting tightrope, and it showed. . . . They were hungry young pups with a view for the kill."

John was even more excited to perform a lip-synched version of "Planet Earth" for BBC's *Top of the Pops* on March 5. Just as the Rolling Stones had been introduced to Britain decades earlier, so it was Duran Duran's turn now. Everyone interested in English music watched *TOTP*. Everyone's mum had been shocked to see flame-haired Ziggy Stardust drape his limp wrist on Mick Ronson's shoulder on *TOTP* almost ten years before. Queen had grabbed a younger generation's attention playing "Killer Queen" on the show. Then there was the wet February night in 1978 when Blondie appeared on *TOTP* blasting "Call Me." Debbie Harry's white-hot stage persona and the locked-in groove of her band pretty much signaled the death of punk and the launch of the new wave, a movement with which Duran Duran would forever be associated, long after the New Romantic ideals faded away. This was still the era when the musical world for young people was defined by *Top of the Pops* and the *Sunday Top 40 Countdown* on Radio 1.

All the young bands and singers were required to pass through these same institutional junctions, eat in the same canteen, and share the same stage. Duran Duran knew that for them, their performance for *TOTP* would be a crucial rite of passage.

The show was taped at the BBC Television Centre in Shepherd's Bush. Duran Duran was wearing new costumes designed by Patti and Jane in Brum. The band was somewhat amused by the program's strange labor ritual, dictated by the all-powerful Musician Union, that had been in place since *TOTP* first went on air in 1964. It was like a comedy routine. The band took their places, not even fully miked up, and pretended to perform their songs while their original recordings played over the speakers. After the long, liquid lunch break, they gathered around a monitor and watched the playback of the "new recording" they had supposedly just made. And that was that. Also in the studio that day, going through the same charade, were rock heroes the Who and also Soft Cell, the new wave group from Leeds with a hit song, "Tainted Love." By then, *TOTP*'s young and trendy studio audience was more involved in the show, being moved by stage managers between the set's three stages and given strict instructions on when to dance and when to applaud.

John recalled that the process was "hard to take seriously. Watching the playback on the monitor after we had been processed by the *Top of the Pops* machine was amusing. Simon had crimped his hair for the occasion. Roger was almost drowned in dry ice. But we were in 'the club' now—a bona fide chart-busting pop band."

⁓

By March 1981, Duran Duran went back on tour, playing to sold-out audiences with lots of girls, in universities and Top Rank clubs in Wales and Sheffield. On March 10, they played the first three singles on the West Midlands music show *Look Here*. The next night, they held a party at the Rum Runner to celebrate the successful tour and "Planet Earth," which was still on the charts and surging in Australia.

Around then, cocaine began to play a larger part in their lives. John later recalled that he was bored when he wasn't with the band or his girlfriend, Roberta. It was then he "discovered the thrills that came from mixing my drinks with drugs. . . . Cocaine was a big part of the seventies rock mythology I grew up with. It wasn't even a secret. I'd read about it in the pages of the *NME*. I had already gotten a taste for coke at the Rum Runner, where it was popular with some of the older clientele. . . . It was all a bit of a laugh, really. No one took it seriously. No one had been to rehab—yet."

After Duran Duran's flash slot on *TOTP*, their booking agent, Rob Hallett, was inundated with invitations for the band to play "Planet Earth" on other programs, both on the BBC and commercial TV. This kept them busy for the rest of April 1981. On April 20, against the better judgment of the band, EMI released "Careless Memories" as Duran Duran's second single, a 45-rpm record with "Khanada" on the back side. The twelve-inch "disco 45" included a faithful cover of "Fame." Despite another slot on the BBC—this time playing four songs live, including their new single—"Careless Memories" struggled for acceptance. The song's insipid "promotional video" barely got on TV. Duran Duran posing on the cover of shameless teen mags like *Jackie* and *Smash Hits* only brought ridicule for the band's look: French sailor shirts, blowzy hair, and thick makeup. *TOTP* broadcast the band miming "Careless Memories," but the kids in the studio weren't impressed. The release was considered generic rock music, as opposed to the futurist overdrive of "Planet Earth." After three somewhat tense weeks, the record's chart position in the middle of May topped out at a disappointing, momentum-killing #37.

Nick Rhodes was angry. There were tantrums. *He'd fucking told them.* Duran Duran's ascent had been fast and furious, but a #37 was a humiliating kick in the crotch. The EMI staff sheepishly assured the band that the next single would be "Girls on Film," and the label's promo people would "do or die." The band's album was scheduled for release in mid-June, and "Girls on Film" would follow in July. Everything depended on its success.

It worked. The album, titled *Duran Duran*, began selling in record stores in every major market (except the United States) on June 15, 1981. (Capitol was still holding off releasing *Duran Duran* in America, waiting to see what would happen in Europe and Australia.) The album's jacket design immediately set it apart from other (usually deeply embossed)

New Romantic record sleeves then crowding the shop shelves; these mostly tended toward being pompous and portentous, even gloomy. (Not surprising considering the band names: Spandau was the prison where Nazi war criminals served their sentences. Joy Division was where sex slaves were kept in Nazi concentration camps. When the lead singer killed himself, the band became New Order, after Herr Hitler's program for what he had in mind for the world.)

For *Duran Duran* and the singles' picture sleeves, designer Malcolm Garrett's studio (Assorted Images) used neat boxes, clear lines, and lurid color for a streamlined approach toward a more corporate-style presentation. The band's portrait on the album jacket was taken by Fin Costello in full New Romantic outfits, makeup, and hair. The inner sleeve featured stills from fashion photographer Terry Jones, plus images from the disgraced previous video and a full set of Simon Le Bon's obscure lyrical intent. After the album took off, Malcolm stayed on with Duran Duran and acted as their art director for all their most important early work.

Two weeks after *Duran Duran* was released, it peaked at a thrilling #3 on the UK chart—great for a new band. At long last, Duran Duran was in the Top 10 for the first time. Champagne flowed at the Rum Runner. Hit-bound single "Girls on Film" and its video then propelled the album like a nitrous oxide hookup. European offshore stations like Radio Luxembourg and Radio Caroline even played deeper-cut album tracks like the long, epic "Tel Aviv," featuring Nick's passionate orientalist journey to points east of Kashmir. The album continued to sell, and as the band's global reach spread, they still enjoyed sustained success in their home country; *Duran Duran* would stay on the English charts for more than two years.

Meanwhile, on the far side of the world, EMI-Japan released a blistering four-song, twelve-inch Duran Duran EP titled *Nite Romantics*. "Planet Earth (Night Version)" was a harder, six-minute-plus dance-floor remix by Colin Thurston and Nick. Even hotter was the five-and-a-half-minute "Girls on Film (Night Version)," with flying timbales, a furious synth-guitar jam, cod-beatnik audibles, and no last verse. The sleeve featured Gered Mankowitz's glamour shots of the band from the April studio session in London: all cheekbones, hair, and attitude. And so began Japan's crazy love affair with Duran Duran.

FILM ON GIRLS

Two somewhat naked young women are awkwardly mud wrestling in a slimy boxing ring, while carefully coiffed and besuited Duran Duran mime a performance of "Girls on Film" on a riser behind the ring. Welcome to the studio set of the band's next video: a soft-core, porn-friendly promo clip for "Girls on Film."

After the humiliation of the whole "Careless Memories" debacle, Paul Berrow decided to go on the down low for the "Girls on Film" video. He hired Kevin Godley and Lol Creme, musicians who'd left their band 10cc and were launching new careers as video directors. Berrow told Godley and Creme that he wanted a super-sexy clip, something naughty, targeting video jukeboxes in American nightclubs in those waning pre-MTV days. Not quite X-rated, he told them, but plenty of tits and ass. So it was pillow fights, mud wrestling, topless models in big eighties hair, and an ice cube touching an attractive and aroused nipple on a bare breast. These steamy details would get the video banned by the BBC when "Girls on Film" was first released in July 1981, but it was still aired in American, European, and Asian markets and helped to brand the band as future planetary superstars.

At the end of June, Duran Duran embarked on what was called the Faster Than Light Tour. The first night, June 29, was at the sold-out, jam-packed Brighton Dome, which came as a total shock to the band. It started with the band backstage, curtains drawn, with Middle Eastern "Tel Aviv" playing as the curtain-raiser. The band took the stage and plugged in behind the safety curtain, and that was when they heard the screaming.

In John's words: "The power of our instruments, amplified and magnified by PA stacks that reach the roof, is no match for the overwhelming force of teenage sexual energy that comes surging at us in unstoppable waves from the auditorium. The power of it is palpable. I can feel it take control of my arms, my legs, my fingers, for the duration of the opening song. It is unrelenting waves of it crashing onstage."

The band couldn't hear themselves as the feverish screams became shriller, more like the shrieking of mythical Irish banshees. They crashed to a halt and looked at each other for support, in disbelief, exchanging anxious smiles. Nick, usually inscrutable, seemed unnerved. The girls crushing down in front of the stage began to get crazy: blouses ripped, people fell down, chairs flew through the air, stretchers carried off fainted lasses. Duran Duran hadn't seen this degree of fan delirium before. Afterward, they asked each other if this was what it had been like for the Beatles.

Pandemonium struck again at the Gaumont Theatre in nearby Southampton when, after a second frenzied scream-fest, the band was caught and mobbed by young girl fans between the stage door and the bus. Long fingernails lanced toward eyes and throats; one girl with a pair of sharp scissors even tried to get a lock of Simon's hair and almost put his eye out. The next night, July 1, the tour had to detour to Rock City in Nottingham after their concert in Leicester's De Montfort Hall was canceled due to the violent riots breaking out across English cities.

The riots had started in Brixton, South London, back in April. David Bowie had actually been born in Brixton in 1947, but by 1981, the area was home to mostly Black immigrants from the Caribbean and South Asia. Prime Minister Thatcher's economic experiments to steer the nation back on course initially led to austerity budgets, deep recession, chronic unemployment, rising prices, and bitter unrest. But that wasn't all. Britain's Black population felt under siege by an uncaring government and especially racist police tactics in their neighborhoods. The April rioting in South London featured Molotov cocktails, street barricades, and newsreels of injured policemen and burning pubs. Alongside stark photographs of Brixton's burnt and shattered streets, newspaper headlines demanded, "Is This England?" Rioting then spread to other cities, beginning in Belfast, where IRA hunger strikers were demanding to be classified as political prisoners. Liverpool's Toxteth slums exploded next in a fury of injury, arson, and destruction that made Brixton's riot look tame. Duran Duran's Leicester show was eventually called off so the police could fight in the streets. Then more riots flared in Manchester's gritty Moss Side, then Bristol, Leeds, Coventry. And it wasn't only Black people who were burning and looting; in the north of England, young skinheads attacked Pakistanis and other South Asian immigrants and fought pitched battles with the police in the streets.

Despite the threat of violence, Duran Duran had a job to do, and they continued to tour throughout early July, playing in Manchester, Glasgow, Edinburgh, and Newcastle (where Andy's entire family came to party with the band backstage). The audiences continued to scream at the band, tearfully shouting out their names, throwing things on stage, treating Duran Duran to astonishing displays of sexual teenage pack behavior. As they traveled up and down the motorways in their blue Citroën, the band was well aware of what was happening in the ghettos and the slums. Birmingham was still quiet, but some felt that the pressure was building among the unemployed youth of its Handsworth suburb, where most of the city's Black population lived.

On July 7, Duran Duran performed on England's other must-see music program, the BBC's *Old Grey Whistle Test*. The next night they were in Liverpool, followed by a major crowd meltdown at the Hammersmith Odeon in West London on July 8. They screamed through the opening bands (Animal Magnet and Our Daughter's Wedding), and when Duran Duran came out, the audience looked to the band like monkeys in the jungle after the bananas had fermented. Headlining the Hammersmith Odeon was one of the three goals John and Nick had aspired to back in 1978; now they were even ahead of the schedule they'd agreed on. The next two of the band's holy grails, Wembley Arena and Madison Square Garden, were now on Duran Duran's horizon.

The crowd was older and more subdued when Duran Duran played the New Theatre in Oxford on Friday, July 10. The university town had so far been uninfected by riot fever; however, while they were onstage, a violent riot broke out in Handsworth, Birmingham, with hundreds of angry protesters throwing petrol bombs and incendiaries at the outnumbered local police. The next day, Saturday, was worse; the BBC grimly reported riots erupting in nearby Wolverhampton, Sheffield, and many others.

Duran Duran was originally scheduled to play the next day, July 11, at the Birmingham Odeon. By then, even though the Handsworth riot had died down, whole streets had been smashed up and looted. The police wanted the theater to cancel, but the Odeon's manager and the Berrows pointed out that demand to see the hometown heroes was so intense that if they canceled Duran Duran's concert, the police might have a second major disturbance on their hands. So, that afternoon, the band signed albums for squirming, shoving fans at the HMV store on New Street. That evening, they played what Simon would remember as the quietest, most subdued show they ever did. It was as if the kids, and the rabidly loyalist crowd from the Rum Runner, were in a state of shock over the riots that had trashed Handsworth over the weekend. It wasn't a good night to get crazy in Birmingham.

Duran Duran wasn't immune to the riots, their causes, and their effects. Three of them still lived at home, and their parents were obviously concerned. A little later, Roger Taylor told an interviewer that Duran Duran was friends with UB40 and other Black bands in Birmingham. UB40 used to rehearse next door to them. Roger recalled, "We'd be singing songs about Rio and girls on film while these guys were writing about racism and poverty and a hard life on the street. It made us think."

The "Girls on Film" single dropped on July 13, 1981, backed with "Faster Than Light." It got on the radio immediately and started to sell, rising to #5 in England by the end of the month, after *Top of the Pops* aired the band miming the song. Then the *NME* published a friendly tour report by Paul Morley, who had been with the band during the riots in Birmingham. Around the same time, Duran Duran's management reminded them that they needed new songs for their second album. One of the first ideas they came up with that summer was the beginning of "Last Chance on the Stairway."

In September, it was back to work, promotion in motion. EMI sent the band to press tours of Spain and Portugal, then to Belgium. The company planned a big showcase for Paris, allocating £10,000 for publicity and another £2,000 on importing two busloads of Rum Runner regulars—many in costumes and full drag—to make sure the still unknown band got a good crowd at a club called Captain Video. Then they were off to a festival in Berlin, followed by a date at Amsterdam's famous Paradiso nightclub on September 12.

Now the five musicians barely had time to unwind before they flew to New York to begin their first North American tour on September 15, an experience that would introduce them to some of their heroes and usher in busy days ahead. MTV had begun playing music videos for the still-tiny American cable TV audience on August 1 without any input from Duran Duran. This would change after Duran Duran became identified with Andy Warhol and Studio 54 during their crazy days in New York City that autumn.

On September 15, a car arrived in Hollywood to pick up Nick and John, who kissed their mothers goodbye, waved to the young fans who'd started hanging around their families' houses, and rode to Heathrow Airport, west of London. Everyone was excited to begin Duran Duran's headlining tour of American nightclubs. Capitol Records executives had taken notice of the band's growing popularity across Europe and the UK and were preparing for similar success in North America. Still, everyone flew economy class on Air India— the cheapest way to get to New York. Andy later claimed he saw passengers cooking meals on paraffin stoves in the aisles.

John, somewhat dazed and confused after a transatlantic flight, felt less than welcomed by the "terrifying-looking" uniformed customs officer who dubiously examined his passport upon his arrival at New York's JFK airport. Of course, John's makeup was a bit blurry, and his luridly dyed hair did seem unusual. He later wrote about his reception:

"Where ya stayin'?" the officer asked.

John had no idea. He called over to the tour manager, Richard. "What's the name of our hotel?"

"The Holiday Inn!" Richard shouted.

The customs guy removed his sunglasses. "The Holiday Inn—where?"

"The Holiday Inn—where, Richard?"

"Long Island!"

"I'm sorry," John said. "I'm . . . in a band."

As he was, seemingly reluctantly, stamping John's passport, the customs man said, "Well, if we need to find you, we'll just put out an APB for a funny-looking guy with purple hair."

John said thank you and—*sotto voce*—"It's *burgundy*, not purple, you wanker."

Instead of heading into the city, the band rented two cars at the airport and headed east to Long Island. Looking out the windows, the band could see the famous Manhattan landmarks—the Empire State Building, the twin towers of the World Trade Center—shimmering in twilight but fading away to their left as the sun was going down. With John navigating, they pulled onto the Long Island Expressway and an hour later deposited an exhausted, jet-lagged Duran Duran at the Syosset Holiday Inn in Hicksville.

Welcome to America.

Most of wealthy Long Island was wired for cable television, and this was where Duran Duran first got a look at MTV—as well as the other forty or so channels then available via cable. It was a dramatic upgrade from the three TV channels back in England. MTV had been narrowcasting for a mere six weeks, but all the essentials were in place: the moonwalking astronaut and his crunchy theme; the hip young VJs introducing the clips; lurid colors, flashy dancers; and about a dozen videos of Rod Stewart in full shag mullet, high-waisted trousers, and chest-baring shirts.

Even though they were still incredibly jet-lagged, Duran Duran could not stop watching MTV.

The next day Duran Duran was interviewed at the studio of WLIR radio in nearby Hempstead. The powerhouse Long Island rock station was an important trendsetter, beginning with punk and on through post-punk, new wave, and New Romantic. Their DJs were already playing "Girls on Film" in heavy rotation and seemed eager to promote the band. That night, the American tour opened with a dynamic rendition of "Girls on Film" at Spit, the old-school punk club in Levittown, before a big crowd of "Stellas and Guidos" (as Italian kids were known locally). The kids knew the main songs from the album and seemed as excited about the band as the fans back in Birmingham. Duran Duran's version of "Fame" also seemed to go down really well with the T-shirt-and-denim-wearing audience. "They didn't look like us," John later said of their young customers, "but you could tell they were ready to."

The next night, Duran played at the Channel in Boston, a mob-controlled club (whose affable and popular manager was murdered a short time later). A guy from radio station WAAF gave the band the strongest pot they had ever smoked, so the show was a little off.

Then, finally, Duran Duran arrived in New York, checking into the St. Moritz Hotel on Central Park South. When they weren't glued to MTV, the band could see the park's maples and oaks bursting out in full autumnal colors. Capitol held a press conference for the band at their offices in Midtown, attracting both editors from teen magazines (*Hit Parader*, *Circus*) and reporters from the *New York Post* and the *Village Voice*. Capitol also told Paul Berrow that the *New York Times* was sending a critic to cover the band's two nights at the Ritz, Manhattan's main venue for rock concerts and raucous dance parties.

When the band arrived at the Ritz on East Eleventh Street, just off Union Square, for the afternoon sound check, they were surprised by how decrepit the old ballroom was. Built in 1886 and barely modernized since electricity was put in, the Ritz was basically a rabbit warren of rickety staircases and anterooms surrounding a Victorian grand ballroom that could hold fourteen hundred people. Without an elevator, handicapped patrons had to be carried inside, and loading in amplifiers and speakers was a grueling ordeal. But the Ritz was known and admired as a friendly and democratic club, and it attracted a diverse crowd.

Back at the St. Moritz, the band changed into their stage clothes. Simon was in one of his two new suits tailored by Antony Price in his King's Road atelier. Following Roger's style, three of the band members wore French sailor shirts in blue and white stripes. All wore scarves and headbands. Trouser legs were stuffed into suede Chelsea boots. Lots of makeup and hairspray completed the New Romantic look. At eight o'clock, everyone gathered in the hotel bar, excited to make their New York debut.

Capitol Records had yet to release their album in North America, but they still sent over two white Cadillac stretch limousines, complete with TV sets and full bars ("a nightclub on wheels," as an impressed John Taylor told his diary), to pick the band up for their gig. They entered the Ritz through a side door, glad to see there was a crowd thronging outside, waiting to get in.

Inside, the club's huge video screen was lit up with Duran Duran's videos. The fans applauded the muddy naked models depicted in "Girls on Film." As "Tel Aviv" played over the PA speakers, Duran Duran walked out to cheering and applause. Simon rolled up the sleeves of his suit jacket, and Duran Duran went to work. John remembered, "It was like we were home, from home. Like at the Spit, the kids knew all the words. The difference in New York City was the higher level of fashion consciousness. These kids looked like us."

After the show, Duran Duran piled into their white Cadillac limousines and were driven to Studio 54 amid its sleazy Midtown neighborhood of porn theaters and dive bars. Cameras flashed as they cut past the velvet rope of desperate souls seeking admittance to the notoriously exclusive nightclub. This easy entry was facilitated by Doreen D'Agostino, Capitol's national publicity manager, who had happily taken the hot English band under her wing. They marveled at the scenes they encountered once inside the infamous disco: deafening music, industrial diamond dust falling like snow on dancing freaks, pretty boys in short shorts, pulsing lights, drugs in the ladies room, oral sex in the balconies, the giant Man in the Moon mobile with the coke spoon up his nose. But the club's ambience wasn't entirely unfamiliar to the band, since Paul and Mike Berrow had modeled the Rum Runner on Studio 54 in the first place. "Studio," as it was known to its regulars, was at the apex of an emerging culture at the beginning of the eighties. The conservative presidency of Ronald Reagan (an analogue of England's Margaret Thatcher), the rise of crack cocaine, and the onslaught of HIV and AIDS were provoking new styles of sharper-edged protest art. This was the era of Jean-Michel Basquiat's nightmarish A-train graffiti tags, Jenny Holzer's one-line epigrams pasted up in Times Square phone booths, and Keith Haring's cartoon stick men enjoying anal sex on downtown subway station walls.

As the band relaxed with glasses of wine, taking in all the decadence and fun, Doreen asked Nick what she could do for him while they were in town. Nick asked her if she knew Andy Warhol, and she replied that she did. Did Nick want to meet Andy? Nick made it clear this was his heart's desire. Doreen told Nick that when they returned to New York after their tour, she would try to make this happen. A bit later, Simon and Andy were driven back to their hotel, but John, Nick, and Roger piled into their limo and had themselves driven around town for the rest of the night, which ended at the McDonald's on Fourteenth Street, where they devoured Egg McMuffins just after dawn.

The second Ritz concert was the next night, September 19. The *New York Times* sent critic Stephen Holden, who usually covered Manhattan's cabaret scene, to review the show. Twenty-five years older than the band, Holden didn't get anything about the band and described New Romanticism as shallow and artless. So Duran Duran's first notice in the mainstream press was less than magic. Noting the New Romantics' "narcissistic concern with clothes and haircuts," the critic described the band's version of "Fame" as superficial. "It showed just how far it must go if Duran Duran is to achieve a meaningful artistic identity. It was hard to tell what was either New or Romantic about it."

Next, Duran Duran played to a dozen college students at the Chance, upriver in Poughkeepsie, New York. The Police had made their American debut there in 1977 in front of a similarly intimate audience (about ten people). A few days later, Doreen D'Agostino escorted the band to MTV's Midtown offices. They met the young Warner guys who'd invented MTV, Bob Pittman and John Lack, whose channel was now seven weeks old and growing fast. The youngish execs were wearing suits, they explained, so that their Warner Cable bosses would actually think it was sane to give them money for the channel. "Who are these guys?" thought Simon. "They're the opposite of rock and roll."

In late 1981, nothing was more talked about in American media than MTV. "I want my MTV" was an underground slogan for those who couldn't get enough of the music videos rotating, repetitiously, day and night. Pittman and Lack sheepishly showed the band the brutally edited and censored version of the "Girls on Film" video they were going to broadcast, drawing groans of displeasure from

Duran Duran. Pittman explained that America was much less sexually permissive than Europe, and the PG (parental guidance) version of "Girls on Film" was the only one that could possibly get on the channel. It was better than nothing. Disappointment aside, the meeting went well, and the band was encouraged to make more videos with MTV's audience in mind. They were all aware they were riding a groundswell of an emerging art form that would change the way people experienced music. Before MTV, kids had to pay to see bands they liked, if only to see how they looked, what they wore. Now bands could reach a few million fans, several times a day, almost for free.

And with that, Duran Duran hit the great American road, with Simon jotting his thoughts in his notebooks in full Jack Kerouac mode. The band was advertised to clubgoers as "Duran Duran—From England!" and the venues were mostly nightclubs that catered to the rock crowd. They started at the Bayou in Washington on September 22, followed by shows at a strip club in Philadelphia and then on to Pittsburgh. After that, it was up to Canada for wildly attended shows in Montreal and Toronto, where they appeared at El Mocambo, the nightclub where the Rolling Stones had famously absconded with the Canadian prime minister's wife. The rest of September saw them in the upper Midwest: two nights in Michigan and then Minnesota, where they got a positive notice in the *Minneapolis Star.* They finished the busy month in Chicago, where they received the most enthusiastic response of their American debut. John and Simon were taken to the Playboy Mansion, where they "scored our first bunnies," according to John. A couple of them even went to see James Brown perform at the Park West on Chicago's West Side.

Several rock critics who saw these concerts remarked how Andy was the hardest-working member of Duran Duran. He led the band and sang the choruses with leather-lunged abandon, all the while running around and jumping off the stage risers. John's sexy poses and Nick's reticence were cool, and Simon's dancing was infectious fun for the fans, but Andy, some noted, was Duran Duran's booster rocket. On tour at least, it seemed to be Andy Taylor's band.

Then it was on to Los Angeles.

Of course, the band and their entourage had to check into the Riot House on Sunset Boulevard in West Hollywood. This was what the LA cognoscenti called the Continental Hyatt House hotel due to the famous mayhem wreaked on the premises back in the misty seventies by such guests as Led Zeppelin, the Who, Elton John, and other big, rich, bored-on-the-road English touring bands.

Duran Duran—from Birmingham—took to subtropical, autumnal Southern California with wide-eyed fervor. The first night of October, they were given a VIP tour of the raunchy rock clubs on the fabled Sunset Strip, including the Roxy and the Rainbow. There was also a long, long shopping trip for albums and cassettes at Tower Records on Sunset, at the time the most famous record store on the planet. Simon wanted to see the nearby Whisky a Go Go, the discotheque where the Doors had been the house band in 1965. The following night, the band headlined at the Roxy, drawing a big (mostly older) crowd, as Capitol was showcasing the band for local radio. Their booking agent, Rob Hallett, had come over with them from London, and he was amazed at the beauty of the girls who'd come to see Duran Duran. It was like someone had called the model agencies and invited the hottest girls in LA to come see them perform. On October 3, the band signed records at Vinyl Fetish Records in Hollywood. Asked by excited high school girls from the San Fernando Valley when their album was coming out in America, the band replied that they didn't know—but thought it would be soon.

Later Paul Berrow recalled how earnestly the band worked on promotion while in America. "They worked bloody hard," he said. "Total dedication from everybody, day and night, seven days a week. The guys were fantastic. There was no 'I don't want to go and do an interview' going on. It was just unheard of. It just didn't happen."

Duran Duran played a second, late show at the Roxy. It had been promoted on the radio and so was crowded beyond capacity. When they returned to the Riot House, the Berrows were bluntly informed by the hotel's irate manager that they were being evicted. Indeed, after a day of heavy boozing, according to Andy, someone from the entourage had poured a bottle of shampoo in the forecourt fountains, sending bubbles down Sunset Boulevard. Then Andy noticed there was a wedding lunch being served below his balcony on a high floor. Soon stale room service food began going over the side before Andy tipped an ice bucket full of water onto the guests. This was no match for Who drummer Keith Moon driving a limo into the pool; they were just being childish rock stars. Still, the hotel staff called the LA County Sheriff's Department, who threatened to arrest them all unless they checked out of the Riot House. No other reputable hotel would take the band, so the rest of their stay in Los Angeles was spent in a fleabag motel in Santa Monica. Andy had to share a bedroom with Nick: "I can remember the sheer horror on his face when a cockroach crawled over him in the night."

⁓

Their American tour was far from over. In October, Duran Duran did a radio interview at KROQ, the most important rock station in Southern California, and then flew up to San Francisco on October 5 to play at the I-Beam on legendary Haight Street. (It was hard hat night—construction workers—at the mostly gay nightclub.) On October 8, they were at Pirate's Cove in Cleveland. The next night, they sold out the Left Bank, a big rock club in Mount Vernon, just north of Manhattan. Duran Duran was on fire now, a shit-hot band in full communion with its young audience of new wavers, post-punkers, and New Romantics.

Meanwhile, Duran Duran was playing a new song ("My Own Way") at the sound checks, complete with Simon's crypto-bohemian lyrics and a blockbuster chorus. Some of the EMI execs had flown over from London for a Duran Duran media showcase at the Savoy Ballroom, the big club on West Forty-Fourth Street. When they heard a demo of "My Own Way," they decided to make it the band's next single, to be recorded as soon as they returned to England.

As she had promised, Doreen D'Agostino called Andy Warhol up at his studio, the Factory, on Broadway just north of Union Square. She told him, "There are five good-looking young guys in town from a great band who want to meet you. They're called Duran Duran, and you'll like them a lot. Also, they wear makeup." Andy Warhol told Doreen to send over some photos of the band and to put him and a few friends on the guest list for Duran Duran's concert at the Savoy on October 10.

Andy Warhol was fifty-three at the time. By then, he was somewhat out of fashion in New York. His major work was behind him, his avant-garde mastery now being eclipsed by brash, much younger street artists like Basquiat and Keith Haring. Little did he know, Andy Warhol was about to fall in love—with nineteen-year-old Nick Rhodes.

By October 1981, Andy Warhol was known as the Prince of Pop and was one of the most famous artists in the world. He had come to New York from working-class Western Pennsylvania twenty years earlier and made his name as a commercial artist by drawing ladies' shoes for newspapers and magazines. When he arrived, the New York art world was dominated by the abstract expressionist clique, filled with macho, brawling alcoholics like Willem de Kooning and Jackson Pollock. But in the early sixties, some New York painters were turning away from abstraction and embracing the plain imagery of advertising and commercial art. Pop artists—Warhol, Lichtenstein, Rauschenberg—produced images that anyone could recognize: flags, comic strips, Coke bottles—exactly the stuff the abstract guys abhorred. Andy Warhol's first silk-screen painting exhibits in New York and Los Angeles were a sensation because he played with the raw imagery of national icons and TV ads: Campbell Soup cans, electric chairs, Elvis, Marilyn Monroe, Jackie Kennedy. "Once you 'got' pop," he wrote, "you could never see a sign the same way again. And once you thought pop, you could never see America the same way again."

Nick Rhodes had idolized Andy Warhol since he was twelve. His admirers called Warhol the first truly American artist, the first who didn't care about validation from Europe. He had revolutionized subject matter, technique, color, and photography. He'd invented slow cinema, happenings, and installations. He pulled rock music into the avant-garde. He declared sobriety and straightness to be boring, and they never recovered.

Pop artists like Andy Warhol were part of a new breed. Their undeclared manifesto held that the postabstract sensibility would be homosexual or ambivalent, not hypermasculine. This would color the Rolling Stones' vivid streak of pop art singles in 1965, as Mick Jagger and Brian Jones came to know Warhol in New York. It would echo down through the Velvet Underground, the band Warhol discovered and produced, and on through David Bowie in the seventies. Now, it was androgynous boy band Duran Duran's turn to be identified with Andy Warhol, who would continue to influence the band for the next few years.

⌒

After the Savoy concert, Andy Warhol and friends were whisked into the crowded green room to meet the band. Warhol had evidently been studying Capitol's luminous eight-by-ten glossies of the band, as he made a beeline straight for Nick Rhodes. Introductions complete, the room grew warmer as the band's girlfriends had also come over from England to savor Duran Duran's big NYC debut. Then it was into the limousines to ride the ten blocks north to Studio 54. Even Warhol was impressed by the band's reception from the club's gnomic doorkeepers, who let them (and a big entourage) sweep in as though they owned the place. Warhol and Nick were shown to a prime table, and camera lights started flashing—king paparazzo Ron Galella was in their faces. The images—sultry new English pop star meets iconic pop artist—would soon grace the *New York Post*, *Women's Wear Daily*, and even *Interview*, Andy Warhol's celebrity magazine. Nick asked Warhol about the Velvet Underground, revealing that Lou Reed's *Transformer* album had meant a lot to him. Warhol responded with something like, "Well, only five thousand people bought that first album, but everyone who did started a band, ha ha." Before the night was over, Warhol invited Duran Duran to come to the Factory and have their pictures taken. Nick kept his usual cool, but inside he was beyond thrilled.

The next morning at nine o'clock, as was his daily habit, Andy Warhol called his friend Pat Hackett, who helped him with his books and literary output. He dictated his diary notes from the previous day, which she would then type and file for later use. As published a few years later, the entry describes Warhol's first exposure to the charms of one of the first boy bands:

> *I wanted to see Duran Duran at the Savoy because their videotape is so good, it's called Girls On Film.* [This from the auteur of classic underground movies like *Chelsea Girls.*] *When I got there the first band was still on. Duran Duran are good-looking kids like Maxwell Caulfield* [actor and star of *Grease II,* a film Warhol saw three times that month]. *And then afterwards they wanted to meet me so we went backstage and I told them how great they were. They all wore lots of makeup, but they had their girlfriends with them from England, pretty girls, so I guess they're all straight, but it was hard to believe. We went to Studio 54 in their white limo and* [club owner] *Steve Rubell was really nice to them. He took them to the booth and gave them drinks. Ran into old friends, met a bunch of new kids and got home at 5:00 (cab $5).*

Andy Warhol started telling anyone who would listen that he had a crush on Nick Rhodes. "Oh, I love that Nick," he gushed to Andy Taylor, "and I got a photograph at home to prove it!" Warhol also suggested to (very butch) Andy Taylor that he should be wearing pearls onstage.

As Simon later recalled, "Andy Warhol had a real crush on Nick, who at the time looked a bit like a younger, prettier version of Andy Warhol. So it was quite funny, really."

John also remembered Warhol with fondness. "Andy Warhol was a sweet man—and he was very kind to us. Later Doreen took us to the Factory. Andy took Polaroid snapshots of us and asked us to sign them. He also gave us signed copies of his book *Andy Warhol—From A to B and Back Again.* So we would meet him again several times over the next few years." The band noticed that their import UK album was blaring over the Factory's excellent sound system, much the way the Rolling Stones had been the Factory's soundtrack in the sixties.

Duran Duran stayed in New York for a few more days, soaking up the city's electric vibes. As Simon reminisced, "New York was an incredible place at the start of the eighties. You had all these amazing nightclubs—the Peppermint Lounge, home of the twist. Studio 54 was in its last days of coolness but still going. There was Paradise Garage. We hung out at Danceteria [where young Madonna Ciccone from Michigan liked to go dancing]. It was incredible. You'd go to clubs and run into Billy Idol. Johnny Thunders. Debbie Harry at CBGB. The whole scene was about being out—and having fun."

After six action-packed weeks in America, Duran Duran boarded an Air India jumbo jet and returned to Birmingham. Nick and John found themselves back in their bedrooms in their parents' homes, a big change after the good hotels and so-so Holiday Inns across America. EMI was clamoring for a new single, so Colin Thurston booked Duran Duran into London's Town House Studios for a week and produced "My Own Way" and "Like an Angel." The former was goosed with John's edgy bass line, très Chic, and Richard Myhill's flighty strings dueling with Andy Taylor's growling lead guitar. "Like an Angel" was a slice of tepid Tropicália, a respectable B-side. Three lovely woodcuts of a matador decorated the sleeve and label, designed by artist Patrick Nagel (who would also create the cover of *Rio* the following year).

The twelve-inch single label read: "© *1981 original sound recording made by tritec music ltd.*" The Berrow brothers still owned Duran Duran.

The single was released in mid-November and reached the UK's Top 20. Nick hated the whole process: "This was the only time we ever had to sit down and say to ourselves, 'OK, we've got to write a hit single now.' It was only released in England, and I think it was one of the biggest mistakes in our career. *Ever.* We'll never do it again." Duran Duran's latest was put firmly in the shade by Human League's album *Dare*, which was England's hottest album that year.

Fourteen European concerts followed in late October, beginning with four shows in Germany, including Berlin, Hamburg, and Münster. Then they ventured to Stockholm for a live broadcast on Swedish television. Back in London by mid-November, they found themselves back at Manchester Square, where EMI garlanded the band with multiple gold and platinum album sales awards from European and Asian countries, just as the single "My Own Way" was topping off at #14 in the UK.

After taping "My Own Way" for *Top of the Pops*, it was back to the road with the Careless Memories Tour. The popular street poet John Cooper Clarke opened for Duran Duran at the Festival Theatre in Chichester the day after they played a wild, sold-out show in nearby Southampton. Raving kids in Birmingham stormed the stage of the Rum Runner in a fan frenzy on December 3. Joined by their opener and fellow EMI band Talk Talk, the tour continued through England as the winter began to set in: Canterbury, Sheffield, the Manchester Apollo. The roads were so slick in Wales that on December 13, the band's car was part of a pileup on the A5. Fenders were bent, but no one was hurt.

A few days later, the crowds outside the Hammersmith Odeon in West London were so turbulent that it took a private security team and a squad of London police officers to escort the band from their van to the stage door. Delirium was the order of the evening on the first night, December 16.

The BBC filmed the second night. Duran Duran takes the stage at nine o'clock to a thousand flashbulbs. Simon steps up to the microphone and asks, "Is there anyone out there?"

He's answered in screams. He begins the song in his posh accent. The tempo is thrilling, the drums miked loud. John's hyperactive bass lines are popping. Next up: "Planet Earth." Simon tells the fans, "It broke the ice for us." It's faster than the record, with Nick's sequencer emulating the aliens landing on Earth (or a child being born). Stately "To the Shore" relieves the tension in the big room, seething with young lust. Andy's guitar attacks "Late Bar" with a certain northern fury. Next Simon says, "Here's a new one," and they launch into "Last Chance on the Stairway," written while they were in California. John's upstage bass solo draws tears and moans from the girls. Clothes, programs, and candy are thrown onstage and land at his feet.

"Khanada" changes the concert's pulse with its drones and balladry. "Night Boat" comes next, a science fiction epic pairing synths and drums. When it expertly segues into "Sound of Thunder," the audience morphs into a hysterical dancing mob. One girl faints in front of the stage. Then another. The air is charged and electric. "Faster Than Light" is Andy's metallic showcase, the harder side of Duran Duran. Simon puts everything into "My Own Way," which he really likes more than the fans do. "Careless Memories"—played hard rock style—ends the set with a wild, Dionysian abandon. "Look out, look out, look out," Simon shouts, and then: "Good night!"

The encore is "Girls on Film." As the lens motor drive starts snapping, Simon calls out, "OK, it's your turn to sing," and the audience roars into the chorus like a Crystal Palace football crowd. No one is really ready for the evening to end, so the band convenes and Simon returns to the microphone. "Do you wanna dance?" Febrile screaming. "How about 'Planet Earth,' the night version? Yeah?" So Nick finishes the concert with an extended synth showcase that sends the happy young fans back onto freezing King Street and into the Hammersmith tube station.

There were a few more dates scheduled before Christmas. The Careless Memories Tour played in Edinburgh and Liverpool before ending with three nights at the Birmingham Odeon. There was a party after the third show at the Rum Runner, and everyone reflected on the amazing ride that Duran Duran had enjoyed in 1981. There was a feeling in the air that night that 1982 was going to be even more exciting.

PART 5

Now it's early 1982, and John Taylor and his best friend, Duran Duran's agent Rob Hallett, leave Hallett's flat in Kilburn and are driven to Chelsea for some shopping. Traffic on the King's Road is blocked by a crush of red Roadmaster double-decker buses, so John and Rob get out to walk the last few yards until they pull into Ebony, where John buys a lot of his clothes. Today, John is there to pick up some fresh cocaine, but it's a Saturday and John has been spotted by some kids, who crowd into the shop until they're shooed out by the manager. The kids then tell other kids on the street that John Taylor from Duran Duran is inside, wearing makeup and dyed hair, looking incredible, and a mob of unruly teens spills into the King's Road. Drug transaction complete, John and Rob find themselves unable to leave the shop. The kids in the street turn into a happy mob, singing "Planet Earth" and "Girls on Film" like football chants, ignoring the police trying to break up the crowd and get stalled cars and their angry drivers moving again. Eventually a police van forces its way through, and John and Rob, along with their Peruvian contraband, are driven away to relative safety.

EMI had been promoting John Taylor above his bandmates as "the face" of Duran Duran, the idea being it was easier for young fans (now called Durannies in the press) to identify with one face instead of five. But, John confided to his diary, this was taking a toll on both him and his family, whose home in Birmingham now always had a bunch of fans hanging around outside, even when John was in London or on tour. The stress and isolation were starting to wear on him as well. The fact was that "Porn Star Johnny," as he referred to himself after a weeks-long sex binge in America, was afraid of being alone, and cocaine and alcohol were good for morale. "I didn't want to be lonely," he wrote, "and the drugs ensured I never was. I'm a pinup on thousands of bedroom walls, but the fear of loneliness is turning me into a cokehead."

It didn't help that the former four-eyed nerd Nigel John Taylor couldn't walk down the King's Road in London without causing a riot.

EMI was still promoting "My Own Way" (Duran's most recent single) in February 1982. The band performed "Anyone Out There" on the *Old Grey Whistle Test* on the BBC, and the ratings for the show were very high. Their label wanted a second album of songs as soon as possible, and the band had just started writing again in Birmingham. Nick had the beginning of the "Save a Prayer" sequence down, and Simon was writing about hungry wolves and tropical girls dancing on the sand. They had recorded four songs ("My Own Way," "Last Chance on the Stairway," "New Religion," "Like an Angel") the previous August in EMI's demo studio in Manchester Square, which provided the foundation for the album. They cut the demo for "Hungry Like the Wolf" at EMI, then "Save a Prayer" at Bob Lamb's studio in Birmingham. The budget was about £65,000, double the budget for their first album. Then, feeling under pressure in England, Duran Duran decamped to a secluded chateau in France to write more new music for what they were assured would be an international breakout album for the band.

New material came together organically as the band was sequestered over a mild French winter with a decent chef and cases of vintage wines. Simon had been inspired by his American experiences while on tour, and many of these adventures became grist for new, ever-ambiguous lyrics in his ever-present songbook.

Also joining the band in France was Andy Taylor's girlfriend, Tracey Wilson. Andy was completely in love with the beautiful and soulful young hairdresser, who was also a champion horsewoman. In France, he told the others he was going to propose to her on February 16, which was also his twenty-first birthday. Paul Berrow coughed and suggested that maybe it would be better business if the whole band stayed single for now. Roger was also getting serious about Giovanna Cantone, who was still working at the Rum Runner. Tracey and Giovanna were also close friends with Nick's girlfriend, Elayne Griffiths.

No one told Andy Taylor what to do, in his private life at least, and so on the evening of his birthday, he went ahead with the plan. He'd been celebrating at the Rum Runner until three in the morning. Tracey had a cold and had gone to bed early in the flat Andy was sharing with Simon in student/hipster/immigrant Moseley. Andy aroused his sleeping beauty, admitted he'd had a few, and asked her to marry him.

According to Andy, "I paused, waiting for a response. . . . Tracey rolled over sleepily. 'OK, I'll tell you in the morning,' she said and went back to sleep. Charming!"

Later in the morning, Tracey told Andy she had dreamed he'd proposed to her in the night. Then she said—yes. Andy went downstairs and found a groggy Simon staring at a sink full of dishes.

"Oh, really?" Simon said when told the news. What he actually meant was, Are you sure? But Andy was certain he'd made the right decision. Later, Simon congratulated him, saying, "It's great, if that's what makes you happy." It was a priority, in Duran Duran, to keep Andy Taylor happy.

A few days later on February 24, the band played "Girls on Film" and "My Own Way" on live TV for the British Rock and Pop Awards. Duran Duran had been nominated in the Best Newcomer category, but at the end of the evening, Human League—then red-hot in Britain—took away the prize.

Duran Duran finished the best album of their career, *Rio*, in the late winter and spring of 1982. (Some think *Rio* is the only great album they ever made.) With Colin Thurston again producing at AIR Studios in London, they also cut a few extra tracks that were used as flip sides of singles. Nick also exploited the sessions as a master class in sound production. He was the first to arrive at the studio and the last to leave once the session was complete, closely marking

Colin's techniques from initial microphone placement to finished track. EMI had told their producer that the company was finished promoting Duran Duran as a New Romantic synth band. What EMI wanted now was a rock-edged dance groove. Their advice: "Think Led Zeppelin and Talking Heads having a baby and calling it Duran Duran."

Most of the songs were inspired, lyrically and emotionally, by the lurid adventures the band had experienced on their US tour: the hot girl with the red sports car in Montreal; the decadent Aladdin's Cave of Studio 54; Warhol's Polaroid session at the Factory; squalid, shameful eviction from the Riot House; plentiful girls, models, paparazzi, limos, drugs, delirium, exhaustion. It was the whole rock-and-roll fantasy come true. Speaking later, Simon revealed that "Rio," both the song and the album, was really all about the way they had felt in America.

The track "Rio," which would open the album, sparkled and then exploded with thunderous echo and metallic guitar chops. The song had been worked out during the American sound checks while on tour. Mountains and rivers fly by under the jet plane at eight miles high, while the bass part comes from the nexus of Harlem and downtown. The saxophone solo was played by Andy Hamilton, a friend from Birmingham. (He would stay with Duran Duran onstage for most of their career.) The climax came with crazy synth patterns and Simon shouting "Alive! Alive! Alive!" before Rio herself dances on the sand and on to her bright future. The title, John recalled, "to me, was shorthand for the truly foreign, the exotic, a cornucopia of earthly delights, a party that would never stop."

"My Own Way" came next, with its directions to the Peppermint Lounge on West Forty-Fifth Street between Sixth and Broadway. Big drums, soaring chorus, and recorded a year earlier, "My Own Way" was remixed to relate to the post-punk-disco aspect of the band's newer songs. "That was as close to pure disco as we would ever get," John explained. "Lonely in Your Nightmare" had Beat-generation lyric aspirations and a windy and moaning bridge; it sounded like the Police circa 1980. John used his new fretless Japanese bass for the first time on the track.

"Hungry Like the Wolf" erupted out of the studio speakers like a blast of body heat, smelling of danger and fear. The malign spirit of Jim Morrison was present like a three-legged coyote, as sound bites of hunters and prey, backed by hard rock rhythms, evolved into heavy breathing, carnal moans, and female orgasms. The first side of the *Rio* LP concluded with "Hold Back the Rain," with Andy's flame-throwing guitar dueling with Nick's ectoplasmic synthesizers in one of the band's better studio jams.

Nick's doomy, organ-wise introduction opened up the album's second side. This was "New Religion," whose spacey four-note riff and casual funk beat framed Simon's double overlapping story lines, which he later described as "a dialogue between the ego and the alter ego." Next would come "Last Chance on the Stairway," written in Los Angeles, the song like a car ride in Southern California and a budding romance that went nowhere as signals were vague and chances were missed. Legendary American beauty Bebe Buell—former *Playboy* model and muse to Jimmy Page plus others—is name-checked in the lyrics. There was even a marimba solo and the mention of "a scene right out of Voltaire."

"Save a Prayer" had grown out of Nick and Andy building chords over a lovely sequencer track in the studio. It would, of course, become one of Duran Duran's greatest hits and its wistful recounting of a close romantic encounter one of its era-defining moments. "Some people call it a one-night stand," declared Simon, "but we can call it paradise." Nick's quite wonderful love theme would be a fan favorite all through the life of the band, even drawing in some famous admirers. Sometime later, Nick was at home in Hollywood when his mother said there was a phone call. "Who is it?" Nick asked.

"Michael Jackson," she replied. It turned out Michael was calling to tell Nick how much he loved "Save a Prayer."

Rio ended with "The Chauffeur," a sinister ditty with lyrics about swarming aphids, the Western Isles, and somehow being left behind—by the chauffeur. The track was composed by Nick during an all-nighter, late in the recording sessions. The lyrics had been written by Simon while he was in Israel in 1978, just after being dumped by his girlfriend. Simon's urgent, steely cries of "sing blue silver" implied for some listeners the sonic surrealism of amplified vocals streaking through the atmosphere of a rock concert. At the end of "The Chauffeur," the album concludes with a brisk jingling of coins. Digital samplers were a few years away, so Nick had to record sound effects live: not only the coins but also the lit match on "Last Chance on the Stairway" and the laughing girl on "Rio" (reputed to be Nick's then-girlfriend, Cheryl).

The members of Duran Duran had all rented apartments in London to be near AIR Studios, but after hours they hung out at the Embassy on Old Bond Street, a private nightclub where the regulars included lesser royalty, rich aristocrats, and rock stars like Freddie Mercury and Roger Taylor from Queen and the Who's Peter Townshend. Cocaine was sometimes on offer behind the manager's bulletproof door. Soon John was one of the club's main attractions, especially after he'd broken up with his girlfriend, Roberta, at Christmas. "He was the absolute star of the place," Andy later recalled. "He was starting to get a staggering amount of female attention, much more than the rest of us. The record company had pushed him into the spotlight because of his looks, and all the wild partying was his way of letting off steam."

One night at the Embassy, Andy and John were hanging out with the Kemp brothers from Spandau Ballet and Steve Strange, now a member of the band Visage. When the club closed, they all went over to Steve's house in Notting Hill, where they found the great Yorkshire singer Robert Palmer lying on the bed in a suit and tie, laughing to himself. Andy thought he'd taken acid. Eventually Robert, who everyone admired, came around, and the night continued until dawn.

Another night, John was in the Embassy's restaurant with pal Rob Hallett when the club's owner, Stephen Hayter, came to their table and invited them to the office. "You're going to like this," he said over his shoulder. "Follow me." Sitting in the office was David Bowie, along with his date, the glamorous socialite Sabrina Guinness.

Bowie: "Hello, boys." Focusing on John, he said, "I've *heard* about you."

John: "Oh! Thank you. Yes, we covered 'Fame.' And Colin Thurston is producing us." The remainder of the night was spent in the presence of their greatest hero. They got back to Rob's flat, elated.

John and Rob spent a lot of time at the Embassy. John usually kept busy signing autographs, but even with all the cologne and makeup, they never seemed to attract any of the young models and actresses who beautified the club. Much later, Stephen Hayter explained to Rob that the reason he and John never scored any girls was because everyone thought they were gay.

$\sim$

Soon, the money started pouring in from record sales and touring. Andy bought a huge flat on top of a Victorian industrial building in Wandsworth, South London. He also purchased a hot little BMW 325 that he didn't have a license—or know how—to drive. The Berrows bought Ferraris. International pop stars Nick and John thought about moving away from their parents in Hollywood. They'd been amused to learn that their so-called rivals in Spandau Ballet, Gary and Martin Kemp, were still sharing the bedroom they were raised in, in their parents' North London council flat.

Meanwhile, they approved the striking cover illustration they'd commissioned from artist Patrick Nagel, whose work Paul Berrow had admired in *Playboy*. This was a smiling representation of Rio, the girl who dances on the sand, set off against a striking magenta background. These were the beginnings of the last days of classic album art, an era when the record store also served as a sort of populist art gallery. Andy Warhol had designed albums for the Rolling Stones, Grace Jones, and Aretha Franklin; Robert Rauschenberg for Talking Heads; Keith Haring for disco star Sylvester.

Patrick Nagel's alluring *Rio* jacket would become the central image associated with Duran Duran over their career. The album's inner sleeve, again designed by Malcolm Garrett, featured complete lyrics and a portrait of the band taken atop the British Petrol building in London, with the musicians dressed in brand-new Antony Price suits. These were also the clothes they wore in the groundbreaking videos they made for a targeted campaign to get them on MTV in America.

Toward the end of the *Rio* sessions, they made a video for "The Chauffeur" with British director Ian Emes, who worked mostly with Pink Floyd. This was a terrible attempt to continue the sleaze of "Girls on Film" and infuse Duran Duran's image with sadomasochistic undertones inspired by Helmut Newton's fashion photography and the neo-noir themes of *The Night Porter*, a 1974 movie with Charlotte Rampling. Following the soft-core vibes of "Girls on Film," the new video deployed naked breasts and writhing women in a carnival of poor taste and crosscut cinema. When Paul Berrow showed the video to MTV in New York, programmer Les Garland told him it was one of the worst he'd ever seen.

"Look," Garland told him, "all the videos we see look alike. They're taped in the same studios in New York and LA with the same dancers by the same directors [who'd switched from making TV commercials]. MTV has almost no Black audience because those areas aren't wired for cable yet, but we have to play 'Billie Jean' because it just looks so different from everything else on the channel.

"If you want to get your band on MTV, you gotta give us something new, something exotic. If you shoot in thirty-five millimeter, that would be even better than tape. Give us something in a jungle or on a mountain or Japan, and you'll get your band on MTV."

Back in London, with the album almost in the can, EMI execs decided that they would try to make a video album for all the songs on *Rio*. This wouldn't exactly happen, but they did agree to rehire Russell Mulcahy, who had directed "Planet Earth," to make clips for "Hungry Like the Wolf," "Save a Prayer," and "Rio."

Explaining that MTV wanted exotic locales, Paul suggested filming in Sri Lanka, formerly Ceylon, the exotic tropical island in the Indian Ocean. Paul had been there, he said; Sri Lanka had open beaches, ancient temples, colorful people, teeming bazaars. He had a fantasy about building some kind of spiritual retreat there. Russell had also worked there, and he added that production costs were lower than almost anywhere else in South Asia. As soon as the album was done, they agreed, Duran Duran was going to Sri Lanka to take the music video to the next level.

In early April 1982, Nick and Andy were finishing studio work for the *Rio* album before following the rest of Duran Duran to Sri Lanka. Unbeknownst to Nick, this would also be the end of his intense apprenticeship with Colin Thurston in the recording studio due to a financial falling-out between Colin and Paul Berrow a few months later. With the album's last details sorted, a chauffeur took Nick and Andy to Heathrow for the long flight to Colombo, Sri Lanka's capital. It was still chilly in England, so Nick was fully dressed in black leather. After a twelve-hour flight, he deplaned into astonishing tropical heat and humidity, thinking, "I'm not really dressed properly, am I?"

There was a man waiting with Nick's name on his sign, and Nick figured the limo would drop him at a five-star hotel where a shower would revive him. The man with the sign pointed instead to a dusty old van. "I said, 'How far is it to the hotel?' He said, 'Five hours.'"

Andy added, "This vehicle was old, and there was no air conditioning, so it acted like an oven in the baking heat. Nick was wilting as he sweated in his leathers while we rattled and rolled along these terrible roads. . . . There were beggars everywhere, many with missing limbs. We'd never seen poverty like this. It was shocking. If we stopped for some watermelon, the car would be surrounded by crowds of little brown children. Nick was almost moaning now. 'Fucking hell,' he said. 'This place is horrible. They're *bastards* for bringing us here.'"

Nick remembered, "We finally arrived in a seaside town called Galle, and it was like a mirage—the most beautiful beach you've ever seen. As I was walking up to the hotel, an elephant passed me on the street. I thought, 'It can't get any stranger than this.'"

Out on the beach, Russell Mulcahy was working with a local production crew, who had tortuously gotten all the necessary permits through the tourism authorities. With a budget of £30,000, Russell's brief was to make three videos: "Hungry Like the Wolf," "Save a Prayer," and part of "Lonely in Your Nightmare." (He'd previously made a clip for "My Own Way" in London, with a bullfighting theme related to the matador woodcuts of Patrick Nagel's jacket for the single release.) Russell's storyboard for "Hungry" was based on Simon's lyrics "I'm lost and I'm found." If MTV wanted exotic stories, Russell would give them Simon Le Bon as Indiana Jones, lost in the torrid jungles and steaming cities of Asia, with serpents, monkeys, and parrots galore, until he finally meets up with his band in the city and tells them what happened to him. The director was quick to discover that Simon was a natural in front of the camera. Most of the young rock stars he worked with giggled during takes or looked at the camera, forcing retakes. As a former child actor, Simon had appeared in commercials since he was five. He'd been on the London stage at fourteen. He knew what he was doing as an actor, knew how to make pursuit and evasion look real. The only problem with Simon was that he had dyed his hair orange, by mistake. Simon was mortified. He wore Russell's gray fedora for much of the shoot.

For the "Save a Prayer" video, Mulcahy focused more on John Taylor, moodily strumming his guitar in Galle's coastal paradise as reddening evening fell on old Ceylon. There was also a spiritual theme to the shoot, limning the song's sexual context, as the band was filmed atop a holy mountain and then perusing massive stone temples of the most antique Buddhist lineage. The "Prayer" shoot provided loads of good (and bad) stories that the band would dine out on forever.

First, there were the elephants.

A local herd had been hired to spice up the videos. Amid much hilarity, the elephant handlers, called mahouts, got Nick and John on their animal. Then they got Simon and Andy up on theirs. Nick noticed that all the mahouts seemed drunk. Finally, Roger got his own elephant, and they began to roll film. There was also this huge female around, part of the herd, who let out a mighty trumpet. The sound technician was taping all this, and he thought it would be funny to play her back through the speakers at full volume. But it turned out to be the elephant's mating call, and suddenly Roger's elephant wheels around, charges through the paddy, and mounts the female with Roger still aboard. Nick laughed while thinking back on the event, noting, "Roger's hanging on for dear life, and all the mahouts are rolling around, thinking this is hilarious. If he'd fallen off, he could have been trampled to death. It was funny as hell but also quite hairy for a moment."

Another scene dreamed up by Russell (and storyboardist Marcello Anciano) called for an elephant to squirt water from its trunk over the bare chest of one of the band. No one volunteered for this supposedly homoerotic scene. Andy said, "In the end, John agreed. After all, we argued, he was the pinup. That scene appears about halfway through 'Save a Prayer,' and we ribbed John over it for many years to come."

Another elephant scene, filmed by a lagoon where the same crew had once worked on a Tarzan movie, went awry when a maddened bull broke free, splashed through the water, charged its handler, and roared off into the jungle. They'd been warned that elephants could kill, and Andy was concerned that the herd might turn on them. He'd been swigging from a bottle of Jack Daniels during the shoot, and to get out of the way, he clamored up a tree and sat out on a branch, about ten feet over the water, prepared to mime playing his guitar. The other elephants were splashing in the water, pissing in the lagoon. A bit dazed, he was shouting, "What the fucking hell are we doing here? Which one is supposed to be fucking Tarzan?" Then somewhat tipsy Andy lost his balance and fell into the lagoon. The filthy water was muddy and dark, and when he surfaced Andy spat out a mouthful of blackened liquid elephant shit. He tried to make himself throw up, but it didn't work. He finished the bottle of Jack, realizing that he might be in for some dark days ahead.

"We're a fucking rock band," Andy muttered to John that night. "What the fuck were we doing out there, pouncing about on elephants?"

When the band and the crew arrived in Colombo to finish "Hungry," filming Simon running through teeming city streets and markets with Duran Duran in hot pursuit, they learned that England had just gone to war with Argentina over the Falkland Islands. The military junta that was running Argentina had seized the lightly defended islands in the South Atlantic, which they called the Malvinas. Prime Minister Thatcher sent a naval fleet to retrieve them. It was an undeclared war but a dangerous conflict all the same. Ships were torpedoed and sunk on both sides; soldiers and sailors were dying for real. They listened to the BBC World Service on shortwave radio, trying to find out what was going on. No one knew what would happen.

On a blazing hot morning, a couple of buses drove band and crew to the ancient fortress of Sigiriya, near the city of Kandy in the middle of the island, to film scenes for "Save a Prayer." This was a mountainous rock formation that had been a fortress, then a royal palace, then a Buddhist monastery. It was a holy place, so a helicopter had to drop Nick and Simon onto the rock in a bucket because it couldn't land on the shrine itself. Nick recalled later, "I must have been entirely insane."

In order to show respect, they were required to be barefoot, but the rock felt like they were walking on hot coals. While the audio track was playing, Simon was yelling, "Fuck you, Russell! Fuck yoooooooou!" When Russell finished the scene, the still-rolling camera captured them hopping around the hot stairs like their feet were on fire.

Down below, the band was filmed, all respectfully barefoot, walking around the temple precincts. They noticed that hundreds of saffron-robed monks were streaming into the area, and many of them seemed annoyed to find some strange tourists—Duran Duran—loitering in their historic sanctuary. It turned out the monks were there for a nationalist political rally, and they definitely seemed annoyed to find these young English guys in their midst. Andy Taylor thought this might end badly.

"By now there were thousands of monks surrounding us, most of them glaring at us in silence. One of the monks came over to us and spoke through our interpreter: 'You are causing grave offense! Leave respectfully—now. You have to go!' We were quickly back on the buses and gone."

A year later Sri Lanka exploded. A civil war between the native Sinhalese Buddhists and the (mostly Muslim) Tamil population (which had been imported from southern India by British colonials to work on Ceylon's lush tea plantations) would last until the Tamils were defeated in 2009. The videos produced in Sri Lanka by Duran Duran in 1982 were among the last to show the paradise-like island nation before it was convulsed by decades of conflict and death.

Duran Duran's last night in Kandy was spent shooting the finale of "Hungry Like the Wolf," with the band (back in their snazzy suits colored in shades of avocado, apricot, and lavender) reuniting with their errant singer in an old café that looked like a scene out of *Casablanca*. And that was it. Russell left for London and the editing desk. Duran Duran flew east, to Australia, via Air Lanka. John later wrote, "We had been in Sri Lanka just eight days, but we had filmed iconic footage that would define Duran Duran for a generation."

After shooting the videos in Sri Lanka, Duran Duran flew to Sydney to begin the band's first tour of Australia, starting in Adelaide on April 15. There was a brief layover in Thailand, during which the band and its twenty-strong road crew disgraced themselves with a night of bawdy inebriation. Only abject begging and bribes saved them from another hotel eviction.

The Australian reception for the young band was warm and friendly. EMI's Australian subsidiary released an EP disc, *Night Versions*, with extended tracks for the discos, and many of the concerts were almost sold out, including the Palais in Melbourne and two nights at the Hordern Pavilion in Sydney. The band loved Australia, where they could walk around unbothered, unlike at home. On their first night, they met local heroes INXS—Australia's biggest band—at Benny's Bar, a Sydney speakeasy where that band hung out in its early days. Simon Le Bon and protean INXS singer Michael Hutchence paired off, compared notes, and would become close friends. The next night, the band held a beach party for the road crew. A model agency sent over a bunch of its younger clients, who began to take an interest in the trampoline set up on the beach. Andy noted, "Everyone was urging the girls to have a go, shouting, 'Come on! It's for the road crew!' Soon young models were bouncing up and down on the trampoline, topless, while the crew were all openmouthed with wonder."

From Adelaide to Brisbane, Australia really loved the band. Radio interviews were long and obsequious. Young fans—80 percent girls—hurled themselves toward the stage, pushed back by burly security guys better suited for rugby. Duran Duran appeared on *Countdown*, the local version of *Top of the Pops*. This show was hosted by veteran radio DJ Molly Meldrum, who had helped "Planet Earth" get to #1 back in 1981. Now he promoted the band's concerts on the air, and the whole tour sold out. Out in Australia's wild west, the band rode to some concerts in open-sided cattle trucks, with the equipment bouncing around in the back. Everything seemed like an adventure.

Before leaving for Japan, the boys went to a big party at Molly's sprawling house. The Australian cricket team was invited, and it got a little rowdy. Soon after, they were taken to the Manzil Room, rumored to be the most dangerous rock-and-roll bar in the world, full of hard-core roadies and bikers and the sheilas who love them. According to Andy, Duran Duran and entourage were asked to leave for being rambunctious. Others said they were thrown out as a precaution before the locals started killing them.

John remembered the tour for its intense sexuality. To him, the Australian girls he met seemed to have few inhibitions about instant hookups. "In Australia I came to appreciate the rather strange phenomenon of meeting a girl in the hotel lobby upon check-in and being in bed with her less than an hour later. What services those girls performed!" He sent a postcard home to his parents in Hollywood: "Absolutely unbelievable. Just like the Beatles. Screaming kids. Had to get a police escort from the radio station and we were on the news as the amazing new sensation. FABBO!! John XX"

Meanwhile, Andy began to feel ill during the band's second show in Sydney. He vomited violently behind the amps just before the encore. His stomach was hurting; it felt as though he'd been poisoned. The hotel doctor told him he had a fever and advised him to get some rest. Andy knew it was those fucking elephants. He started to hate the band's management for making him sick.

Duran Duran arrived in Japan on April 23, met by a few hundred frantic girls and a flying squad of interpreters, promoters, publicists, and security agents. The vans carrying them to their hotel were shadowed by speeding taxis full of excited young fans who were hanging out of cab windows, screaming at them. In John's van, Rob Hallett remembered, the lads were bemusedly singing "I Love Rock and Roll." It was every English underground club band's fantasy to have such an adoring fanbase, now presenting itself as reality TV. But there was a downside to Japanese adulation. John thought that compared to the looseness of Australia, Tokyo felt like being in prison, albeit one with superior room service. They spoke on the radio via interpreters, were herded around by the publicists, and were minded by their guards. They were shown the stupefying spectacle of Tokyo's Ginza district at night, with futuristic neon displays that made Times Square or Piccadilly Circus look lame. Like all visiting rock bands, they were ceremoniously given new Sony Walkmans, the innovative cassette players that, for the first time, allowed people to listen to music of their choice while on the go. (The Walkman was so influential that in 1983, cassettes outsold vinyl recordings for the first time.)

The Japanese tour included five concerts in late April, playing mostly in auditoriums, starting with Nippon Seinenkan Hall in Tokyo. They traveled to Osaka and Nagoya by bullet train, where security struggled to get the band to their cars in train stations mobbed by huge crowds of fans, who seemed to be equally screaming and crying. The brief tour ended with two more shows in greater Tokyo, at Sun Plaza and Shibuya Kokaido. On an off day in Tokyo, John and Roger went shopping in the Harajuku district. Along for the ride was their friend and driver Simon Cook and their security squad. As they meandered through the warren of market stalls and restaurants, John was recognized; there weren't that many tall Anglo pop stars in finery and makeup wandering around Harajuku that afternoon. Soon they were being followed by a few dozen kids trying to speak to them and get autographs. Simon Cook said they had to get out of there. The Japanese guards looked worried and started whispering into their headsets. Just as the scene was beginning to crack, they backed a car down a side alley, bundled John and Roger into the rear seat, and roared off as a couple hundred crazy kids were about to mob their vehicle.

Simon's experience was different. He was told that Western models working in Tokyo liked to congregate at the bar of the Four Seasons Hotel, so off he went. "In Japan, all I was interested in was finding women. I'd take them back to my hotel. I spent all my time in the clubs, or in my bedroom, bonking. It was all front. You grab your balls, close your eyes, swagger up to the girl of your choice, and just go, 'Hi, baby.' That's it."

"The Japanese processed us," John later wrote. "The promoters controlled the experience, as if we were a potentially dangerous substance that must not be allowed to contaminate the calm and order of Japan. They were happy we were there, but they would be even happier when we left."

By early May, Duran Duran was exhausted. Everyone but Andy—who went home to see his fiancée—went to relax on the idyllic Caribbean island of Antigua for a week's holiday at the English Harbor resort. It was off-season in the West Indies, so they had the beach to themselves. John took up windsurfing. They sent their cool suits to the cleaners. Everyone (except Nick) was tanned by the intense sun of the Leeward Islands.

Back in chilly London's Manchester Square, the EMI staff loved Russell Mulcahy's thrilling footage from Sri Lanka. There was nothing like these images on music television, nothing like them on MTV, and they wanted more—as soon as possible. "Don't come home," the band was told on the eve of their return to London, because Russell, Paul Berrow, Andy, some models, and a film crew were flying out to Antigua to shoot a new video for "Rio."

According to Russell Mulcahy, it was Paul Berrow who said, "I want to go yachting in Antigua."

"So," Russell said, "we wrote a video about yachts."

Andy arrived in Antigua a day after the rest of the band. At the airport departure lounge at Heathrow, he had noticed a chic young woman who looked exactly like Rio, the illustrated girl on Duran Duran's album jacket. This turned out to be Reema, a beautiful half-Lebanese model from London's Model One agency. Like Andy, she and two other girls were flying to Antigua to work on videos with Duran Duran. Of course, as they gained altitude, Andy told her that she didn't look anything like Rio. Reema just laughed at him. After a glass or two of champagne, Andy put his seat back and smiled thinking of John and Simon, who would surely be subtly competing for awesome Reema's attention in the coming days.

Nick said that they shot the "Rio" clip in only two days. The film crew splashed colored dyes on models lolling in the gentle surf. This was Russell appropriating imagery from a sexy portfolio book called *Foxy Lady*, by the Belgian photographer Cheyco Leidmann. Ironic, low-budget attempts at James Bond film homages tried to evolve from storyboard to production. There was a parody of the scene in *Dr. No* in which Ursula Andress emerges from the Jamaican froth with a diving knife strapped to her leg; in the Duran Duran spoof, knife-strapped Reema beats up Roger on the beach when he accosts her. Armed with a pathetic toy rifle, John makes an amphibious beach landing that ends in a champagne cocktail. Simon was filmed falling into the aquamarine bay in various clumsy positions. He smashed into the dock on the last take and hurt his back, but it was the one they ended up using.

They also chartered a majestic sailing yacht named *Eilean*, attached a camera to her bowsprit, and prepared to go to sea on a windy day in the Lesser Antilles. The band were back in their fruit-colored suits, freshly laundered shirts, and skinny ties. Hair and makeup were wild to the wind as the captain laid on full sail and the *Eilean* began to race across the choppy ocean. The captain had warned the band and film crew not to lark about on the boat. Falling off into the churning sea was dangerous, possibly even fatal. There were strong currents in these waters, not to mention poisonous jellyfish.

Soon Simon was manfully belting out the "Rio" choruses, standing and sitting on the heaving bow, as the band hangs on (for dear life) behind him on the racing sailboat. John and Andy were filmed miming the song's saxophone solos, after which—very unscripted—John upended Andy and pushed him off the speeding boat and into the sea.

Andy came up sputtering. He was wearing an Antony Price suit, not a lifejacket, and he wasn't much of a swimmer. He managed to grab the line attached to the dingy trailing the yacht, holding on for dear life.

Their furious captain came about, dropped a sail, and rescued Andy. He gave them a bitter scolding, saying that Andy could have been killed if he'd come into contact with the keel or the rudder. This put a damper on the morning—there were sniggers about possible floggings at the mast, maybe even an HMS *Bounty*–like keel-hauling— but Russell Mulcahy had the footage he needed, including poor Andy walking the plank. The film crew agreed over a pint that John was a jerk for tipping Andy off the boat.

Nick hated making the *Rio* video. He was seasick and miserable, and he later said that everyone on board threw up during that shoot on the water. "For us, it was like, 'Wow—we can get the record company to pay for us to go to the Caribbean and make a video!' Of course we were going to go; we were kids. You'd never make a video like that now, but for the times they reflect, they were very much in context. The funny thing is, it looked like we were having a great time, but it was appalling. There wasn't one of us who didn't lose our lunch on that shoot.

"God, I hated that boat. Wrecking my nice suit with those dreadful waves splashing everywhere? Really! Tie the damn things up and serve cocktails on 'em. Boats: they're best tied up—just like women."

Simon noted, "We portrayed a James Bond fantasy. John in combat gear, me in a white dinner jacket on the boat, with the phones and wearing flippers. We were making arseholes of ourselves in the Caribbean. The boat was the closest we ever got to the superstar affluence thing. . . . It was like, 'Hey, look at this! This is fantastic!' And it was something nobody had seen."

Much later, Nick told an interviewer, "We were only on that boat for possibly three or four hours. And now that image is engrained upon a generation of early MTV viewers. When we were making those videos, we thought they would appear on *Top of the Pops* in England and then get shown for a couple of weeks on MTV. We didn't expect they'd still be around, thirty years later. It was hard to get away from the image of us in suits on that boat."

Before returning to England, Russell Mulcahy also shot a video for "Night Boat," depicting scantily clad white female zombies terrorizing Duran Duran in the scary dark night of the tropics. Despite its over-the-top camp, the "Night Boat" video was almost never broadcast anywhere.

Back in London, the campaign for *Rio* was well underway. After the single was released on May 4, Duran Duran mimed "Hungry Like the Wolf" on various UK television shows. Then Andy came down with nausea and fever, and he was taken to a National Health Service hospital, where he lay in a crowded ward and his condition worsened. Moved to a private hospital, he was diagnosed with a nonspecific virus and then sent home after five days. Upcoming concerts in Europe were pushed back until September. Andy blamed their management, and the elephants of Sri Lanka, for his illness, and he never really forgave them.

"Hungry Like the Wolf" was topping the charts now, pounding its way into the British Top 10. When they mimed the song on *Top of the Pops*, Simon was shown emerging from the dancing audience, as if he were one of them, in a blue shirt with a Chinese glyph. Andy was in leathers, John in a headband, Nick almost unnoticed in back. Asked about the song, Simon referenced Jim Morrison's major influence on him. "He was the Lizard King, wasn't he? The animal spirit god. That idea meant a lot to me, from when I started writing, and I tried to get it into our music. While we're standing there, wearing suits and lip gloss, there's this writhing, scaly thing inside us. That other image was just a decoy."

Two weeks later, on May 15, "Hungry Like the Wolf" reached #5 on the UK singles chart.

Meanwhile, EMI was preparing to drop the *Rio* album worldwide, but there had been a glitch. In Los Angeles, the Capitol Records staff listened to *Rio* and envisioned their Christmas bonuses flying out the window. The album tracks sounded too soft for American car radios, and the A&R staff claimed they couldn't hear a hit single in the US market.

Andy recalled, "Capitol promised to put a lot of backing behind us—if we remixed the *Rio* album for the States. [They said,] 'Don't do it—and we won't.'" This was a no-brainer because Duran Duran already knew from touring that they needed to change their sound to a harder-rocking format if they wanted massive success in American arenas. "Not that we had much choice," Andy said, "but we were in agreement."

John mourned the death of their vision: "That was the end of Duran Duran, our original idea—an underground club band."

Andy added, "We remixed *Rio* with the help of an American sound engineer [in Los Angeles]. It gave the album a smoother, cleaner sound that went down better with US audiences, who were used to slightly [cleaner] sound than we'd developed in the UK."

No one told Colin Thurston about this, and he might have been surprised to see the producer's credit on the American release of *Rio*: "Producer & Engineer—Colin Thurston. Remixed by David Ker-shenbaum." (Kershenbaum had worked on UK new waver Joe Jackson's records.) Thurston later said he might have taken his name off the album if he'd known. Colin would never again work in the studio with Duran Duran.

As *Rio* moved quickly up the European charts—it would get to #2 in England by May 22—Duran Duran began moving away from their association with New Romanticism. As they did interviews with the European press to explain their subsequent touring delay, John insisted that the band wanted to build its own identity apart from "any broader movement."

"That New Romantic label came in so the press could box away a selection of bands. It didn't have a lot to do with the music. It was more looking at photographs of bands. We were a New Romantic band before anybody had actually heard us. They just took one look at us and seemed to think we'd fit into that category. But the bands have started to grow away from each other. Duran Duran is not just a New Romantic band any longer; they're a band to themselves. Likewise Spandau Ballet and Ultravox."

Simon added, "It's obvious as soon as people come to see us, or buy the record, or find out what we're actually doing. If they do know anything about the New Romantic movement, they can distance us immediately because we've got so many differences. We like to play live and get in front of the people. We try to reach them rather than just sell them records. And then there's the fashion thing. We're not particularly theatrical-looking, are we?"

⁓

The Falklands War ended on June 14, 1982, when invading British forces—paratroopers and Royal Marines—accepted the surrender of the Argentine garrison defending the islands. The Falklands returned to British control, where they remain to this day. About a thousand men had died on both sides. The Royal Navy's victorious fleet returned to Portsmouth a month later amid unforgettable scenes of patriotic fervor not seen since Winston Churchill was prime minister. The ugly little war—which made no impact on Duran Duran whatsoever—would result in the reelection of the Iron Lady as prime minister in 1983. The hapless Argentine generals would be overthrown soon after. But victory in the Falklands did mean that Duran Duran was promoting their new music during the rest of 1982, while England basked in rebooted imperial glory and general hope for a better future. Duran Duran wasn't the World War II–era Vera Lynn, but they were what England had at the time.

⁓

Then they were off—for weeks and weeks—throughout the summer, on a long North American tour, playing the new *Rio* music in clubs, theaters, and "sheds"—large outdoor amphitheaters, usually in the suburbs of major cities. Some concerts, they opened for bands like Split Enz. They played in New Jersey, Long Island, and at New York's Dr. Pepper Summerfest on Pier 42, on the Hudson River. They also played outdoors in Philadelphia and then made their American TV debut miming "Rio" and "Hungry Like the Wolf" on the local teen pop music show *Dancin' on Air.*

Meanwhile in Manhattan, MTV's Les Garland was thrilled when Paul Berrow showed him the new videos shot in Sri Lanka and Antigua. The band's exoticism, storytelling, and colorful, boyish humor were exactly what Garland had ordered earlier in the year.

"Clear the decks," Garland ordered MTV's staff. "We're about to become the Duran Duran channel!"

The *Rio* tour continued at a breakneck pace throughout July 1982. After playing the Peppermint Lounge in Manhattan, their friend Robert Palmer came by to see them. He and John shared a pack of Kent cigarettes. Later, John ran into Blondie bassist Nigel Harrison at the Odeon café, downtown, and they bonded over their shared first name. Harrison sadly confided that Blondie's upcoming tour might well be their last. John proposed that Duran Duran open for them, like they did back in 1980.

Duran Duran sold out the Paradise rock club on Commonwealth Avenue in Boston. Then it was off to Canada: Le Club in Montreal; Massey Hall in Toronto. Simon sang in a tight knee brace, having torn a ligament in Montreal. After that, traveling by train, they played for two weeks in the Midwest, including First Avenue in Minneapolis, where Prince reportedly came to see them, and then back through Canada and the northwestern United States. On July 27, they opened for Dwight Twilley at the Greek Theatre in Los Angeles. The dancing audience of eight thousand wouldn't let them go, so Duran Duran played two encores. It was the biggest crowd they had played to in America so far.

After the show, they learned they weren't going home after all. Blondie wanted them for a dozen shows, beginning at the Starlight Amphitheater in Kansas City, Missouri, on August 2.

Southern California is blazing hot in the summer, and the dry heat may have affected the band, because some of them got new girlfriends.

But first, Andy Taylor married Tracey Wilson on July 29 in a small ceremony at the Chateau Marmont Hotel on Sunset Boulevard in Hollywood. The wedding had been postponed for videos and Andy's intestinal upset, but he and willowy Tracey finally tied the knot. John—wretchedly hungover—was Andy's best man. The band looked fabulously handsome in rented top hats and proper morning suits; there was a massive wedding cake, and pizza was served. The champagne bill was eye-watering.

The other members of the band weren't lacking love in their lives, either. A bit earlier in the summer, the band had been invited to a cocktail party on a Capitol executive's sailboat docked in Marina del Rey, on the coast south of Santa Monica and Venice. There, Nick made the acquaintance of one Julie Anne Friedman, a young model, aspiring actress, and heiress to a midwestern retail fortune. She was considerably taller than Nick, but that's what he liked: a bigger, imposing, beautiful young woman. It was love at first bite for Nick and Julie Anne.

Then there was Bebe Buell, the most beautiful of the rock courtesans (or groupies, as they used to be called). She was a thirty-year-old former teen model who had been a *Playboy* Playmate of the Month in 1974. She also had a liaison with Led Zeppelin's Jimmy Page the following year and was close to Rod Stewart and Mick Jagger. Then Bebe had a daughter in 1977; the daughter would grow up to be actress Liv Tyler, fathered by Steven Tyler of Aerosmith. Duran Duran had first met Bebe during their earlier shows in Los Angeles. Simon fancied her and had even name-checked her on "Last Chance on the Stairway"—"Bebe, dance with me"—but now it was John Taylor to whom she gravitated when they crossed paths again at the Club Lingerie on the Sunset Strip.

John was fascinated with Bebe; he found her to be a wise, witty, and profoundly sexy older woman. She told him she was in the process of getting a band together, and she played him the four-song EP she'd recorded the previous year with Ric Ocasek and the Cars in New York. Bebe was looking for a record deal and was open to amorous friendships with gorgeous English rock stars. She found John to be amusing, especially his compulsive need for takeout cheeseburgers from McDonalds.

Around the same time, an undercurrent of tension began to run in Durania. John was competitive, and he watched Nick's new side project—producing a young London band called Kajagoogoo—in progress. Earlier, Nick had been approached by Christopher Hamill, a waiter at the Embassy, who called himself Limahl—an anagram of his name. The demo tape he persuaded Nick to accept contained "Too Shy," which Nick recognized as a surefire radio grenade. He and Colin Thurston eagerly started producing the album. Kajagoogoo was then signed by EMI; Nick would finish producing their record when they returned to London.

John was jealous; he wanted his own side project now. Maybe he could produce Bebe Buell's debut album. He told her he'd work on it when they got back to England.

After opening for Blondie in Kansas City, the band toured Illinois, Iowa, and Minnesota. Blondie was on their last legs. Their recent album (*The Hunter*) had flopped. The guitarist had been replaced. Many of the ten-thousand-seat sheds they were playing were only half full. As the opening act, Duran Duran was playing in summer daylight, without much in the way of lighting, to fans just arriving and trying to find the beer concession. Then, almost every night, Duran Duran crowded behind the mixing desk to watch Debbie Harry start the show by singing "Rapture" as she rode a glass elevator down to the stage. John Taylor later said that "it was interesting to watch and learn, up close, the level of stagecraft and theatrics needed to play to the bigger open-plan American venues."

They also noticed that band leader Chris Stein looked unwell. He and Debbie Harry seemed secretive, reclusive, and every night they rushed away immediately after their show.

EMI released the "Save a Prayer" single in England on August 9. A remixed "Hold Back the Rain" was the flip side. Two weeks later, the single rose to #2, narrowly missing the top of the UK charts.

Back on the road, they hit Chicago, Detroit, Cleveland—all opening for Blondie. By then Julie Anne Friedman had joined the entourage and was traveling with the band. This was a first for Duran Duran, and not everyone was thrilled, especially Andy, newly married, who'd sent his bride back to England because he thought Duran Duran had an unspoken pact about girlfriends. Nick didn't care what anyone thought; he didn't like Julie Anne being out of his sight.

On a steamy Saturday, August 14, the tour reached Giants Stadium in New Jersey, the biggest venue Duran Duran had played yet. The massive football field was located in the Meadowlands, a reclaimed tidal swamp across the river from Manhattan. The early evening haze was thick as Duran Duran took the stage. Backstage, they were delighted to meet David Johansen, former singer of the New York Dolls, who also performed that night. But this was nothing compared to Debbie's special friends who came backstage after the show: Nile Rodgers and Tony Thompson from Chic.

John Taylor almost lost it, especially when Nile told him, "You guys are awesome!" John responded, "Man, we fucking *love* you! *You're the reason we're here!* You guys are the reason I started playing bass!"

Tony Thompson, probably the best drummer in the business, replied formally, "Why, thank you, my good man." Everyone laughed. Tony then doled out rails of high-octane cocaine, and they were off to Studio 54. In the car, Nile—very dark, charismatic, funny, wearing long dreadlocks—told the tale of how he and bassist Bernard Edwards couldn't get in the club back when it opened in 1977. Apparently, a Black man could only get into Studio 54 if he was famous or a drag queen, and the men in Chic were neither. So after being turned away at the door, they wrote a funky, angry dance number called "Fuck Off," which later became "Le Freak," one of Chic's biggest hits, with its classic refrain, "Ah, freak out!"

Now Nile practically "owned" Studio 54. His habit was to take over a stall in the ladies' room as his private booth and coke parlor. John remembered that "the DJ played 'Planet Earth' when we walked in with Nile. It was a crowning achievement for a band born out of the Rum Runner club scene," back in Birmingham. John and Nile Rodgers shook hands, making a pact to work together someday.

Duran Duran's last concert with Blondie was on August 21 in Philadelphia's JFK Stadium. The late-summer heat in South Philadelphia's flatlands was oppressively humid and still. Phil Collins's Genesis had been added late to the bill, so the huge venue was only about a third full. Afterward, they thanked the guys in Blondie for the great exposure to their audience. No one could foresee that in three years, Duran Duran would be back at JFK Stadium, riding a #1 single in the United States, headlining the American Live Aid concert. As for Blondie: their album bombed, their tour lost money, and they canceled a subsequent European tour. After Chris Stein got really sick, Blondie, the best of the American new wave bands, formally broke up in November 1982, after six years.

While in New York, Duran Duran stopped in to visit their friend Andy Warhol. On Monday, August 23, Warhol noted in his diary: "The Duran Duran kids came by [the Factory] and brought some bigger and taller girlfriends," referring to Nick and Julie Anne, plus John and Bebe. John was hatching a plan to bring Bebe to London and record a new version of T. Rex's "Bang a Gong," with Chic's Tony Thompson hitting the drums as hard as John Bonham had in Led Zeppelin. Maybe they could get a single out—an instant worldwide smash—even before Kajagoogoo!

Simon and Nick taped a promo for MTV, and then Duran Duran flew Air India home to England. "Save a Prayer" hit #2 in the UK. No Duran Duran record had gotten on the American charts yet, but that was all about to change.

In September 1982, EMI record executives in London were getting worried about Duran Duran's lack of success in America. *Rio* was doing well in Europe, Australia, and Japan, but the album just wasn't selling in the United States. Capitol had serviced and reserviced "Hungry Like the Wolf" to American FM rock powerhouses, but the DJs still weren't playing the record. Paul Berrow told EMI that Capitol's LA execs were less than preoccupied with getting Duran Duran radio airplay, infatuated as they were by the label's recent signing of Missing Persons, a cool local band. (Missing Persons had a red-hot girl singer—Dale Bozzio—fronting the band half naked in a see-through plastic bikini, whereas the veteran Capitol execs had never been excited by Duran Duran's low-spark, New Romantic pose.) The implicit threat was that if Capitol couldn't break Duran Duran in the United States, the band would sign with Sony or Polygram when its contract expired. Manchester Square reminded their colleagues at Hollywood and Vine that it had been a (long) while since Capitol had a planetary hit record and that *Rio* was supposed to be it.

Staff producer David Kershenbaum was brought back to the studio to remix four album tracks, three from *Rio*. His mission was to make Duran Duran sound like Van Halen on an American pickup truck radio. John was shocked by this strategy. He thought *Rio* was perfect as it was and hated that they were giving in to raw commercialism, but Nick and Andy were all for the remix. They listened in the studio as the drums got more wallop, the guitars got saber-toothed, and the trademark synthesizers were mixed down, to be less astral. Worldwide disco hit "Hungry Like the Wolf" sounded better immediately, transformed into thudding dance rock with louder female panting and more orgasms. "Girls on Film" got a complete rethink into an extended night version with a big jam rundown on the fade. "My Own Way" was remixed for dancing. A note on the jacket said, "Hold Back the Rain" was "composed of five quatrains addressing camaraderie . . . [and] best describes the feelings the quintet share for each other during their long and grueling world tours."

Capitol didn't want to replace the original *Rio* tracks with the new mixes, so they released them instead as a new twelve-inch EP titled *Carnival* late in September. There had been no pictures of the band on the *Rio* album jacket, an honorable mistake. *Carnival* had five gauzy shots of happy, snappy Duran Duran, plus some data about the tracks for the American fans.

Carnival was the third attack Capitol's weary promo staff had tried to launch Duran Duran onto American radio, but now it actually worked. Rock stations from Maine to Arizona began playing the remixed "Hungry Like the Wolf," and it would become Duran Duran's first American hit record. Early in October 1982, *Carnival* appeared on *Billboard* magazine's "Hot Hundred" chart at #98—for one week only, the first Duran Duran record to chart in America.

It was a late-summer Tuesday in New York. MTV's Les Garland and his staff were screening new videos coming into the channel at their weekly meeting, choosing some for rotation on MTV and laughing at the (many) inept or pathetic clips presented to them. Garland later recalled, "Then our director of talent and artist relations came running in and said, 'You have got to see this video that's just come in.' MTV wanted to break new music, and 'Hungry Like the Wolf' was the greatest video I had ever seen."

After that, neither Duran Duran nor MTV would ever be the same.

Back in London, Duran Duran prepared to tour Europe, performing the concerts that had been postponed when Andy got sick. Simon did a round of interviews, replacing John as the band's spokesman.

EMI and Tritec Music wanted to move the band away from the almost passé New Romantics, and Simon, with better education and training, was more in line with what they thought an eighties rock star should look and sound like. So he was interviewed on *The Big Breakfast* morning program by Paula Yates (girlfriend of Irish singer Bob Geldof, of the Boomtown Rats), the bosomy presenter whose shtick was to interview rock stars while lying in bed with them. In print interviews for *Smash Hits* and *The Face*, Simon talked about touring Japan and America and was rhapsodic about his Sony Walkman, which he predicted would change the way the world listened to recorded music. EMI then released a seven-inch picture single, *An Interview with Simon Le Bon*.

Now John was *really* jealous. First Kajagoogoo, now this. He went to see Dave Ambrose at Manchester Square and broached the idea of him producing legendary beauty Bebe Buell cutting T. Rex's balls-deep "Bang a Gong" with an all-star band under his—John's—direction. Dave's response was temperate: "Really, John? Can she sing?"

John said he wasn't sure, but she'd made a demo with the Cars back in New York. Dave said he'd take it up with his colleagues. Then, somehow, the British tabloids got wind of the story and luridly recounted Bebe's amorous adventures with the elder statesmen of rock before young John Taylor came along. Soon John and Bebe were no longer dating, which was awkward, but John still wanted to remake "Bang a Gong," and he was determined to make it happen sometime in the future.

On September 23, Duran Duran flew to Stockholm, Sweden, to kick off their European tour. After the show, they picked up a big touring bus and worked their way through the Scandinavian capitals, sleeping primarily on the bus's cramped bunk beds (tight conditions that seriously imposed on the burgeoning affair John was having with the Berrows' cute younger sister, Amanda). He was also worried he might still have the case of crabs he acquired on the road in America. At some point he realized that if he was walking around with STDs, maybe he shouldn't still be living with his parents.

Then it was on to Norway, two concerts in Finland, and the Falconer Theater in Copenhagen on September 30. "Save a Prayer" was a huge single in Europe, and the northern kids sang along as if for their lives. Early October saw the band playing all over West Germany, starting in Hanover and Hamburg, before arriving in West Berlin to play at Sektor, Berlin's biggest club. On October 6, they showed up in Munich during the infamous Oktoberfest and checked into the Hilton hotel.

Because they weren't playing that night, they went to see Kool and the Gang. The room was full of American soldiers, which reminded Andy of his time performing at American air bases. Afterward, the promoter suggested they check out the Sugar Shack, a basement after-hours club, because Roxy Music would be drinking there. Andy went back to the hotel to be with Tracey, but John and Roger went along with their minder, Simon Cook, and were invited to drink champagne with Bryan Ferry in the club's VIP area. John told Bryan all about waiting in the rain outside the Birmingham Holiday Inn to get his autograph back in 1975.

"I must have scored some blow before the concert," John recalled later, "because all I can remember of it is a blur with a beat." At the Sugar Shack, John started getting itchy. "My drug craving was keeping me restless. I could not keep still." He was ricocheting around the room, bouncing between the bar, the toilet, and the lounge, making a nuisance of himself. John's maquillage and magenta hair drew disapproving attention to his wasted condition. A group of men in leather jackets left the club. "Then," John later wrote, "the night turns black."

No one knows for sure what happened at Munich's Sugar Shack early that morning. Roger Taylor said he thought someone might have said something. All anyone remembered was that some locals left the club and returned a bit later with baseball bats and started swinging while shouting homophobic curses in guttural German. John hid in the toilet with Bryan Ferry. Roger was smashed in the head and knocked out. Simon Cook took several sharp blows but fought back. He even chased the assailants up the steps and out into the wet, early-morning street. When the fight was over, they rushed John back to the hotel. Roger went to the hospital.

A little later, John came to Roger's room. Roger was just back from the hospital, his clothes drenched in blood. A roadie told John that there had been a fight at the club. John didn't understand how he could have missed it because he was thére. Then he saw Amanda Berrow tenderly pressing an ice pack on Roger's skull wound. This sent John into a drunken jealous rage, and he stormed back down the hall to his room. On the way, John deliberately smashed his right hand through a wall-mounted glass lamp, gushing blood everywhere. The crew took John to the hospital, where doctors sewed a dozen or so stitches in his wrist and hand to close the wound.

Back at the hotel, John instructed the roadies to wake up Andy, who found John wrapped in bandages and crying. Simon Cook, bloody and bruised, told him, "They came at us with baseball bats in the nightclub and beat the hell out of us." Now they had to get out of Germany fast, before the press found out that Duran Duran was attacked in Munich—a humiliating public relations disaster. "No one has got to know about this," Cook said, taking charge. "We'll pay the hotel bills, no fuss, dead quiet. We'll catch the earliest flights we can get." Later that day, the band slunk out of the Hilton and onto their bus, then to the airport and back to London. Somehow, the British tabloids never found out what had happened in Bavaria.

John knew he was in disgrace. Due to his injuries, he couldn't play the bass guitar, so they canceled concerts in Germany, Holland, Belgium, and France. A few tense days later, John faced his bandmates and their management, with his heavily bandaged arm in a sling, in the Rum Runner's upstairs office. Paul Berrow warned him that an unfortunate "accident" like this must never happen again. There was too much at stake; a lot of money had been poured into Duran Duran. Meanwhile, Duran Duran was #1 in Portugal, and they weren't canceling three sold-out shows; someone else would play the bass. John would be along for promotion and photo calls, but they were looking for someone to sub for John onstage. John could only say he was sorry; he wasn't even really sure what had happened.

A few days later, they arrived in Lisbon. At a crowded airport press conference, John was amused by the band pretending to respond like the (cheeky) Beatles and the reporters seeming to imitate the press interviewing the Beatles in *A Hard Day's Night*.

John later wrote, "And I was back in my role as swinger in chief, not going to let anything get me down. Only that evening, standing alone at the side of the stage, watching *my* band perform without me, did I pause for any introspection. My stand-in was a thorough pro, who had no difficulty learning my parts. The conclusion was gut-wrenching. I was not an irreplaceable component of the machine anymore."

Fortunately, John's hand improved enough that he was able to rejoin the band at the beginning of their sold-out, month-long tour of the United Kingdom, beginning in Caird Hall, Dundee, Scotland, on October 30. A few days later, "Rio" was released as a single in Europe and America, backed with "Hold Back the Rain." The record was played constantly while the band performed in Leicester, Liverpool, Manchester, and Newcastle. "Rio" hit #9 in England by mid-November. In America, Capitol turned on the heat, getting the now completely remixed *Rio* album into the big chains like Strawberries, Tower Records, and HMV. This was also when the "Rio" video got into heavy rotation on MTV, with its images of colorfully suited Duran Duran surfing aquamarine waves like young ocean gods, like the guys on *Miami Vice*, like the coolest band in the world.

Duran Duran finished off their epic year of 1982 with "Rio" as their fourth UK Top 10 and five massively sold-out concerts at the Hammersmith Odeon in West London. Demand for tickets was so intense that kids without seats came to Hammersmith anyway just to get next to the energy on cold November evenings. The band got dressed in their hotel and were driven to the venue in limos. It took two lines of helmeted London cops to get the band into the Odeon and right onto the stage, where the amps were ready and buzzing and 3,400 teenage kids—mostly girls—down front were already foaming.

The last show was filmed by Eric Fellner, the future Oscar-winning producer. There was also a new engineer in the sound booth, Ian Little, who was helping Duran Duran on their upcoming single, "Is There Something I Should Know?"

As filmed, the concert starts with "Rio" and a blast of white light. Simon wears baggy trousers, high-top sneakers, and a blue Chinese shirt. The stage set is dominated by red and black columns, with risers big enough for John and Andy to leap from. Andy Hamilton comes on to play Lady Rio's blistering saxophone homage. Next comes "Hungry Like the Wolf"; Simon prowls the stage with lupine cunning, an actor acting out a Graham Greene jungle mystery. Amid torrid screaming, the band takes it down a couple of steps, beginning with the foghorns of "Night Boat," in which Simon channels the shade of Jim Morrison in a leather jacket and just the right slouch hat.

The live version of "New Religion" is much funkier than the record, with scratch guitar and churchy projections. There's a brief intermission, with Simon telling the kids, "Here's a song that means a lot to us." [Screaming.] "It's a love song." [Louder screaming.] He's talking about "Save a Prayer," during which the camera catches Nick in his only stage move of the show, twiddling the slider of his Roland synthesizer to produce the little yodel of the song's wistful prayer. "Save a Prayer" is the evening's best singalong, with a rapturous group swaying down front and in the balconies.

Then Simon asks them, "Do you wanna dance?" Yeah! It's bang into "Planet Earth" and pandemonium in the stalls. A naturally big guy, Simon is all clunky with rubbery moves, more athletic than graceful. Andy Hamilton on sax navigates through the Odeon's now humid atmosphere. "Ba ba ba, ba-ba ba ba-ba—this is Planet Earth," sing thirty-four hundred besotted kids along with Simon and Andy.

Duran Duran keeps the crowd dancing with "Friends of Mine" and Andy's blazing power chords, more punk than romantic. He's jumping off his riser bare chested, now sporting a brown flat cap. Roger Taylor mans his drums like a tank commander in his cockpit, deploying intensely furious concentration and drive. "Careless Memories" explodes into hard rock, electric energy released from a capacitor. Then the show slows to a cover of Cockney Rebel's 1975 ballad "Make Me Smile," a song that would then disappear until it made it to a Duran Duran single B-side two years later.

After the band walked off, the Hammersmith Odeon started to shake as the kids clapped and yelled and stamped their feet. The encore was "Girls on Film (Night Version)." Outside in the November rain, a thousand kids blocked King Street. Eventually the band got through a crush of police cars and headed back to the hotel, exhilarated and fulfilled.

Two days later, their mimed tape of "Rio" aired on *Top of the Pops*. The band was on a stage set with the kids in front, very enthused. The director focused more on Nick this time as Andy Hamilton faked a twisting, histrionic sax solo that seemed to crack up the band.

For the rest of November, it was back to the tour, starting on the southern coastal cities of Brighton and Southampton. The boys played in Cornwall on November 21 before several Midlands concerts. Three shows at the Birmingham Odeon sold out in seconds, so a fourth was added. A record signing at the big HMV on New Street drew turbulent crowds like a high-stakes soccer match.

In December, Capitol released the remixed "Hungry Like the Wolf" single in the United States. Some of the senior executives from the era of the Fab Four remembered the days when Beatles singles held the top four or five chart positions in the same week. Maybe they could move Duran Duran product like this too. Their promo guys were now seriously urging the radio DJs (and the MTV VJs) to please refer to Duran Duran as "the Fab Five."

By Christmas, "Hungry Like the Wolf" had climbed to #3 in America, and all three *Rio* videos were in heavy rotation on MTV. The last two months of 1982 saw the still-fledgling cable channel and Duran Duran almost merging in a continuum of glamour and fame. Even without radio play, they were selling tons of records in markets where kids saw them on MTV. Fans who lived in places not yet wired for cable television complained bitterly that they couldn't see Duran Duran, Michael Jackson, and Toto.

So it was obvious who should headline MTV's epic year-end broadcast on New Year's Eve.

After months on the road, the members of Duran Duran were happy to go home and spend the holidays with their families. Simon was with model Claire Stansfield, his beautiful Canadian girlfriend. (There were also tabloid newspaper stories that month that had Simon flying back to Sri Lanka with another girl.) But their vacations were short-lived; a few days later the band was back in New York to star in *MTV's New Year's Eve Rock 'n' Roll Ball*, live via cable from the Palladium (then a nightclub) on Fourteenth Street in Union Square, a short walk from Andy Warhol's Factory.

Duran Duran played for an hour to a full, dancing house, really rocking, and for an enormous cable television audience estimated to be about eight million viewers, the channel's highest-rated show yet. A bit later, John Taylor was having a drink in the bar when Andy Warhol cruised by. "Andy wandered over," John remembered, "sipping his drink through a straw. He leaned in to my ear and whispered, '*You* should be the singer.'"

"No thanks, Andy," John replied.

Duran Duran in New York's Central Park during their first visit to America in 1981. From left: Roger Taylor, Simon Le Bon, John Taylor, Andy Taylor, and Nick Rhodes. *(Photo by Michael Putland.)*

Duran Duran around the time *Rio* was released. *(Photo by Michael Putland.)*

Diana, Princess of Wales, meets and greets Simon, John, and Andy at
the Prince's Trust Rock Gala at London's Dominion Theatre in July 1983.
Duran Duran was Diana's favorite band. *(Photo by Getty Images.)*

Rhodes with early and
ditions of London's *Daily*
July 23, 1983. The
changed its headline
heir critic slammed the
s performance. *(Photo*
inia Turbett.)

aylor *in excelsis* during
g Blue Silver Tour in 1984.
by Denis O'Regan.)

The paparazzi had a field day as Nick Rhodes married Julie Anne Friedman in London on July 18, 1984. Press accounts noted the groom wore more makeup than the bride. *(Photo by Tony Weaver.)*

Nick with Andy Warhol and Tina Chow celebrating Warhol's birthday, July 1985. *(Photo by Ron Galella.)*

John Taylor escorted model
Renée Simonsen to the
Golden Globe Awards in
Los Angeles in January
1986. *(Photo by Ron Galella.)*

John Taylor with Amanda
de Cadenet around the
time they married in 1991.
(Photo by Albane Navizet.)

Guitarist Warren Cuccurullo replaced Andy Taylor in Duran Duran for fifteen years. He is seen here with Simon at the Whitney Museum of American Art's exhibition "The Warhol Look: Glamour, Style, Fashion" in November 1997. *(Photo by Catherine McGann.)*

A reunited Duran Duran meet the press at Webster Hall in Manhattan in August 2003. *(Photo by James Devaney.)*

Nick Rhodes and model Meredith Ostrum at the London premiere of *The Aviator* in 2004. *(Photo by John Furniss.)*

Simon and Yasmin Le Bon at the *Liaisons Au Louvre* benefit in Paris in 2008. Duran Duran is the only band ever to play in the Louvre. *(Photo by B. R. Petroff.)*

Duran Duran accepted MTV Europe's Video Visionary Award in Milan in 2015. *(Photo by Anthony Harvey.)*

Prince William, son of Diana Spencer and future king of England, gin and tonic in hand, chats with Nick, John, and Simon at a benefit for Counterpoint, the prince's charity combating youth homelessness at London's Roundhouse in November 2019. *(Photo by Dominic Lipinsky.)*

PART 6

In January 1983, Duran Duran was nearing the apex of its trajectory through the higher atmospheres of imperial pop domination. Serious sterling was coming in, not only through record sales, touring, and publishing but also through teen-targeted merchandise that included branded clothing, fan accessories, pencil cases and lunch boxes, cosmetics, candy—almost anything their new merchandiser, Michael Warlow, could think of to slap on a colorful band photo. In England, the musicians now needed minders and bodyguards to move around in public. They were everywhere in the media, especially in magazines. Culture Club's Boy George complained that they were on so many covers of *Smash Hits* that the teen mag should be renamed *Duran Hits*.

They also began attending awards ceremonies as honorees. At the 1983 British Rock & Pop Awards, Duran Duran won Best Group, with Simon named Best Male Vocalist. *Rio* won Best Album.

In need of a new single, they quickly wrote and recorded "Is There Something I Should Know?" The song was a plea from a lover—"Please please tell me now"—wanting more information from someone who's holding back. Russell Mulcahy shot the video featuring the band in Kraftwerk-like blue shirts with tucked-in white ties on a geometric set of stairs and angles. There were also babies crawling around, a scene on the steps of the Bank of England, a bit in a forest, and flashbacks to Sri Lanka and Antigua, just so no one would forget the days of yachts, models, male pouting, and big shoulders.

The plan was to use the new single to anchor the American release of *Duran Duran*, the band's two-year-old first album, just before the summer, while *Rio* was still selling well in North America. Then they would make their third album, embark on a massive world tour at the end of the year, and, after that, just keep on going, getting bigger and bigger, like the Beatles and the Stones.

But along with praise came the downside. There began to be criticism of Duran Duran's video imagery, especially in America. The pastel cocktail of yachts and models depicted in the videos was considered disrespectful in light of the hard times that some people faced in England and abroad. Some of this criticism stemmed from the band's wide (over)exposure in the media. Tabloid journalism was all about selling newspapers and airtime while building someone up and then selling even more papers and airtime while tearing them down. Duran Duran's video fantasies gave their enemies plenty of ammunition to vent class-based anger and frustration toward the band. One writer portrayed Duran Duran as "over-exposed egomaniacs and male bimbos, silly playboys living absurdly lavish lifestyles, imprisoned by the screams of even sillier teenage girls and apparently hated by everyone else." It didn't help that John Taylor told a *Penthouse* magazine interviewer that his idea of a great woman was "someone who could tie me up and whip me and make great bacon sandwiches." Later on, when *Smash Hits* asked John what kind of appliance he'd like to be, he said a refrigerator, so he could stay cool.

Their musical peers weren't supportive either. Boy George regularly slagged the band in the press. "They were selling champagne and yachts," George complained. "Who did they think they were selling them to?"

Even Johnny Rotten had a go: "And as for you poor little cows who buy Duran Duran records, you need serious help because these people are conning you."

In America, *Time* magazine attacked MTV as shallow, violent, and racist, referring to MTV stars Duran Duran as "an affable, uninspired British band currently aglow with success."

Some of this was jealousy, of course. Nick told interviewers that his band was seriously misunderstood. "Our videos became larger than life," he explained. "People believed, 'That's what they must do all day, hang out on yachts.'"

John stoutly maintained that the *Rio* videos "are totally at odds with who we are as a band." Simon found it annoying "that suddenly we were put into this pigeonhole."

"The success of the *Rio* videos drove us crazy," John said later. "Every interview we did—and we did thousands—would begin, 'These videos of yours are really amazing! Whose idea was it?' Then the phrase 'video band' started coming up, and it would set us off."

Not everyone, however, was so judgmental. Joe Elliott from Def Leppard later remembered, "We got on well with Duran Duran, but we were jealous of them because they shot their videos on yachts, with beautiful suits and women covered in war paint. We did ours at [derelict] Battersea Power Station, and our women were in cages. As much as they were all heterosexuals, you could understand why gay men would fancy them, especially Nick Rhodes. I mean, even *we* fancied Nick Rhodes."

Andy remained philosophical. "People thought *Rio* was about a lifestyle we aspired to—yachts and models. Here we are on-screen with a materialistic image that we would become associated with, but this was the early eighties, and it wasn't an obvious route to go down. Punk had shunned crass materialism, but as the rock writer Dave Rimmer said around that time about Duran and other bands, suddenly it was like punk never happened."

Looking back, Nick recalled that while other bands were singing about the dark side of Mrs. Thatcher's Britain, Duran Duran had a different idea and made it happen. "In the eighties a lot of what we did was misunderstood because we'd been living in the same gloomy years of high unemployment and miners' strikes and civil unrest as everybody else. But our answer was that we have to get away from this, and make it a little brighter, because it didn't seem to us like a particularly promising future."

⌒

Nick stayed in New York for a while after the new year. On January 7, 1983, Andy Warhol recorded in his diary, "Nick Rhodes of Duran Duran came to the office and he brought his girlfriend, Julie Anne. He's 23 and she's 23. He was wearing twice as much makeup as she was, although he's half as tall." Nick then returned to England to finish coproducing Kajagoogoo's album for EMI before getting Duran Duran's brand-new single ready for release.

"Is there something I should know?" is a question to which the answer should always be yes, but this new song provided no direct answers. But it *did* have an earworm guitar hook and Simon's lyrics pleading with someone dangerous. "And fiery demons all dance when you walk through that door / Don't say you're easy on me / You're about as easy as a nuclear war" recalled Simon's earlier notion of Duran Duran being the band you'd be dancing to when the atom bombs started raining down. Simon and Andy had written the song quickly in an apartment they shared on Green Street in London, and it owed a lot to Lennon and McCartney's "Please Please Me." EMI loved the record because it deliberately sounded a little like the Beatles circa *Rubber Soul*. The marketing department thought it would be Duran Duran's first UK #1 single when it came out in March.

But as things turned out, it would *not* be Nick Rhodes's first #1, because Kajagoogoo's album *White Feathers* was released in February, and the childish but catchy "Too Shy" single hit #1 in England on February 19. This gave coproducer Nick Rhodes enormous satisfaction, and he graciously accepted the jealous teasing from his bandmates in Duran Duran, who so far had only gotten to #2.

Meanwhile in America, "Hungry Like the Wolf" was charging up the American charts while riding the airwaves. Syndicated programs like *American Top 40 with Casey Kasem* and *The Dick Clark National Music Survey* played "Hungry" all winter, with hundreds of local radio stations following their lead. So "Hungry Like the Wolf" reached *Billboard* magazine's #3 position in the United States on February 26, and *Rio* was awarded a gold album on March 1.

Around the same time, John hooked up with sultry Birmingham beauty Janine Andrews one cold night at the Rum Runner. As an ardent James Bond fan, John was fascinated to hear Janine's funny account of her recent acting role—a bit part—in the still unreleased new Bond film, *Octopussy*. They later moved on to John's new flat in upscale Edgbaston, where he had recently relocated after his mortification at bringing sleazy American body lice to his family's home in Hollywood. John and Janine were a hot item that winter of 1983 in Birmingham, an affair that didn't last but would have important ramifications for Duran Duran later on down the road.

Mclarch 1983 went by in a blur of TV appearances, the band miming "Hungry" and the unreleased "Is There Something I Should Know?" on *Oxford Road Show* on BBC2 and *The Saturday Show* on ITV. EMI released the *Duran Duran* video album on all three contemporary formats: VHS cassette, LaserDisc, and Sony's Betamax. On March 20, "Is There Something I Should Know?" was issued as a single 45, backed with the moody instrumental "Faith in This Colour," everywhere on Planet Earth except the United States, where chugging "Careless Memories" would be the single's flip side. These tapes had been remixed by Ian Little and Alex Sadkin, the highly regarded Island Records staff producer who had famously worked with Bob Marley and Grace Jones and more recently with the hairy English pop group Thompson Twins.

And suddenly, for the first time, a Duran Duran single debuted at #1 in the UK. Everyone was excited. "Is There Something I Should Know?" stayed on top of the English chart for the next three weeks as the band flew to New York to try to capitalize on major American attention. Capitol would also be releasing the band's first album (for the first time) in the United States that spring, issued in a new sleeve with updated photos. The inclusion of "Is There Something I Should Know?" made the original *Duran Duran* album too long, so "To the Shore" was left off the American album release.

By March 1983, Duran Duran no longer crossed the Atlantic sitting in Air India's economy seats for eight hours. Now the band and its Tritec management began to fly British Airways' four-engine delta-winged supersonic jetliner Concorde, which flew at Mach 2 (1,350 mph) at fifty-five thousand feet, so high that passengers could see the curvature of Planet Earth. The four-hour flight landed them at New York's JFK airport ready to roll. Beginning on March 14, the band reported to NBC's studios at 30 Rockefeller Plaza, where they joined the cast of *Saturday Night Live* as that week's musical guests. The band and the comedians got on so well that the musicians were included in a few skits; however, almost none of these sketches made it to air on March 19, when Duran Duran performed on both the dress rehearsal and the live broadcast. *Saturday Night Live* was the band's first major exposure on an American broadcast network. Andy Warhol came to the cast party afterward, as Nick's guest, saying, "I feel like I'm in this band."

Earlier that day, the band was scheduled to sign copies of their new video album at Tower Video in Times Square. Both New York rock station Z-100 and new wave station WLIR on Long Island leaked word of this, and by noon a thousand fans had stopped traffic along rain-washed Broadway. The band's cars were mobbed; they barely made it inside the store without being torn apart by hysterical kids of both sexes. The fans lined up inside were hardly less crazy, pushing and shoving each other to get their VHS cassettes signed by all five

Durans. Outside, a Channel 7 film crew was jostled and harassed as it tried to film the deteriorating scene. As a threatening sky began to pelt down rain, the police captain monitoring the scene estimated the braying and singing crowd outside to be about twelve thousand teens. He called in the cavalry in the form of a dozen riot cops on horseback as the rest of the signing was canceled. It took an hour to disburse the kids, while a shaken Duran Duran had to be spirited out of the store's shipping door and through a series of back service alleys in a cold spring downpour.

Duran Duran met up with Andy Warhol a few days later at MTV's studio on Long Island. Nick and Simon were to be guest VJs for an hour, playing their favorite videos and bantering about music, with Warhol putting in a surprise appearance. The rest of the band would come on at the end of the hour.

It was all on tape. Nick was in a sharp suit and sported long, bushy hair; Simon was in a yellow top that looked like a child's bib. After signing on, they introduced David Bowie's brand-new song, "Let's Dance," as the first video of their shift. (EMI was keen on this because Bowie's new *Let's Dance* album had just been released on their EMI America label.) When they came back, Simon and Nick chatted about Bowie, his five-year retirement from concerts, and even his next single, "China Girl."

Next came a hallucinatory series of state-of-the-art videos, from Michael Jackson's "Billie Jean" to Blondie's "Rapture" to the Eurythmics' "Sweet Dreams." After a commercial break, MTV found Andy Warhol sitting between Simon and Nick, who commenced a mock-surreal dialogue about being followed by a guy with a camera while a silent Andy (in his platinum fright wig and butch dungarees) kept snapping the motor drive of his camera like the beginning of "Girls on Film."

Videos by Roxy Music, Robert Palmer, and Kate Bush and Peter Gabriel's "Shock the Monkey" finished the set. Simon could be seen twirling around as they returned with the whole band. Nick introduced "the whole Taylor family—Roger, Andy, and John." Then Duran Duran presented MTV with a framed gold album of *Rio*, which Simon hung on the studio wall. At last, it was time for the "MTV World Premiere Video" of the new video for "Is There Something I Should Know?"

The historic synergy between English band and American cable network was now sealed and secure. It was also Andy Warhol's debut on national cable TV, but the event is strangely absent from his published diaries. He did, however, show up at a contrived Duran Duran "rehearsal" and taped them for *Andy Warhol's TV*, his primitive video show on a local New York public access cable channel.

In April 1983, recognizing that the band and its cohort were all exhausted, Tritec Music signed a three-month lease for an old chateau close to the village of Valbonne, near Cannes in the south of France. The house had a recording studio, plus a chef and a well-stocked cellar, which wine connoisseur Nick Rhodes appreciated. The idea was to keep the band working while they relaxed in the lavender-scented hills above the glamorous Riviera city. This was also the onset of a year in tax exile to avoid the crushingly high income taxes successful musicians had to pay if they lived in England. Andy said, "Our advisers told us that rock and roll can be very fickle and we shouldn't bank on always being so fortunate. 'You might have one or two more successful albums ahead of you, and then it could be all over.'"

These words turned out to be somewhat prophetic. For the next twelve months, there would be only a strictly limited number of days when Duran Duran could go home.

There was a lot to accomplish in France. EMI wanted the next Duran Duran album as soon as it could be written and recorded, so producer Alex Sadkin and engineer Ian Little (who had worked with Roxy Music) were also in residence while the band was trying ideas and cutting demos. The instruments were set up in an airy top-floor attic with cables running downstairs for electricity. The recording console was in a mobile studio parked in the chateau's courtyard. Besides trying to write, the band had to almost completely overdub the Hammersmith Odeon concert before its BBC broadcast. Then there were slightly rusty band rehearsals for European concerts that summer. Meanwhile, individual band members were flying between Nice and London to fulfill commitments. John Taylor appeared on the TV show *Pop Quiz*. The whole band came back to mime "Is There Something I Should Know?" for *Top of the Pops*, then returned later to Birmingham for a cover shoot for the teen magazine *Jackie*.

Because of all this, progress at the chateau was decidedly slow. The band usually started working around four in the afternoon, and the sessions would only last a couple of hours. John spent most of the evenings in Cannes nightclubs, which were gearing up for the intensity of the annual Cannes Film Festival in May. Eventually, the French sessions did produce a couple of new songs, including one called "Seven and the Ragged Tiger."

Often the whole entourage would go into Cannes for the evening. When they heard that Russell Mulcahy was making an Elton John video on the town's main boulevard, La Croisette, they all trooped into town to have some fun.

Elton John was happy to see Duran Duran. They were making a clip for his song "I'm Still Standing," which Elton told them was about him still being in business while the New Romantics seemed to be taking over. Meanwhile, the video shoot had gone a bit wobbly because Russell had fallen into the bay with a fully loaded camera the day before. Duran Duran found Elton John in the bar of the Carlton Hotel, where they spent a languid cocktail hour getting Rocket Man loaded on vodka martinis. "Oooo, you *are* lovely boys," Elton kept telling them as another silver bullet went down. After a half-dozen martinis, Elton went upstairs and destroyed all the furniture in his suite in a drunken rage. When he came to, he asked his assistant what had happened.

"*You* happened," the PA replied. The hotel then presented a whopping bill—the furniture pieces were Empire antiques—to Russell Mulcahy, which doubled the cost of the video shoot.

Back at the chateau, not much recording got done because some preferred snorting cocaine around the swimming pool as the fragrant *printemps* in the south of France got more beautiful. Andy said later, "Looking back, it was the start of the megadamage because my cocaine use began to accelerate, and John had developed similar habits of his own. We were living the high life to the full, and soon we were partying in Cannes every night."

John added, "We did get a handful of tracks going in France. We had a groove called 'Spidermouse' that became 'New Moon on

Monday.' Simon sketched out verses for one called 'Seven and the Ragged Tiger.'" The seven were Duran and the Berrows. "The ragged tiger was the phenomenon that was beginning to swallow us all up—fame."

EMI publicists now dispatched a stream of print journalists to Valbonne to interview the band in their idyllic Provençal chateau, and Channel 4's popular show *The Tube* sent host Jools Holland and sexpot presenter Paula Yates to film a segment with them. Thinking back on the experience, John laughed: "Here we were, recording in the south of France, pretending we were the Rolling Stones, when we were only making our third record. We'd just barely moved out of our parents' homes."

Andy Taylor recalled that it was around this time that cracks began to appear in various relationships. It was one thing for John to arrive in the Côte d'Azur in his brand-new VW Golf GTI; it was another for Paul Berrow to top John with an even newer (and much more expensive) rust-gold Ferrari. Andy started wondering why their management seemed to be making more money than the band. The Berrows owned a big portion of the rights to Duran Duran's music rather than being paid a percentage like regular talent managers. Everyone knew the Berrows had developed the band, but were they taking more than their rightful share—especially when they didn't even write the music?

Andy later wrote, "There was nothing illegal about it, but Nick and I were both uneasy. But Simon was close to the brothers, hatching plans to buy a big yacht and race it around the world. Roger avoided any kind of confrontation if he could, and John was the least financially astute of all of us. So nothing was said, but the situation began to grate on me."

One night, during the Cannes Film Festival in May, Paul drove his Ferrari into town and parked outside a nightclub. When he returned, he found that someone had smashed all the car's windows. Some thought this amusing. Andy also developed a serious problem with Nick's girlfriend, Julie Anne, who liked to gossip. She told Andy's wife, Tracey, that she had seen him flirting with a model seated next to him in first class on a recent flight from New York. Andy and Nick had a furious blowup over this, and Andy later said that the rift between them never properly healed. He started referring to Julie Anne as "Yoko Ono" behind her back.

⟋⟍

Early on in June 1983, "Is There Something I Should Know?" hit the Top 10 in America, reaching the #5 slot. The *Rio* album remained on the *Billboard* Hot 100 album chart for the next two years, selling about six million records.

On June 6, John escorted Janine Andrews to the premiere of *Octopussy* at the Leicester Square Odeon in London. John was used to cameras flashing when Duran Duran appeared at these things, but it was nothing like the frantic heat lightning of dozens of paparazzi when the guests of honor—the Prince and Princess of Wales—arrived on the red carpet, welcomed by producer Cubby Broccoli and the current James Bond, Roger Moore.

John was eager to hear the new Bond theme, having grown up listening to the legendary songs associated with the series: Shirley Bassey belting out "Goldfinger"; lively, episodic "Live and Let Die" by Paul McCartney and Wings; Carly Simon crooning "Nobody Does It Better" (from *The Spy Who Loved Me*). So he was disappointed to hear *Octopussy* represented by "All Time High," written by perennial Bond movie composer John Barry, with lyricist Tim Rice, and warbled by American singer Rita Coolidge. John was even less impressed by the film itself, one of the weaker 007 mash-ups inspired by Ian Fleming's stories. Still, it was cool to see his girlfriend up on the Odeon's huge screen, if only briefly.

It would be even cooler, John mused, if his band could write and record the theme for the next Bond film, which was already in production. There had to be a way to make John's dream come true.

As *Rio* and repackaged *Duran Duran* were headed for gold and plat-inum sales awards in America, EMI's Dave Ambrose was pressuring Tritec Music Ltd. for another album from the band. Being tax exiles, Duran Duran couldn't record in England. No one wanted to return to France, where musical inspiration had been in short supply. Also, the chateau's studio had proved unreliable and exhausting since the musi-cians had to run up and down three steep flights of stairs when they wanted to hear a playback in the mobile studio. So it was decided that the band would return to the lazy zephyrs of summer in the Carib-bean Sea, specifically George Martin's AIR Studios on Montserrat, a British Overseas Territory in the Leeward Islands. Martin had opened the studio in 1979 as a tropical branch of his London operation. AIR Montserrat was also recommended by Alex Sadkin, who had worked there with Grace Jones and Robert Palmer. For yacht-obsessed Simon and the Berrow brothers, an added perk was that they could go sailing on days off.

Tritec booked the studio for five weeks, and the band settled in to separate villas. Summer is off-season in the Caribbean; there were hardly any tourists around and few distractions, so Duran Duran imported their own Sony TV sets and VCR players in enormous wheeled cases usually used for concert equipment. They rented the little Suzuki jeeps that the locals drove, explored the island's narrow roads, and visited its dormant volcano, La Soufrière. Duran Duran arrived in Montserrat with some of the ideas developed in France, and they got to work and cut the first tracks of "The Reflex" by the end of June, fueled by the remaining bottles of the case of champagne ordered to celebrate John's twenty-third birthday.

Alex Sadkin said later he was surprised at how little the band's writers really had this time around. The truth was that everyone was burned out from being in the band, and it was hard to focus on creativity. They did have the beginnings of funky "Union of the Snake" and the great chorus of "New Moon on Monday," but there wasn't much left to work with after that. But at least Sadkin could hear these three as strong singles, and he could make do with the rest of what Simon, Nick, and Andy came up with next. Sadkin also knew Duran Duran's third album was going to be very hard to produce.

Those closest to the band noticed that things were changing between the members as well. With their girlfriends around, some of the old camaraderie was missing. Paul Berrow later told an interviewer about this period: "At first it was military—videos, tour, album, tour—but what do you do when you get there? [You] get a girlfriend, and a demanding one almost certainly—and then the whole entity changes. The band comes together for just work and then goes away again to a new set of friends. There's conflict among the merry men."

Nick also appeared to be under some sort of strain. He and Julie Anne had dinner one evening with Simon and Claire Stansfield, and Nick excused himself early and went back to rest at the villa he was sharing with Andy and Tracey.

The newlyweds were watching videos in bed later when Julie Anne banged on their door. "It's Nick," she cried. "You've got to come see this."

As Andy later remembered, "Nick was in a terrible state, sitting in a chair, clutching at his chest and gasping. He was pale and sweating, and he seemed to have trouble breathing. He looked like he was about to have a heart attack, which is clearly what he feared was happening. I was terrified for him." Eventually Nick was flown to Miami, where he was diagnosed as having had a panic attack complicated by high blood pressure brought on by stress. When he returned to Montserrat, Nick gave up whatever was getting him through the night, save only red wine. The others then noticed that he gradually became a different person, easier to talk to and less intimidating with outsiders. Photographer Denis O'Regan, who was closer to the band than most, observed, "The thing with Nick, it was difficult to tell whether he was on drugs or not. He's always been that persona, which is a little bit out of the ordinary."

In mid-July, booking agent Rob Hallett called and said they had to come back to London for a charity performance before Prince Charles and Diana, Princess of Wales. Duran Duran, Hallett reported, was Diana's favorite band! "You'll all be introduced to Charles and Di in person before the gig," they were advised, "so everyone will need to be on his best behavior."

This was huge. "Bloody hell," Andy thought. "It must all be true about Diana being a fan of ours." Everyone wanted to meet Lady Di.

The Prince's Trust was Charles's private charity, set up in 1976 to help troubled youths gain employment and better their lives. The trust's first fundraising concert had taken place in Birmingham the previous year, headlined by Status Quo, a veteran English band that Charles liked. This year's concert would feature Dire Straits at the prince's request, but then it was suggested that Duran Duran, as the UK's biggest band, would guarantee a sellout. The Montserrat sessions were put on hold. The boys flew first class on Pan American back to London to play for the most famous woman in the world—and their biggest fan.

Their other biggest fans, about three thousand girls and some photographers, showed up at Heathrow at seven thirty in the morning to welcome Duran Duran home. From Heathrow Airport, the band was driven to the Grosvenor House, the luxury hotel overlooking Hyde Park. The bandmates' families gathered there, and Andy even had a reunion with his brother and the mother who had abandoned them when they were children. The next morning, they awoke to find a press encampment outside the hotel and traffic on Park Lane disrupted by photographers trying to get pictures of the band. Duran Duran had their own security guys, all ex-military, who warned them not to carry drugs to this gig, as the police cordon around the theater would be like nothing they'd ever seen.

Tottenham Court Road, in the heart of London's neon-lit theater district, was jam-packed on the warm summer evening of July 20, as the heir to the British throne and his dazzling young wife (who at twenty-two was the same age as most of Duran Duran) stepped out of a Rolls-Royce and into another star-bursting flashbulb storm in front of the Dominion Theatre. Duran Duran had entered earlier by the heavily guarded stage door and found the theater locked down by security, their dressing rooms inadequate, and no time for a sound check. They'd rehearsed a bit in Montserrat for this (and worked on their tans), but they hadn't played live since the winter. So their opening set was a disappointing, stop-start affair with tuning problems and buzzing amplifiers. Someone had told Simon he was Diana's favorite, so the sunburned lead singer, who hadn't been onstage for months, over-egged the pudding and looked a bit clumsy, at least according to the next days' papers.

After the concert, the band lined up with Dire Straits to meet Charles and Diana amid a mechanized rattle of camera motor drives. Andy was startled to see Diana, wearing a cute sort of sailor's bib over her flowing summer dress, seem to hurry through her introductions to Dire Straits and then march straight over to John and hold out her hand.

"Ma'am, this is Duran Duran," the equerry said.

"I don't need any introductions to *these* boys," Diana happily blurted. "I know *exactly* who they are!"

Andy recalled, "We felt as if Diana was telling the world, *This is my band!* as she shook hands with John. She knew our names, what we were about, everything." Diana made sure to smile and make eye contact with all of them. But when she then seemed to linger in front of Simon, John's inner self was screaming, *"Look at me!"*

Prince Charles, on the other hand, seemed as though he hadn't been to a rock concert before. He told Simon, "I never knew you had to be so fit." The prince told Roger, "I rather like your gear."

Nick recalled, "They commented on our tans and chatted to us about Montserrat. They seemed to know a bit about us. And Diana looked great—really pretty."

John later remembered their big date with Lady Di: "I don't know if it was the jet lag or the perfume, but I had tuning problems throughout and played horribly. . . . The performance was of little importance; it was all about the photo op. That picture of me and Simon with Diana went around the world." As an added bonus, it made his parents happy and proud.

The next morning, the front page of London's *Daily Mirror* read "Diana's delight" and featured the photo of her speaking with bronzed Simon, John, and Andy. When their reporter filed his copy slagging the band's unpolished performance, the headline for the later edition was changed to "Diana's let-down," but the priceless photo of the princess with Duran Duran remained on the front page.

Sometime later, the band learned why security at the Prince's Trust concert had been unusually strong. The Irish Republican Army had killed Prince Charles's mentor, Lord Mountbatten, in 1979 by blowing up his boat. This time around, informers had warned MI5 that IRA assassins would try to bomb the Dominion Theatre on July 20, murdering prince and princess, Duran Duran, and maybe even Dire Straits as well. Andy later wrote that the Irish bomber was in fact a double agent who foiled the plot; on a subsequent TV appearance, the faux bomber said that Duran Duran had no idea how lucky they were.

On July 23, before returning to Montserrat, Duran Duran went home to Birmingham to play a charity show in Aston Villa's soccer stadium, Villa Park. This event was a complicated maneuver by Paul Berrow that ended badly for Duran Duran.

The idea was that the band was supposed to finish their third album in September and then begin a major international tour in November, running well into 1984, bringing them into every major concert market then available, selling more tickets than U2 and the Stones, and making them stand out as the most popular rock band in the world. Tritec Music Ltd. was marketing these concerts as the Sing Blue Silver Tour after Simon's allusive lyric in "The Chauffeur." Planning had been going on for months. The Berrows now wanted Duran Duran to play what amounted to a paid rehearsal for the tour while they were in England for the Prince's Trust Rock Gala. Duran Duran was booked into Villa Park, which held forty-two thousand. The set designers got to work on production details. The sidemen and backing singers who would work the tour were flown in. So was the American support act, Prince Charles and the City Beat Band, a funky Chic-alike (on Virgin Records), whose very hip leader (Charles Alexander) played the Lyricon wind synthesizer that Nick admired. So were Duran Duran's friend Robert Palmer and his band, also from America. This was because none of the other big English bands invited to play—Eurythmics, Culture Club, Thompson Twins—had any intention of opening for Duran Duran in Birmingham.

Paul Berrow wanted to cover these expenses for their tour rehearsal, but he didn't want to get paid for the concert because of the band's tax exile situation. He needed a charity that would receive whatever remaining profit the concert made after Tritec had paid off expenses. Rob Hallett had once interned for Mencap, a charity that helps young people with learning disabilities. Mencap excitedly accepted this proposal after Rob reportedly told them they might receive £80,000 if the show sold out. It looked like a sweet deal all around. Duran Duran would be playing for all their original fans while getting ready for its biggest-ever tour, supporting a most worthy charitable project.

Like Duran Duran, Aston Villa Football Club was riding high in 1983. The team had won the Football League Championship in 1981 and the European Cup in 1982. In 1983, they won the European Super Cup after defeating Barcelona. Roger Taylor was happy at the sound check because his childhood dream was to play in the goal for Aston Villa, and here they were. But only about eighteen thousand fans arrived to hear Duran Duran and the support bands. Peter Powell introduced Prince Charles and the City Beat Band at six o'clock. Robert Palmer followed with an hour of sophisticated rock, including hits like "Sneakin' Sally Through the Alley" and "Some Guys Have All the Luck."

Duran Duran, all dressed in white, took the stage at 8:40 as a blazing sun began to set behind the stage. The new touring troupe now included sax soloist Andy Hamilton, percussionist Raphael DeJesus, and Chic's B. J. Nelson and Charmaine Burch singing backup vocals. Their stage production included massive black gates that opened to reveal the columned set as the band charged into the new opener, "Is There Something I Should Know?" But something went wrong, and one of the gates failed to open all the way. The stage manager signaled Roger to stop playing while the problem was fixed. Then they had to restart the concert.

"Good evening!" Simon yelled after the opening number. "It's great to be back! We're going to play a little song for you now about those cute little furry animals. . . . So all you little bunnies better run, because—we're . . . *hungry like the wolf!*"

Next came brand-new "Union of the Snake," which they'd played for the first time for Diana a few days earlier in London. Simon, a bit breathless: "Well, we've been twice around the world now, and where did we end up? *Right here*—back home where we started. . . . Great to be back; thank you for coming tonight. We'll play a slower song now . . . which we hope will spread a little bit of evening calm."

The rest of the show followed the basic set list for the upcoming world tour: "Lonely in Your Nightmare," "New Religion," "Night Boat," "Friends of Mine," and "Save a Prayer." "Planet Earth" now came midset, before "My Own Way" and "Hold Back the Rain." Le Bon favorite "Careless Memories" got Villa Park's sparse audience up and rocking, and then "Rio" had them singing like a soccer crowd. For the encores, John and Andy returned to the stage in Aston Villa jerseys, and they rushed into Iggy Pop's "Funtime." The show closed with the night version of "Girls on Film." It seemed like the entire Midlands jammed Broad Street trying to get into the after-party at the Rum Runner, which ran very late. John and Robert Palmer ended up drinking in the club's VIP lounge, which was where they began talking about doing something together outside of Duran Duran.

After a few days at home, the band flew back to Montserrat to work on album tracks at AIR with Alex Sadkin. Meanwhile, a furor broke out in the newspapers when it was disclosed that the Mencap show hadn't made any money. Attendance had been half of what was expected, and expenses were astronomical since Tritec Music had linked tour production costs to the concert's gross receipts. The Mencap concert had actually lost money, so there was nothing coming to the host charity. Seeking to prevent a public relations disaster, Paul Berrow sent Mencap a compensatory check for £5,000. Thinking this might be a joke, the charity didn't cash the check, instead framing it, mounting it on the office wall, and notifying the press. Then the charity's president went on morning TV and said words to the effect that no one knew where the money went. It would take almost two years for forensic accountants to agree that nothing illegal had occurred. By then, the five musicians and their two managers had each donated £10,000 to Mencap as a show of good faith amid as much publicity as could be squeezed out of the papers.

Andy was particularly outraged by the negative press Duran Duran had to deal with. They already had an image problem in England, where they were sometimes depicted as a vapid, lightweight boy band. Instead of helping a popular charity, now they were portrayed as greedy tax exiles. Andy was vocal in his criticism of their management's handling of this fiasco and even complained to a reporter dispatched to Montserrat by *Melody Maker*. This was Steve Sutherland, an old Duran Duran supporter, who could be counted on to file positive dispatches from the tropics. The journalist duly reported that Nick Rhodes stayed out of the sun, that John Taylor appeared to be bored and uninspired, that Roger Taylor had a great tan but seemed tired, that Simon Le Bon was relaxed and upbeat, and that Andy Taylor had found the island's best dive bars and could often be found in them. At AIR Studios, Sutherland heard eight new Duran songs, unmixed, with only guide vocals "in various states of disarray." "Union of the Snake" might be the new album's first single, he wrote. "['The Reflex'] is sharper and more brutal than anything they've recorded before." He noted that Chic's veteran singers B. J. Nelson and Michelle Cobbs were also on hand in Montserrat to sing with the band—"na na na na"—on "The Reflex." Alex Sadkin told Sutherland that they were a long way from completion and were having technical problems with the studio itself.

Andy hated the studio's speakers and also complained that the tape machines were running either fast or slow. Equipment seemed to fail at an unusual rate, causing nerve-wracking delays because replacements had to be airlifted from London. These complaints ended up in a tense meeting with the AIR engineers, who told Duran Duran they were whiny and unprofessional. "It's *you guys*," they were told. "You guys are not working. Our studio is perfectly fine."

This deteriorated into bad blood. "Payment of bills was questioned by both sides," John recalled. "We received a stern letter from AIR London telling us we were no longer welcome at their UK facilities."

Alex Sadkin suggested moving the sessions to his home base, Island Records' Compass Point Studios in the Bahamas. "I'm not going to another fucking desert island," sputtered Nick. No one wanted to return to France, and England was out because they were tax exiles. And so, at the end of August, Alex Sadkin packed up his reels of tape, and Duran Duran flew to Sydney, Australia, on the other side of the world, to try to finish their difficult, even tortuous, third album, *Seven and the Ragged Tiger*.

Duran Duran and entourage touched down at Sydney's Kingsford Smith Airport at the end of August 1983. They were met by a polite but serious customs search and asked if they were intending to immigrate. Then it was off to shared penthouse flats, a suburban mansion for the Berrows, and a rented villa for Tracey and Giovanna. This was spring Down Under, and the weather was fair along the city's famed harbor and beaches. Sydney is Australia's financial and cultural capital and far away enough from England that rock stars like Duran Duran could be out in public and unbothered by the sophisticated Sydneysiders, as the locals were known. Even so, their presence was only secret for a short while; within days, the *Sydney Morning Herald* and the *Daily Telegraph* reported that Duran Duran was in town.

They were there because Sydney was a bit like home for Duran Duran. "Planet Earth" had been #1 in Australia during the heady New Romantic days in the spring of 1981, and they had friends in the city. Their concerts in the Hordern Pavilion that year were the first sold-out arena shows they had ever played, and they loved the young audiences. Sydney was supposed to be a fun time for the band, while slightly writer's-blocked Simon struggled to create and record lyrics for their new tracks. But there were other problems as well; the singer told friends he was having second thoughts about his feelings for Claire Stansfield. Simon and his beautiful girlfriend were reported to be in the process of buying an apartment together in her native Toronto, but he was increasingly unsure where their relationship was really going. Simon's big blue lyrics book reflected some of his romantic ambivalences and don't-knows in those trying days in Sydney.

EMI's recording facilities in Sydney, Studios 301, were located at 301 Castlereagh Street and were considered slightly inferior to AIR Montserrat. But Nick and Alex Sadkin liked the studios' speakers immediately, which was a big relief, as a change of studio can make tapes sound very different to where they'd been recorded. Even Andy found Studios 301 to be OK. Duran Duran had another month to finish their new album; then they would rehearse the new songs, build a solid set list, and stay on the road well into 1984.

No one knew all this would almost kill Duran Duran.

~

Nick Rhodes and Alex Sadkin spent September 1983 working on the dozen songs they'd brought with them from Montserrat. Nick bought a new Fairlight sampler from the Australian manufacturer and used it to record and manipulate sounds and mix them onto existing tracks, giving their music an even more techno feel. "I thought the thing was never going to get finished," he said later. "There's a lot of pretty songs on there, but then underneath there's this sort of not quite controllable hysteria."

They knew the first single would be "Union of the Snake," which was close in sound and feel to David Bowie's "Let's Dance." It had a hint of reggae in the guitar and a wild, Bowie-esque sax solo. Simon's new lyrics continued his anxious, son-of-the-Beat-generation themes: "There's a fine line drawing my senses together / And I think it's about to break." If Simon's snake reminded anyone of something, it was confirmed by "The Reflex," another song of phallic imperialism set to a stripper beat and coyly describing events attending the male biological urge: "The reflex is in charge of finding treasure in the dark / And watching over lucky clover, isn't that bizarre? / And every little thing the reflex does / Leaves you answered with a question mark."

"New Moon on Monday" (the projected second single) was an echo of Duran Duran's love of Roxy Music, the vocal sung more Bryan than Ferry. Its soaring and inspirational chorus would make it a perennial fan favorite, even with its strange, *musique concrète* bridge that sounded like space stations colliding with asteroids.

The new album's less popular tracks included "Cracks in the Pavement," sounding like an homage to the Police with a carnival vibe, hopping rhythm, and a cool coda. "If I had a car," Simon sings, "I'd drive it insane." "I Take the Dice" is mysterious: "For a kiss or whisper, you pull out a desperate prize." There's a heartbeat rhythm to "Of Crime and Passion" along with the radar sounds of Nick's synthesizers and Simon's words about passion's rage. The mood continues on "Shadows on Your Side," the darker side of pop fame with echoes of Jim Morrison's poetry. "Tiger Tiger" is a pastoral drone, evoking a jungle painted by Rousseau with hidden tribes playing rattles and sticks. "The Seventh Stranger" finished the new album with a somewhat tepid ballad and a less-than-magic guitar solo. There was also a trance-like, hypnotic drone called "Secret Oktober," pretty and lush, a future single B-side.

While work continued at Studios 301, John seemed to be enjoying Sydney's nightlife with desperate energy. His basic parts were already recorded; he'd changed his style to play fewer notes and get more feel out of his bass guitar. At the same time, he was fighting with his girl-friend. He'd given Janine an engagement ring, but she kept giving it back to him after their arguments. Cocaine was plentiful in wealthy, polyglot Sydney. The so-called designer drug MDMA, or ecstasy, was also up and coming in the dance clubs where John hung out. After an uncontrolled nosebleed, John spent a night in the hospital with a suspected perforated nasal septum. Another morning, while driving home from a nightclub where he had eaten a little white pill a strange girl had passed him, his rented BMW spun out on the Sydney Harbour Bridge and smashed into the railing. John wasn't injured, but it was embarrassing when the accident was reported in the newspapers.

John was also sick of making this album. It had been months of torture in three studios. Andy felt the same way. "The third album was a laborious plod," he sadly recalled. The agony was drawn out further because Simon's beatnik muse had disappeared and good lyrics were hard-earned on the tracks.

During this time, John shared a majestic penthouse apartment with Alex Sadkin on George Street, with distant views of Sydney's swan-shaped opera house and the Harbour Bridge. One morning, while John was shaving, Alex told him that in the studio the previous night, the song "Seven and the Ragged Tiger" had morphed into a new song called "The Seventh Stranger." The new arrangement meant that John had to return to the studio and redo his bass parts. John blew up. He later wrote, "I freaked out. I picked up a heavy glass and threw it at the shower door, smashing it into a million pieces.

"Fuck, Alex—this is *bullshit!* That song was *finished! I'm* finished! I am fucking *done.*" Ever the diplomat with stoned rock stars, especially bleeding ones, Alex explained that it wasn't a big change, wouldn't take long, and would make a better ending for the new album's second side.

Later that day, John (his bandaged hand raising eyebrows) and Andy were in the studio, finishing their parts on "The Seventh Stranger." Andy was fed up too. "That's it," he told John, bitterly. "I'm having no more of this. I am off."

Wait—was Andy leaving the band? John was startled. Andy was generally considered to be Duran Duran's true grit. Andy's guitar chops were the balance against Nick's synths that made the band great. Maybe, John told Andy, it was time for them to do a project together—outside the band. They could get the best guys in the world to play with them, like Tony Thompson, the former Chic drummer, a man who could be mentioned in the same sentence as John Bonham. They'd first discussed the idea one night back in Cannes, where Tony was playing drums on David Bowie's Serious Moonlight Tour. If they had some good songs, a side project with them and Tony Thompson and a singer could possibly be as big as Duran Duran.

John later said this was the beginning of a split in the band that would only get worse over the next year. It was "Andy and I on one side; Simon, Nick, and the Berrows on the other. Roger did a balancing act." Andy couldn't leave now, John reasoned, because Andy was the only one he could get stoned with. Alcohol and drugs were beginning to assume control. John later lamented, "One of the worst effects of this was that I didn't want to be around Nick anymore, my oldest friend." Nick didn't snort cocaine or trip on ecstasy. In fact, Nick was openly contemptuous of the run-down state John and, to a lesser extent, Andy were usually in. Indeed, John was, he later wrote, "caught up in a vortex of fear, arrogance, loneliness, and extraordinary popularity."

Andy noted that "John's destructive demons were surfacing once more. He crashed his car on the Sydney bridge. While Nick, Simon, and I worked on the top of the songs, John would go off and party on his own. We had a lot of fun together as a band when we were on the road, and going out drinking together in clubs was great fun, but problems would occur when we were in the studio."

It got worse when fans found out where they were working. "Recording at EMI in Sydney turned out to be hell. We were mobbed there, and security had to fight our way through whenever we went in and out. It was flattering, but after a while it began to wear us down." There were stories about the band being asked to leave hotels because teenage girls blocked the entrances. Even steady drummer Roger was annoyed. "You go to a restaurant, and it's in the paper. You can't scratch your bum in public."

Soon, native Australian Russell Mulcahy arrived in Sydney, having just directed new videos for the Stones and Billy Idol. They shot a video for "Union of the Snake" featuring demons, a bellhop, an elevator to hell, snakes and parrots, flashbacks to Sri Lanka, horsemen, and fire. Mulcahy and his film crew would catch up with Duran Duran around the world for the next few months, documenting the Sing Blue Silver Tour for an eventual concert movie.

The Australian summer days grew longer into October, when Duran Duran had finally completed the laborious, obsessive, soul-destroying mixing of *Seven and the Ragged Tiger* and were preparing to release their new music to the world. Alex Sadkin and Nick Rhodes spent so many compulsive nights on the album tracks that they had only twenty-four hours to record and mix "Secret Oktober," the flip side of "Union of the Snake." Glamorous Manhattan photographer Rebecca Blake flew in to take the cover photograph of the band: dressed up, slicked back, and glowering before the massive, fluted stone columns of the State Library of New South Wales. Then an actual Bengal tiger was imported for the album jacket and the tour program. This was locally reported to have cost £65,000, or about $100,000, but designer Malcolm Garrett only ended up using the tiger's eye and a bit of its massive bum on the actual LP sleeve. The design also featured the band's various logos including the DD, the crescent moon, and the vaguely fascist-looking triple-X glyph, plus a Chinese-style antique map indicating snow-capped mountains and the many rivers Duran Duran would soon have to cross on their long journey home.

Back in New York, Capitol Records and Tapes (and now CDs) snuck the "Union of the Snake" video to MTV prior to the single's radio release, drawing furious protests from radio programmers who resented the cable channel's encroachments on their territory. Unfortunately, this also might have affected the song's chart position when it was issued to all markets on October 17. A few days later, the band and entourage gathered for an Aussie barbecue at the suburban mansion rented by Paul and Mike Berrow to await the phone call reporting its chart position. Last time there had been massive cele-brations when "Is There Something I Should Know?" debuted at #1. As the vintage champagne cooled in silver buckets and hamburgers sizzled on the grill, Paul took the call with high hopes. But "Union of the Snake" had only made it to #3. They all looked at each other. No one said they were disappointed—the competition was Culture Club and Billy Joel's "Uptown Girl"—but John Taylor vividly remembered the champagne warming up and the burgers getting cold.

⌒

Tour rehearsals and production meetings began at the Sydney Show-grounds in mid-October amid intercontinental promo efforts. They mimed "Union of the Snake" for *Top of the Pops* and taped segments for various American networks desperately trying to catch up with MTV, such as NBC's *Friday Night Videos*. ("Union" would reach #3 in the United States.) The band members were also interviewed by their early local champion Molly Meldrum for the *Countdown Aus-tralia* program on the ABC (Australian Broadcasting Corporation). Then, on November 12, Duran Duran flew to Canberra and opened their epochal Sing Blue Silver arena tour at that city's National Indoor Sports Centre. When singing "The Chauffeur," Simon would stretch the word "sing" until the halls seemed to sparkle with a shiny syn-ethesis, and the fans would fire up their plastic lighters like tiny stars in the galaxy.

So beginning in November 1983, Duran Duran embarked on what would be the original band's grandest and farthest-reaching campaign, spanning across Australia, Japan, England, the United States, and Canada. Over the next five months, the now eight-piece stage ensemble played to more than 750,000 people, and their hard-won album, *Seven and the Ragged Tiger*, reached the top of the English charts. But the charts and the tour were nothing compared to the huge income from merchandise. Tritec's merchandise director, Michael Warlow, had licensed hundreds of Duran Duran products, from toys and clothes to a board game (*Duran Duran into the Arena*) and even to branded Duran Duran batteries in Japan for kids to use in their Walk-mans. The Sing Blue Silver Tour pushed membership in the official Duran Duran fan club to upward of six hundred thousand fans, an unusually large number in the eighties and something that attracted much comment in trade journals. Duran "merch" was a goldmine. There were one hundred thousand Duran Duran fans in Japan alone, where only Michael Jackson (and his pet chimpanzee, Bubbles) had a bigger fanbase. Michael Warlow joined the tour to supervise the merchandise sales, which set unprecedented sales records for swag in both the United States and Japan. And this was doubled by the huge mail order business generated by the glossy Duran Duran fan club newsletter, "edited" by planetary heartthrob and pinup John Taylor.

Warlow remembers those days: "They were a good group of people. Michael Berrow had brought me in to develop their marketing, and the guys were a bit younger than me, in their early twenties. You took to them immediately. As a band they were flexible and interesting, with a keen sense of who they were and what they were doing. They were incredible at meeting and greeting their fans at the shows. They had this amazingly close bond with early MTV, which gave them the widest possible audience for a band of their time—which helped us sell lots of stuff to the kids. What I liked about them was that what they really wanted the most was credibility from other musicians and the press. They wanted the respect due to all the labor they'd done. That's what was truly important to this lot."

From Canberra to Sydney and then Brisbane, with local band the Little Heroes in support, Duran Duran sold out every show. When *Seven and the Ragged Tiger* was officially released on November 21, Duran Duran was in Melbourne, on the other side of the continent, for two concerts. After the first show, at a party at Molly Meldrum's house, John discovered a prerelease copy of INXS's new single, "Original Sin." The song sounded great, and he noticed the credits read, "Produced by Nile Rodgers. Engineered by Jason Corsaro." They played the single a few times. If the presiding genius of Chic could make INXS sound this good, John thought, why not Duran Duran too?

The last shows were in Adelaide and Perth. Although Roger, John, and Nick had earlier accepted an award for Australia's Most Popular International Act, press reviews were mixed, with some critics seeing through the fan pandemonium and noticing missed cues, clumsy dancing, and new songs that sent fans to the bathrooms. One writer described "Union of the Snake" as "more clunky than funky."

Barnstorming rock band Duran Duran was back in England by December 1, 1983. They had enjoyed Australia's high summer, but now it was almost Christmas back home, and the atmosphere was icy and gray. Everyone caught colds and felt sick. To maintain tax exile status, the band now had to perform fourteen concerts in eighteen days. Any time off was spent on album and tour promotion: TV talk shows, radio interviews, in-store album signings. Outside the band, Nick bought a posh London house. Andy and a partner opened a trendy (if short-lived) wine bar called Rio in Whitley Bay. Toronto newspapers also confirmed that Simon had finally bought a luxury flat there with Claire.

On December 3, *Seven and the Ragged Tiger* reached #1 on the UK album chart, the first (and the last) time this happened for Duran Duran. The teen mags like *Smash Hits* loved the new album, but hardly anyone else seemed to agree. A *Sounds* critic complained, "*Seven and the Rancid Ravings* is so assuredly awful that it breaks new ground in badness. . . . A nervous disorder of people near to cracking up." In America, reception was hardly any better. *Rolling Stone* gave the album two stars out of five. The punk magazine *Trouser Press* called it "a sorry collection of half-baked melodies, meaningless lyrics," and "over-active studio foolishness."

The band had been in London for a few days when word reached their highly eligible bachelor, John Taylor, that there was a beautiful new model in town. Her name was Yasmin Parvaneh, the daughter of an immigrant Iranian family. Everyone in London was talking about her beauty, her intelligence, her sense of humor. Despite his on-and-off romance with Janine Andrews, John fancied a date with the willowy Yasmin, but the modeling agencies had strict policies against handing out their girls' phone numbers to rich rock stars. Sadly, John's amorous attentions were turned elsewhere. But not long after, Simon stole Yasmin's number at a photo shoot, hurriedly copying it from her modeling agency's face book while the photographer went to the bathroom.

The British leg of the Sing Blue Silver Tour began with two concerts at the Manchester Apollo on December 6 and 7. Next came Queens Hall, Leeds, on December 8, with the band Australian Crawl opening the shows. Traveling in luxurious tour buses, they next played the Royal Highland Exhibition Hall in Edinburgh on December 10, where Paul Berrow informed them that *Seven and the Ragged Tiger* had reached #8 in the United States and had sold about a million copies in its first month on the American charts. After that, it was back to Leeds on December 11 before arriving home in Birmingham for two nights at the newly opened Birmingham NEC (National Exhibition Centre) on December 12 and 13, followed by a scant two days of rest and interviews with music press flown in from North America.

Rolling Stone was America's premier music publication, but the magazine had been less than enthusiastic about Duran Duran from the beginning. Editor and publisher Jann Wenner was ambivalent about his own closeted sexuality (he would come out as gay ten years in the future), and he had held Duran Duran, whom he secretly considered very sexy, generally at arm's length: scant and snarky coverage, niggling record reviews, and general disrespect for the band's tight connection to hated MTV, which *Rolling Stone* considered to be dangerous competition. But junior editors pointed out that Duran Duran's new album, which they admitted wasn't actually that great, was a Top 10 record in the United States and had sold more than a million units. Not only that, but Duran Duran was also touring America in early 1984, and some shows in major markets—the Northeast, the Midwest, the Mid-South, and especially California—were already sold out. Cleveland's WMMR, one of the country's most important (and closely watched) FM rock outlets, was currently playing five album tracks from *Seven and the Ragged Tiger*, mostly because of fan requests. Every time Jann Wenner ran into Andy Warhol at a dinner party or gallery opening, Warhol teased him about being too old to appreciate Duran Duran. So, almost reluctantly, as if propelled by inexorable market forces, *Rolling Stone* assigned music editor James Henke the task of covering the band's two-night return to Birmingham. In return for a backstage pass and access to the band, Duran Duran was guaranteed the cover of *Rolling Stone*.

The writer got to town while the band was working up north, so he first interviewed the Berrow brothers in their office at the Rum Runner. Michael gave him the band's back story—teenage Nick Bates and Nigel Taylor turning up in 1978, saying they had a band and were looking for a gig. Meanwhile, Paul Berrow was on the phone arguing with producers from *The Tube*, England's coolest music television program. They were going to film the first night in Birmingham and then talk to the band the next day. They wanted to interview the band by the hotel's swimming pool to get that azure *Rio* kind of shot. Berrow said no way—that era was passé—and suggested the lounge of the tour bus. They ended up in the hotel restaurant instead, but Paul Berrow didn't want Duran Duran shown drinking wine on camera.

The following evening, James Henke was chatting with Simon, who was standing in the aisle of the tour bus as the band was driven to the NEC. The writer had already heard that "Charlie" (as Simon was known to Duran Duran insiders) was also called "Lardo" (behind his back, of course) because of his recent weight gain in Australia. Now, as if on cue, Simon sneezed hard and accidentally popped the two buttons holding up his black stage trousers, studded up the legs with silver conchos like Jim Morrison used to wear.

Down came the trousers to his ankles. Those nearby snickered at Simon's tight blue underwear. This was an emergency because they were almost at the venue. The band had taken to dressing for the stage in their hotel so they could run in and out of the arenas to avoid being mobbed. Quickly, Simon stripped off his trousers and gave them to their two Australian wardrobe girls, who sewed the buttons back on. The reporter found the pantsless rock star to be a

less-than-magical sight, describing "an honest-to-God teen idol wearing only a vest, a T-shirt, and blue underpants. Le Bon, you see, is
no John Travolta when it comes to physique. Not a slob, just slightly
chubby legs, a little bit of a gut."

As the support band Australian Crawl came off stage, the writer
checked out the fans (dubbed "Durannies"); the sold-out arena held
11,500 of them, and they were excited to see their hometown band
gone international. "When the lights went down, the crowd went
nuts. It's the kind of scene that's been played over and over again in
pop music, from Frank Sinatra to Elvis Presley to the Beatles to Rick
Springfield. Girls crying. Girls fainting. Girls screaming. The audience created such a din that even if one could hear the band's music,
it was impossible to concentrate on it." Andy Taylor would later say
that they could go onstage and just fart because it wouldn't make any
difference.

But the writer ended up with a certain grudging respect for his
subject. "These guys believe in putting on a show," he noted. "And
on this British tour they were putting on their flashiest show yet:
nine musicians on stage, flashing lights, six illuminated Roman columns across the back of the stage. Sure, its grandness smacked of
pretentiousness, the extra musicians seemed to serve little purpose,
and Le Bon's tortured singing and klutzy dancing were at times an
embarrassment.

"But Duran Duran delivered all a fan could ask for in the way of
music: an hour and a half long set, replete with the group's numerous
hit singles and their latest smash 'The Union of the Snake.'" At the
end of the evening, the highlight of the concert for *Rolling Stone*'s cor-
respondent was when Simon stopped dancing, grabbed at his waist,
and rushed to the side of the stage, where a seamstress from Sydney
was waiting with needle and thread. Lardo had popped his buttons
again.

Most of the band was staying in their tour hotel in Birmingham,
but Andy was in his comfortable suburban house in nearby Wolverhampton with (newly pregnant) wife Tracey and both their brothers,
which was where *Rolling Stone* interviewed him. About getting into

Duran Duran, Andy said, "The band was quite blatant. They said, 'Look, we're fucking poseurs, man. We want a good-looking fucking poseur band, with no apology.' That was good for me—I liked dressing up and wearing makeup." But that already felt like a lifetime ago. Adoration had gotten old, and besides, Andy stopped getting much fan mail after he married Tracey. Asked about their upcoming American shows, Andy replied, "It's funny, but a year ago this time, we couldn't have sold eggs in America." It was MTV that had changed their fortunes, Andy said. The writer mentioned the harsh criticism the band had incurred for their escapist fantasy videos. Why the globe-trotting, model-escorting image when millions in England were in dire straits? Why the fast-forward to being Rod Stewart? But Andy just laughed at this—*Smash Hits* and *The Face* didn't give him this crap—and after some polite, evasive banter, he showed *Rolling Stone* the door.

Next, the writer sat with twenty-one-year-old Nick in their hotel bar, a faux pub called the Plough and Harrow. Nick spoke in his aristocratic drawl, a languid voice that many tried to imitate but few rarely got. "I have *immense* ambition," he said, "and I had a very vivid impression of what I wanted to do. I'm a Gemini, and I believe in *immense* detail."

Nick was asked about the *Rio*-era videos, and he brought up his friendship with Andy Warhol, whom he said was all about image rather than substance. According to Warhol, it didn't matter what they wrote about you, Andy had said, as long as you could measure it in column inches. Nick said, "I think the image was obviously very important to us, after the music. Let's face it, everybody who's been massive in the last twenty years has had a *bloody strong* image."

Then again, Nick sighed, "maybe we should have worn masks. . . . Look, we don't play our music for thirty-year-old bank clerks."

~

"I think that's all bullshit," spat John Taylor a bit later in the Plough. The writer had just suggested to John and Simon that "five well-dressed playboys jet-setting around the world" wasn't quite the coolest image for a band in 1984. "I mean," John continued, "we do get criticized for exotic video locations. But does [film producer] Cubby

Broccoli get criticized for doing the same thing in James Bond movies?" So did Duran Duran want to be rock and roll's answer to 007? John admitted that the image thing had gotten out of hand. "OK . . . videos in Sri Lanka . . . Duran Duran here and there. . . . Yes, our videos gave the impression that we were frolicking on beaches and going sailing in the afternoon. We were trying to give that sort of young, jet-setter, playboy image, which was great at first. Well, maybe we have made a few mistakes, and I think that was one of them. But I don't regret having done it."

Simon insisted that Duran Duran had nothing to be ashamed of. "That's what people do," he averred. "They work and have parties. That we fly around the world is because our work is all over the world. And I like parties—any excuse for a party."

Simon was adamant that Duran Duran was a positive influence on its audience. In fact, he started to sound like Margaret Thatcher: "We present kids with a very obvious example of people who've done something to get out of the dumps. We've been called decadent, but I wouldn't agree. We're very optimistic. I don't think the world is crumbling. I think it's just a matter of people doing things for themselves and not putting too much weight on the politicians' shoulders and letting them live your life for you.

"Kids in England have been brought up with the attitude that somebody would give them a job, that they'd never be unemployed, that they didn't need to create a job for themselves. That attitude is what we're up against. That's what we're subverting—that whole social attitude of being looked after by the state. I believe in looking after myself. I think I can do it better than anyone else."

The writer conceded that Duran Duran's music was not the usual teenage fodder, with Simon's Beat poet sensibility ruling out standard love songs. Simon explained that *Seven and the Ragged Tiger* was even a sort of concept album: "It's an adventure story about a little commando team. The seven is for us—the five band members and the two managers—and the ragged tiger is success. Seven people, running after success. Ambition—that's what it's about.

"People seem to be coming around to our point of view," Simon concluded. "I was once quoted as saying we'll be the band to dance to when they drop the bomb. But I've got a very strong sense of the survival of the species. I believe in genetics and breeding. That's a very important part of evolution. But, I'm not a snob. Ask anybody." He laughed. "Well, anybody who matters."

On December 17, the boys were photographed for the cover of *Rolling Stone* at the Chelsea studio of David Montgomery, a friend of Andy Warhol's. Montgomery's portrait of Jimi Hendrix had been used on the *Electric Ladyland* album, and he was the first American allowed to take an official portrait of the queen. Montgomery shot Duran Duran dressed for winter, on an all-white set decorated like a surrealist film by Jean Cocteau, with disembodied arms and legs protruding from the walls.

The next evening, Duran Duran began a sold-out, five-night run at Wembley Arena in North London, bringing the five-year-old prophecy—Wembley by 1983—to fruition. (Some historians of the short-lived Republic of Durania contend that these arena concerts at Wembley in December 1983, with special consideration for the production's early computer-enabled stage lighting, constituted the apex of the original band's musical career as a live band.) The concerts garnered mostly positive reviews in the London newspapers, a rarity, and after Christmas, the tax exiles would leave England yet again. The next few months playing around the world would be the hardest work Duran Duran would ever do, and afterward the band would never be the same.

John and his on-and-off fiancée Janine had reunited over the holidays. As a 007 fanatic, John liked dating a Bond girl, but he also admired Janine, liked her proud cheekbones, and felt comfortable with her. He told *Smash Hits*, "We're both very down to earth. We spend Christmas at each other's mums and dads. The papers go on about my 'Page 3 Girl,' but it's nothing to do with jet-setting. It's not like that at all."

On Christmas Eve 1983, John and Janine were in John's bachelor pad in Edgbaston and were hungry. Janine called in a takeout order from their favorite curry house in Moseley: chicken bhunas for two, please. But they didn't deliver. So John grabbed his keys and Janine her sable jacket. They sat in John's frigid Aston Martin DB5 for ten minutes, waiting for the engine to warm up. Sean Connery, John's preferred James Bond, drove a silver Aston Martin DB5 in *Goldfinger*, the second Bond film. Only a few hundred DB5s were manufactured between 1963 and 1965, and John's twenty-year-old vintage car had recently cost him a fortune.

The Aston Martin was unreliable, but it was still cool. The engine purred like a leopard in estrus as they headed toward Moseley. A carol service from the cathedral was on the radio. The wet streets and decorated shop windows of Birmingham flashed by. The curry house was the only shop open. A few sketchy Moseley types were hanging around on the street. It started to rain. Janine didn't want to be left alone in the Aston Martin, so she followed John inside. When she closed the car door with the keys in the ignition, the doors locked. There they were in the rain—pop star and Bond girl—holding their Christmas dinner in paper sacks. Fortunately, one of the Moseley types was experienced. Soon John and Janine were back in his flat, waiting for Santa Claus.

PART 7

Duran Duran was in Paris in January to film the video for "New Moon on Monday," first working in a studio in riverside Bercy and then within the stone walls of the nearby medieval village of Noyers, northeast of the city. Russell Mulcahy was busy elsewhere, so his colleague Brian Grant directed. The storyboard featured the band members as anti-fascist resistance fighters whose decadent cabaret (featuring a onetime Miss France, cast by the band) disguises a subversive clandestine press. Nightriders with torches carry most of the optics, and the band looks young and silly. Nick thought the video was awful and made no narrative sense, but MTV put the clip into heavy rotation when "New Moon on Monday" was released on January 14, with "Tiger Tiger" as the B-side.

But the single only reached #10 in America, a disappointment. Back in London, there began to be concerns about the band in Manchester Square. Neither "Union" nor "New Moon" really caught fire like their earlier records. As Dave Ambrose recalled, "The budget for *Seven* was terrifying, and when the first two singles didn't really take off, I started getting very anxious." Alex Sadkin may have been a great studio engineer, but Ambrose didn't think he knew how to coax great songs from a band like Duran Duran. Also, he noted, "there are some insecurities that come out when you've got unlimited budgets. You can end up overmixing, and it can take a terribly long time."

But *Seven* started getting gold album awards in major markets, then platinum, as the Sing Blue Silver Tour continued in Japan, beginning at the Sendai Sports Centre on January 17. It was winter in Japan, and everything was covered in icy, frozen snow. With a film crew documenting the tour, they continued through Nagoya and Osaka and sold out several nights at the legendary Budokan martial arts arena in central Tokyo, where again they were stalked by hard-core Durannies and moved through writhing mobs of girls by muscular escorts. "Playing the Budokan—that was a big deal for us," John said. He also remembered that they started playing much harder, with Roger goosing the tempos and the guitars turned way up. "We were louder, angrier, more aggressive, and darker than [the fans] could possibly allow themselves to imagine."

There were no drugs to be had in Japan, nothing except for rather strong pep pills available in pharmacies. The law was strict. Udo Artists wouldn't help them or any of the rock bands passing through Japan. Even Paul McCartney had spent nine days in jail (and was later deported) in 1980 when he tried to bring some weed through customs at Narita Airport. "It was all drinking," John recalled, "and that meant things could get violent." John trashed his hotel suite after their concert in Fukuoka. That was a Sunday matinee, where the road crew had to keep sweeping the stage amid a constant fan barrage of stuffed animals, plastic toys, bouquets, love letters, underwear, cans, coins, whatever could be thrown at the band.

Meanwhile in New York, Tritec Music hired Nile Rodgers to remix "The Reflex" with the same modernist funk energy that had blasted Bowie's "Let's Dance" into a planetary club smash a year before. Some Capitol execs worried that boy band Duran Duran faking the funk would turn off their core audience, but John told Nile to ignore them. The new album depended on the success of this remix.

The last show in Japan was back at the Budokan on January 25. It took the hall crew an hour to clear the stage of all the junk the fans had thrown. Andy's car was also mobbed outside the venue. A scrum of a dozen little girls shrieked at him, their faces pressed against the windows, smashing their tiny fists on the roof and yelling. The fans in front were crushed against the car, and some started to panic and faint. When they returned to the Four Seasons Hotel, the car was covered with lipstick.

Three days later, the road crew built the band's touring stage in the Saddledome in Calgary, so they could test the equipment before the grueling, forty-four-concert North American tour leg began on January 30. Coca-Cola was sponsoring the tour; as fans filed into the arenas, they were greeted by a massive red scrim across the stage advertising Coke. There was a pre-tour party with soda marketing executives and their children, where the band was presented with logo-themed tote bags and other swag. Asked to say a few words, John mentioned that he preferred Pepsi to Coke, and a dead silence sent Paul Berrow and merch guy Mike Warlow heading quickly for the doors.

After Calgary, the band boarded their chartered four-engine Viscount turbo-prop airliner that would convey them through wintry storm systems and gut-churning air pockets for the next few weeks. Andy grabbed a large white stuffed bear as he was leaving the stage in Calgary, which would become his cherished airplane seatmate as Duran Duran flew across the North American continent in 1984. Duran Duran played through Western Canada before crossing into Washington State to play in Seattle on February 2. Their Canadian opening act, Images in Vogue, were stopped at the US border and denied entry, having no valid work permits. Other bands opened for Duran Duran for the remainder of the tour.

John considered the Seattle Center Coliseum to be the band's first headlining concert in an American sports arena—"not a style we were familiar with, close to British arenas like the NEC and Wembley, but much, much bigger." Even before the band went onstage, fainting girls were carried off due to panic attacks and dehydration. Duran Duran was used to mob scenes and mania by then, but the mad teenagers in Seattle shocked them all over again.

⁓

"Duran Duran / The Fab Five" splashed across the cover of *Rolling Stone*'s 414th issue, dated February 2, 1984. The story headline called them "Middle Class Heroes": "Thanks to their videogenic good looks and a string of hit singles . . . Duran Duran are causing a sensation reminiscent of the early Beatles. . . . With sex and style Duran Duran savor their American dream." No one liked the rest of the five-page story, which felt rather argumentative with the musicians forced to defend themselves from intimations of irrelevance, but it did mark the first time an American music magazine had put in the time and effort to try to explain who Duran Duran was. (In a simple twist of fate, the back cover of *Rolling Stone* featured an advertisement for Revlon's new Hydrocurve II contact lenses. The young woman wearing the product was a stunning Danish model named Renée Simonsen, who would soon be swept into Duran Duran's social solar system.)

Julie Anne Friedman was traveling with Nick throughout the tour, and not all his bandmates were thrilled. But at the same time, Nick was the Controller—their leader, more or less. Between shows, Nick and Julie Anne huddled alone in hotel suites. Nick also developed a hobby out of distorting MTV videos using the color levels on the hotel television sets and then photographing the screens with a Polaroid instant camera. Simon and Andy did a lot of promotion, such as appearing on the syndicated American music program *Solid Gold*. Andy missed his pregnant wife. John looked forward to seeing fiery Bond girl Janine Andrews in LA. Roger was the hardest working and the most seriously fatigued.

On February 6, they headlined the first of two nights at the Los Angeles Forum, sharing the visitors' locker room with the New York Rangers hockey team, who were in town to play a matinee against the LA Kings. They were also photographed backstage with Liza Minnelli, whose role in the movie *Cabaret* had been an inspiration to Nick and Nigel (and Stephen Duffy) ten years earlier. Mike Warlow later estimated that they sold over a million dollars' worth of Duran Duran merchandise per night at the LA Forum, all in cash. People backstage noticed huge satchels stuffed with money being looked after by their own security detail.

Later that night, John and Janine quarreled in his Beverly Hills hotel suite, whose furnishings were then destroyed. In the early hours, John knocked on the door of photographer Denis O'Regan, an old friend of the band's, who was documenting the tour. A furious Janine had returned her diamond engagement ring to John, who was distraught. He handed the ring to O'Regan, asking him to look after it until he was himself again. In the morning, the ring was deposited in the hotel's safe before tour manager Richard Ames took charge of it.

Denis O'Regan was a big, bluff Irish guy with a twinkle in his good eye for shooting touring rock bands. John remembered that "he was there as a constant observer—when things went right and when things went wrong. Sometimes we loved it; other times we hated it. But we knew this world tour was an experience we never wanted to forget."

O'Regan compiled a detailed optic record of a big rock tour: airport waiting rooms and baggage claims; hotel lobbies, autograph seekers, motel rooms, arena locker rooms; TV studios, backstage corridors, loading docks; interviews, press conferences, photo ops, meet-and-greets; hockey rinks, civic centers, municipal auditoriums, halls and gardens, coliseums, forums, and domes; limo convoys stopping at the golden arches for Big Macs and Quarter Pounders with cheese; sound checks, rehearsals, hair and makeup, mob scenes; frozen northern cities seen from penthouse hotel suites; dressing room buffets, pizza deliveries; landline telephones, butane lighters, Sony Walkmans; airplane interiors, backseats of limousines, heaving scrums of fans, big hair, more big hair; Ronnie and Jo Wood, Nile Rodgers and Bernard Edwards, Liza with a Z; Atari game consoles required in Duran Duran's dressing room per the group's contract rider with the promoter; the bandmates shooting targets in the basement range of the FBI Museum in Washington, DC. Altogether, Denis O'Regan shot about five thousand images of the Sing Blue Silver Tour.

After Los Angeles, the tour headed to three shows in Texas followed by another in Louisiana and two in Missouri. On February 20, it was so cold in Minneapolis that their plane had to circle above twice while the runway was deiced. At the foot of the ramp, two Lincoln Continental stretch limousines were tied together by cables because one's battery had died. Then it was on to the Dane County Coliseum in Madison, Wisconsin, on February 21; two concerts at Chicago's Rosemont Horizon on February 23 and 24; and finally Cobo Center in Detroit on February 25. Duran Duran had played five shows in six days, and everyone agreed they were starting to sound a little like the ragged tiger they were selling. Andy wasn't shy about grumbling that everything had gotten too big. The entourage and road crew numbered about 150 people. He felt, he said, like a mouse in a maze, his life controlled by talent managers, booking agents, and corporate sponsors.

Roger was so beat there were hushed conversations about finding another drummer to finish the tour if he collapsed, but in the end, Duran Duran's throbbing V-8 engine managed to stay the course.

Duran Duran flew to Chicago in a blizzard, white knuckles gripping armrests all the way. "Charlie" Le Bon had a sore throat. Everyone was reading *Roman*, the recently published tell-almost-all autobiography by director Roman Polanski. Their cool new opening act was a band called Chequered Past, a newly formed LA supergroup consisting of Sex Pistol Steve Jones, old friends from Blondie Nigel Harrison and Clem Burke, and Tony Sales on bass guitar. Their lead singer was Michael Des Barres, an actor who appeared on TV shows like *Miami Vice* and who had fronted Detective, the seventies LA band signed to Led Zeppelin's label, Swan Song Records. Chequered Past didn't have much in the way of actual songs, but Steve Jones's blazing electric guitar attack scorched the fresh faces of teenage Duran Duran fans who arrived early enough to witness their short set. The two bands got along well, and there was much hilarity between the dressing rooms before and after the concerts.

The tour moved on to Cleveland and then Pittsburgh's Civic Arena on February 28. This was the same night as the Grammys, where Duran Duran won two awards—not for their music but for their videos: Best Short Form Video (*Duran Duran Video 45*) and Best Long Form Video (*Duran Duran Video Album*). The band couldn't accept in person because they were playing Pittsburgh in a blinding snowstorm. (The band appeared on the awards broadcast via live video link.) Andy complained this was a stupidly lost opportunity to be seen by fans as a happening, world-beating English band in its fucking glory—live!—on American network television, coast to coast. But no. The Berrows hadn't even told them they'd won. The others had never seen Andy so angry with their management.

Then again, Andy complained a lot. Duran Duran, he said, was working too hard, with little or no rest between gigs. Simon's voice was almost shot, and there were still weeks to go on the Sing Blue Silver Tour. The fine vintage wine and cocaine bills were astronomical. The weather was antarctic. It was winter in America, and everyone was cold. It wasn't like England; it was *really* cold. They were doing their jobs, but Andy strongly felt as though these had to be the last days of the band, and he wasn't afraid to say it. He was also quite open about saying the sooner they ditched the Berrows, the better for Duran Duran.

After weeks of growing tensions, Andy and Nick had a bitter row about Nick's girlfriend, Julie Anne, a constant presence on tour who got on Andy's nerves. Nick didn't want to hear it. "This is how it is *fucking going to be*," he told Andy through clenched teeth. And Andy sensed the end of the band was now in sight.

Duran Duran and Chequered Past played in Virginia and West Virginia in March 1984. Their little turbo-prop plane bounced over and around the wintry mountains of Appalachia like a yo-yo. Billy Idol was added to the bill at the immense Carrier Dome in Syracuse, New York. (Everyone was glad to see him—someone from home— and his great guitarist Steve Stevens. They also loved "Rebel Yell.") Then it was back over the border to Canada, where the temperature dropped below zero. Russell Mulcahy shot live concert footage for the video for "The Reflex" at Maple Leaf Gardens, Toronto's famous hockey rink. John recalled, "The phrase 'video band' kept coming up [in interviews], and it would set us off. For the 'Reflex' video it was like, *Let's do a* live *video*. What we were saying was, 'Listen, we're *not* a video band, OK?'"

It got even colder the next night at the Montreal Forum and again the next night at the Civic Centre in Ottawa. After that, they flew down to Philadelphia and back up to Portland, Maine. (Tritec's theory seems to have been that since it was unlikely that Duran Duran would tour like this ever again—Nick would never put up with it—they were playing both the major venues and the so-called sec-ondary markets at the same time. Too bad if it killed the band.) It snowed so hard in Connecticut on March 13 that Billy Idol couldn't reach the Hartford Civic Center, so Duran Duran went on before a sold-out house with almost no one in it. The next night, the also sold-out Centrum in Worcester, Massachusetts, was only about half full. Another show in Virginia preceded a blessed day off; the fatigued musicians of Duran Duran boarded their plane and flew to New York City, where prophecy would be fulfilled when they headlined a sold-out Madison Square Garden on March 19 and then again two nights later. But it was far from the dream they'd imagined. As John later said, "This was the tour we'd been dreaming of back at the Rum Runner office. We'd tell the record companies, 'We want to play Madison Square Garden by 1984.' And we did. But it had gone way beyond our control. Be careful what you pray for."

The first Garden concert had sold out in a half hour. Most of the tickets went to the scalpers—another "secondary market" for con-cert tickets. A second show was added, and these seats went even faster. The band was confined to the (musician-friendly) Berkshire Place Hotel because a few hundred kids were camped outside on East Fifty-Second Street, teeth chattering in the Manhattan spring while they sang "Girls on Film" and "Save a Prayer" until the wee hours, annoying the hotel's other guests. Andy was mobbed and jumped on whenever he tried to leave the hotel, so the band started going out through the kitchens instead. There had also been a scare when Simon and Nick thought they saw someone point a gun at their limo on the way downtown for drinks with Andy Warhol at One Fifth Avenue's hotel bar.

The New York concerts represented a big milestone for the band, and their parents and girlfriends had all flown in. Among the back-stage guests were Duran Duran's heroes Nile Rodgers and Bernard Edwards. Nile had joined the band onstage for Chic's "Good Times" as an encore. Nile then introduced them to his date for the evening, Madonna Ciccone. She was tiny, contained, wide-eyed, and obser-vant. Her album *Madonna* had come out the previous summer, and her single "Lucky Star" was big on MTV. Nile was producing her next record, "Like a Virgin." Madonna was very complimentary to the band, but even so, John was annoyed because she didn't fall for his postconcert charms. Less than a year later, Madonna would sell out Madison Square Garden herself, causing riots wherever she went.

Simon's vocal cords were raw after bellowing "Girls on Film" and "Hungry Like the Wolf" night after night. He sat out the New York press conference organized by Capitol Records on March 22. The next day, Duran Duran flew to Charleston, South Carolina, beginning a southern US leg that would see these intrepid troupers play seven concerts in eight days, covering Florida, Georgia, and North Carolina. Then there was blind outrage when the band was told that Capitol and EMI were objecting to Nile Rodgers's brilliant, popping dance-floor remix of "The Reflex," the next single to be released from *Seven and the Ragged Tiger*. To Capitol's (older) A&R veterans, "The Reflex" remix didn't sound like Duran Duran. They had never heard a Black producer exploit digital sampling technology on a commercial single by a White rock band before.

One night, the phone rang in Nile Rodgers's Manhattan apartment. It was Nick, calling from the road. Nile could hear that Nick's monotonic British drawl sounded upset.

Nick: "Nile, we have a problem."

Nile: "What's up, Nick?"

Nick: "Erm . . . Capitol *hates* the record. The remix."

Nile: "How do you guys feel about it?"

Nick: "Nile, we *love* it, but Capitol hates it so much they don't want to release it. They say it's too *Black* sounding."

Nile was used to racism in the record industry and everywhere else, so he tried not to get angry. "The Reflex" was an obvious #1 in the current US market.

Nile: "Fuck them. If you guys like it, tell them to kiss your ass and put the fucking record out anyway."

Nile later wrote, "Then Nick said something that even my too-Black ass had never heard before (or since, thank God)."

Nick: "The label said that if we forced them to put the record out, they'll want to take points back on our deal because it's going to cost a lot to promote it, and it's not fair for them to bear the extra cost of a record that won't sell."

Nile: "Tell them OK. Yeah—give them the fucking points back if it doesn't sell. Fuck 'em, Nick. I've never heard anything so ridiculous."

⌒

On April 2, Duran Duran played at the Capital Centre in Maryland, near Washington, DC. Simon dedicated "Save a Prayer" to local hero Marvin Gaye, who had been killed by his father the day before. The next night, they played Nassau Coliseum on Long Island, where girls threw underwear onstage with their phone numbers attached. (Andy would later claim that no band member slept with a fan during the entire tour.) Press reviews noted the unbridled screaming teenage ardor in the crowds, especially when John appeared on the video screen over the stage. Two nights later, they played in New Jersey, then in New Haven, Connecticut. On April 9, the band sold out the Myriad Convention Center in Oklahoma City, where Russell Mulcahy screened the new "Reflex" video for their approval at the venue.

Duran Duran won their battle with their label, and Nile Rodgers's remix of "The Reflex" was released as a single on April 16 in the United States, with a concert take of "New Religion" on the flip side. It was an instant radio hit and crossed over into other pop formats. On April 21, "The Reflex" became Duran Duran's first American #1 single, justifying their defiant faith in Nile Rodgers and their own commercial instincts. The single was released in Britain on the same day with a live version of glam band Cockney Rebel's "Make Me Smile" as the B-side. A week later, "The Reflex" hit #1 in the UK. It even got a positive review in the *NME*, which usually treated Duran Duran like unwanted stepchildren.

The last days of the Sing Blue Silver Tour were played out in California. John started doing drugs during the shows, snorting rails of cocaine laid out on the tops of amplifiers ("I crossed a line," he later wrote, "when I started getting high onstage"). Three nights at the cavernous Oakland Coliseum near San Francisco yielded scenes for the concert film that would be called *Arena*. The *San Francisco*

Chronicle's review of the April 12 concert used the words "hysterical" and "rowdy" to describe Duran Duran's young audience.

There were other kinds of hysteria in San Francisco. One night, Andy was awakened by a phone call in the Four Seasons Hotel. Tour manager Richard Ames told him that John had injured himself and his suite was full of blood. Andy flew down the hall to find John bleeding heavily from his foot and incoherent, crying, holding himself and rocking back and forth. Veteran Duran Duran minder Simon Cook was tying a pillowcase around John's leg as a tourniquet. There were broken vodka bottles on the blood-soaked carpet. It looked to Andy that John had deliberately walked on shards of heavy glass, some of which were still embedded in his foot. Help soon arrived, and John was taken to the hospital, where he received more than forty stitches and multiple injections. Andy was the band member closest to John because they were cocaine buddies, but John offered no explanation for what had happened and vehemently denied intentionally harming himself. The incident was quickly hushed up so their insurance company wouldn't find out. No one wanted to point out this was the third time John had seriously cut himself. John later confessed to *Smash Hits*, "It's the worst I've ever been."

The last two concerts of Duran Duran's tour took place at the San Diego Sports Arena on April 16 and 17. Someone thought it would be funny to hire an exotic dancer to tease uptight Nick onstage during the last encore, "Girls on Film." The stripper tried to drape herself over Nick, usually impassive behind his Roland keyboard. Nick smiled as the girl wiggled her breasts at him. Julie Anne, standing nearby, was absolutely livid, but the rest of the group thought it was pretty funny.

Coca-Cola threw an end-of-tour party at the Chateau Marmont. It was something of a staid corporate event until one of Duran Duran's percussionists pulled a knife on someone he thought was trying to pick his pocket. A violent struggle followed as they pried the blade away from him. No one had ever seen a party empty so fast. It would be a while before Coca-Cola sponsored another big rock tour.

Afterward, Simon and Andy flew back home from Los Angeles; they were completely exhausted and slept for most of the trip. Simon reportedly asked Andy if he was leaving the band, but Andy replied that he just wanted to get back to his pregnant wife. Both Andy and Simon were stopped by customs officers at Heathrow, led off to a private area, and strip-searched for drugs. Andy recalled them saying, "Bend over. Got anything up there?"

⁓

The Sing Blue Silver Tour had been an epic journey through time zones and continents, attracting one of the richest young audiences in history, moving tons of merchandise and records, finally ending in the planetary success of "The Reflex" and then worlds beyond—unless one of them tapped out, quit, or died. No one knew then that Duran Duran's original lineup wouldn't tour again in America for another twenty years.

April 1984. An early spring brought the return of Duran Duran to a slightly different English pop scene from the one they'd left. Boy George was firmly on top now. He'd won a Grammy for Best New Artist. Culture Club had been given a Brit Award for Best New Single ("Karma Chameleon") and Best British Group. Nick's beloved *Tatler* magazine ranked the Boy as the most famous person in Britain, a notch above HM the Queen at number two. But it was on with the show for Duran Duran. The hardworking troubadours found themselves once again miming their latest single, "The Reflex," on *Top of the Pops*. Tritec Music decided to cancel the upcoming European leg of their world tour when it became clear that the musicians didn't want to do it. "Those boys were *knackered*," Mike Warlow said. "In England that means they were too damned tired to go right back to work." So all the merchandise—Duran Duran watches and bobble-head dolls—was put in storage. EMI was advised there would be no new Duran Duran album of original songs in the immediate future. The label settled on a Christmas release of a live tour album with a new single as an extra track.

The new single would be called "The Wild Boys." EMI liked the sound of it.

Once again, their perpetual tax exile forced Duran Duran out of England. In May, they made promotional visits to European cities where they would have played in their canceled tour: Rome, Berlin, Monte Carlo. On May 7, they performed at the Montreux Pop Festival in Switzerland. At the end of the month, they attended the Cannes Film Festival, hoping to build up goodwill for their forthcoming concert film.

Simon was in London at the end of the month, breaking up with his girlfriend, Claire. At a photo shoot, he had stumbled across pictures of nineteen-year-old model Yasmin Parvaneh and then copied her phone number from the agency's face book. Simon called Yasmin, whom he'd never met. She thought it was someone playing a joke and hung up on him. But he kept calling and charmed her into accepting a movie date. She thought she was going to a regular cinema but instead found herself walking the star-studded red carpet with Simon at the glittering premiere of *Indiana Jones and the Temple of Doom* in Leicester Square. The Prince and Princess of Wales were the guests of honor. Yazzie (as she was called) was more than impressed when Diana waved to Simon. Their pictures were splashed all over the London newspapers the next day, which was when Claire realized her romance with Simon Le Bon was really over. But after only two weeks, Simon ended things with Yazzie too, telling friends that she wouldn't sleep with him.

Videographer Russell Mulcahy wasn't thrilled with the concert footage he'd recorded in Oakland. He decided to reshoot sequences in a more controlled environment, so on June 13 and 14, they set up at the Birmingham NEC and played before an audience of two thousand fans who got their free tickets through Birmingham's *Evening Mail* and London's *Evening Standard*. The *Mail* reported that some fans fainted from dehydration during the hours-long shoot. Others were bruised from being crushed up against the stage. A week later, Russell shot studio scenes at Twickenham Studios in South West London. A local legend has it that someone from the film crew walked into a nearby pub and tried to hire someone to pose with a live tiger for £100. The punters just laughed at him.

By 1984, nearly all the first wave of music video directors were ready to move on to feature films. This was a group that, in addition to Russell, included names like Julien Temple, Steve Barron, Mary Lambert, John Landis, and Bob Giraldi. Rather than wait for a major movie studio to hire him, Russell bought the movie rights to *The Wild Boys*, William S. Burroughs's 1971 sci-fi novel about technologically adept packs of homosexual teenage warriors who enjoy setting their enemies on fire just for fun. In Burroughs's torrid vision, human civilization would be doomed by 1988, as the Wild Boys mutated into humanoids able to reproduce without women.

Duran Duran was first told about Russell's acquisition back in Sydney while they were working on their album. Russell got them copies of the novel and asked them to write a song called "The Wild Boys" as the movie's main title theme while he worked on a treatment for his contacts in Hollywood. The movie deals all fell through, so Russell kept making videos. But the band liked the sound of "The Wild Boys" as a song title and worked on a demo at Nomis Studios, a rehearsal room in West London. Andy said the demo took them about ten minutes. They all liked that "The Wild Boys" was a much, much harder and abrasive sound than fans of Duran Duran were used to.

Even though they agreed about the new song, no one in Duran Duran seemed thrilled to see each other after a few weeks apart. "It was a tight squeeze, getting all our egos into the tight space," John recalled. Nick began making spikey sampled sound effects (sirens, gunshots, war drums) while Simon adapted some of the novel's dark ideas into lyrics referencing hunger, bloodstains, and murder by the roadside. The wild boys—feral orphans—"never chose this way," Simon wailed empathically, vocal cords straining with emotion. With "The Reflex" still selling well around the world, EMI agreed to Duran Duran's strong suggestion that protean Nile Rodgers be flown into London to produce the track.

Nile (who'd just finished Madonna's "Like a Virgin") listened to the "Wild Boys" demo and said he didn't think it was exactly dance-floor material, but he was happy to work with the band again during July 1984. "It was the first time in my life," Nile later wrote, "that I was so completely absorbed in the lives of superstars." By this, Nile meant people who needed bodyguards to move around London. Nile was taken to all the right nightclubs by John, who was usually received like royalty. Even the gangsters, hoodlums, and hard men stepped back when John and Janine walked into the club with Nile, decked out in full dreadlocks. Nick and Julie Anne took him on pricey shopping excursions in Chelsea and Knightsbridge. Nile recalled, "Nick hooked me up with Manolo Blahnik, who was turning out a men's collection, and the queen's hatmaker, Philip Treacy." Andy, "a solid musician, a highly opinionated dude with a fiery personality," took Nile to his local pub for a pint. Roger was "the most laid-back in the band." Simon? Well, Simon was off sailing somewhere, they told him, eyes rolling back in their skulls.

One afternoon, John took Nile for drinks at a private club in St. James frequented by pop stars. Fans were waiting outside, and John signed a few autographs so they could get in unmolested. Inside, Paul McCartney was sitting at a table by himself. "Not a soul bothered Paul when he left," Nile recalled. "But John Taylor was swarmed by screaming fans. He needed a bodyguard to protect him. The tumult was one step down from actual sixties Beatlemania."

John remembered, "Once again Nile was working his Synclavier magic, editing the groove, retuning Simon's vocals to create something otherworldly, taking the song we'd written to another level. It felt like a big boy's song." Andy told an interviewer how proud he was of "The Wild Boys"—a newer, bigger, hard rock sound for Duran Duran.

The band was working late one night at Maison Rouge Studios on Chelsea's Fulham Road when a riot started. The studio was close to Stamford Bridge, the Chelsea F.C. stadium. Duran Duran fans staking out the studio mentioned to Chelsea soccer fans, who were boozing at the local pub, that the band was working inside, and the hooligans were offended by the thought of these "poofters and benders from Birmingham" near Stamford Bridge. A hostile crowd formed outside the studio and began chanting obscenities. Inside, Nile reported, the scene was chilling. Someone threw a bottle at Maison Rouge, and the police were called. Nile was astonished that he and the band had to be escorted to their cars through a drunken, baying mob by a flying squad of cops to a din of homophobic jeers, bottles, and airborne debris. Then again, it wasn't always great being in Duran Duran.

July in London means the tennis tournament at Wimbledon, where all the best players in the world compete (unless it rains), and large crowds feast on fresh strawberries and heavy English cream. One night, John escorted Janine to a post-tournament party hosted by actor Michael Caine at fashionable Langan's restaurant in Mayfair (which Caine co-owned). Gentlemen's Singles champion John McEnroe was also a guest, along with Ladies' Singles champion Martina Navratilova.

James Bond uber-fan John noticed Albert "Cubby" Broccoli sitting nearby and asked Janine to introduce him to the powerful producer who held the movie rights to 007.

John recalled, "We got to chatting. I said, 'When are you going to have a decent theme song again?'"

Cubby Broccoli knew about Duran Duran. They'd just had a #1 hit in the UK. He replied, "Well, do you want to write the next one?"

"Absolutely!" said John, who was then driven home to his new house in Knightsbridge. With the help of his bodyguard, he stumbled his way through the annoying fan encampment outside his front door, called the other guys, and blurted that he thought they might get the new James Bond theme. The name of the movie—just finished production—was going to be *A View to a Kill*.

John Barry was one of the most successful and honored English composers of movie music. He had scored a hundred films and almost all the James Bond movies, beginning with *Dr. No* in 1962. Presently, he had recently finished the music for the blockbuster *Out of Africa* and was just beginning work on Cubby Broccoli's new Bond film.

The day after the party, John Taylor was driven to Broccoli's production offices on South Audley Street in Mayfair. Sitting behind his massive desk, the producer put in a call to Barry at his home in Oyster Bay, on Long Island. "John Barry was an idol of mine," John recalled, "and I was excited to speak with him. He had a deep, drawling Yorkshire accent."

Cubby Broccoli explained that John Taylor of Duran Duran was in the room and said that he wanted him to work with Duran Duran on the new film.

There was a pause, and then Barry said, "Uh-huh . . . all right."

He didn't seem too happy to hear this news, but the producer was firm. He explained that Duran Duran was the most popular band in England and maybe the world, and he told Barry, "I want you to make this work, John."

Barry invited John Taylor to meet him in New York in August, and so began a unique and ultimately very successful collaboration between composer and rock band.

Russell Mulcahy had spent blood and treasure trying to turn William Burroughs's novel *The Wild Boys* into a feature film, but the material was too strange for Hollywood and the British film industry. Instead, he decided to recycle some of his unused storyboard ideas to make a video for Duran Duran's "The Wild Boys" single. EMI agreed to a budget that John Taylor later claimed was the most expensive music video yet made. To realize the subhuman anarchic grandeur of Burroughs's visions, Russell hired the immense soundstage at Shepperton Studios in Surrey, just outside London (which had been remodeled by George Lucas for the early *Star Wars* films).

Russell pitched the video's action in optic opposition to aquamarine seas, sailing yachts, and sultry models. The "Wild Boys" set at Shepperton featured a postapocalyptic dystopia of robots, stygian mists, and flickering TV screens. Students wrecked their classrooms. The wild boys were portrayed by half-naked acrobats and dancers; they were spray-painted to look like bloodthirsty warriors—"wild boys always . . . *shine*"—dancing-troupe style and looking fierce. The band was allowed only brief cameos in the video with the exception of Simon, who was strapped to a windmill and dunked in a tank of cold water every time his sail came around. The general effect was gritty, violent homoerotica in a hopeless world, one without women and girls, in the age of AIDS.

Not exactly "Rio."

Looking back, Russell explained, "The video alone was a four-day shoot, and they must have spent about a million pounds. Sting was [in the studio] next door filming *The Bride*, and he came over to our set and went, 'Holy fuck!'"

According to Simon, "I remember standing in this enormous studio with all this scaffolding, and there were about twenty guys jumping out of trampolines and coming out of the walls."

Russell noted, "Celebrities kept turning up to gawk at this extraordinary set, with a giant windmill that had poor Simon strapped to it. The windmill would go around, and Simon's head would go underwater into this chilly tank. It did break down at one point, and people had to jump in and lift his head out."

John recalled, "When a gasping Simon was brought to the surface, the cameras were still rolling. This made for scintillating viewing."

Russell had seemingly cast every freak in London for the video. There was the tallest man in England and a young guy who looked extremely old. There were a lot of dwarves; one of the girl dancers was terrified of them and kept having nervous breakdowns whenever they were near her. Acrobats were flying around the set on various dubious contraptions, and accidents happened.

Perri Lister (then Billy Idol's girlfriend) was a beautiful young dancer and choreographer. She appeared in videos for Billy and Def Leppard as well as Duran Duran. "Russell had me topless, painted gray from head to toe, and my hair was painted white. At six in the morning, they would stand there and spray-paint us. We'd all been up for most of the night. There was this one scene where a guy flew across the ceiling [and crashed]. Everyone heard this ghastly sound— *ka chunk!* I think he broke his collarbone."

The crash stayed in the video.

Russell remembered, "There's a scene where we put Perri among all the dystopian, *Mad Max*–looking boys prancing away. I asked her, 'Can we see a tit? One tit?' She said, 'Darling, at this price, you're going to get two!'"

At the time, the "Wild Boys" video seemed to some like a massive ego trip, dripping with overindulgence. Andy wanted to know how their management could have approved such a folly—"a lot of boys camping it up in loincloths." But John felt that the expense might have been worth it. "'The Wild Boys' was more than just a video," he later wrote. "It was an amalgamation of musical, music video, and cutting-edge remix with a production design that rivaled any Hollywood movie." He also said that they kept looking over their shoulders and finding Michael Jackson "chasing our tails and hungry to take the video-king crown off of us."

Duran Duran, he said, had to fight back. So their accountant came to the set to tell them that he'd withdrawn £90,000 from each of their accounts to pay for the way over budget "Wild Boys" video. When the video shoot was finished, the band stayed on the soundstage for another few days to film extra scenes for *Arena*, their new concert movie. Actor Milo O'Shea, who'd played Dr. Durand-Durand in *Barbarella*, filmed some scenes as Dr. Duran Duran, who was supposedly suing the band for stealing his name.

Nick later said of the Shepperton days, "Everyone was still on good terms. Everyone was pleased with 'Wild Boys,' but then we finished a film of the tour, which was the last thing in the world that we wanted to do, and of course we ended up hating it."

While they were at it, the band mimed "The Wild Boys" for *Top of the Pops*.

Late in July, twenty-four-year-old Roger Taylor chartered a Boeing 727 jet and flew a plane full of guests to Naples, Italy, where he married Giovanna Cantone, twenty-two, his sweetheart from the Rum Runner and virtual sister to the rest of Duran Duran. After a choppy evening cruise in the Bay of Naples, where some guests became seasick, the newlyweds spent their honeymoon at the pyramids of Giza. When they arrived back at their new Victorian home in Maida Vale, West London, they found Duran Duran fans waiting for them on their front steps. One had even broken into the house and left a love note for Roger in the kitchen.

A few weeks later, twenty-two-year-old Nick married twenty-five-year-old Julie Anne Friedman at the Marylebone Registry office in London. Friends threw confetti as the couple posed for photographs at the top of the Registry stairs. Everyone wore pink to the wedding. Nick was married in a pink velvet morning coat and matching top hat, and press reports described him as wearing more and heavier makeup than the bride. His best man was his ex-girlfriend, Elayne

Griffiths, who had worked at the Rum Runner. The slightly rowdy, champagne-drenched reception at the Savoy Hotel, where pink flamingos posed for photos in their pens, attracted the cream of London's hip crowd and was said by certain magazines to be *the* celebrity wedding of 1984. (Press accounts of Nick's posh wedding barely mentioned the bride, usually described as "an American heiress.") Simon's date was Claire Stansfield, but it was also rumored he was still seeing Yasmin on the side. The couple's honeymoon was a long cruise in the wine-dark Aegean Sea. They returned to their new mansion on Gilston Road in Chelsea, filled with Nick's huge collections of rare books, art deco furniture, and art by Warhol, Keith Haring, and Jean Cocteau. Nick's Picasso paintings remained in storage because it cost too much to insure them at home.

Simon, on the other hand, was sailing with Paul Berrow on a rented yacht off the coast of Sardinia in an event called the Swan World Cup. Simon's sailing friendship with Paul meant that he was less ready to change management than the others in the band, who were fed up—especially Andy, who was talking openly about starting a different band entirely with John.

Andy's wife, Tracey, gave birth to the first Duran Duran child, Andrew James Taylor, on August 20, 1984, and forced him to reconsider his priorities. "I began to wonder if things might actually be better outside the band," Andy said later. "We'd had a fantastic time and enjoyed enormous success, but was it starting to take an unacceptable toll on all of us?"

⌒

In September, Duran Duran returned to New York City, where their concert album was being sequenced and mixed by Nile Rodgers's engineer, Jason Corsaro, at the Power Station Studios, the famous converted Con Edison electrical relay station on West Fifty-Third Street. John Taylor attended all the sessions, which were often paused for refreshment when Mick Jagger or Bryan Ferry (recording his solo album) stopped by. On September 14, Duran Duran attended MTV's Video Music Awards, where Nick and Simon presented an MTV Moon Man statuette to Cyndi Lauper for "Girls Just Want to Have Fun." John, flush with cash, bought an upper-floor apartment in an unfinished new building on Manhattan's Upper West Side. Coincidentally, Boy George also bought a flat there, on the same floor as John.

The "Wild Boys" single was released on October 26, with "Cracks in the Pavement" as the flip side of the record. The single had six different sleeves, one for each member and one with the whole group. It reached #2 in both the United States and UK, behind "Like a Virgin." The heavily edited *Arena* "live" album came out in November, consisting of ten concert tracks and "The Wild Boys." Most critics felt the album sounded inert and canned, with very little stage presence and almost no audience reaction. But *Arena* duly climbed to #4 in America and #6 in England. Tritec Music failed to get a theatrical release for the *Arena* film, and the best they could do was to get it screened on MTV. The same fate met *Sing Blue Silver*, the tour documentary. VHS sales of *Arena* were affected by generally poor reviews that dumped on the film's nonmusical narratives, which were then cut from a shorter version, retitled *As the Lights Go Down*. At the same time, Tritec self-published a softcover portfolio book of Denis O'Regan's tour photos, edited by Mike Warlow. The ten-dollar *Sing Blue Silver* book was sold mostly through Duran Duran's fan club and then distributed to airport newsstands. By the end of the year, it had sold about a quarter million copies, making *Sing Blue Silver* one of the best-selling books of 1984.

A few months later, Russell Mulcahy's "The Wild Boys" clip won the Brit Award for Best Music Video.

THE POWER STATION

Like other musicians in its generation, Duran Duran grew up listening to Bob Marley proselytize on behalf of his hero, Haile Selassie, emperor of Ethiopia, whom Bob's Rastafarian sect described as the living embodiment of God. But Selassie had been overthrown and murdered in 1975, and a communist government drove Ethiopia into the parched soil of the Horn of Africa. And indeed all over Africa, the rains had paused, and endemic drought set in. Famine's horsemen were on the loose and running riot.

Fast-forward to autumn 1984, in London, where BBC television was covering the Ethiopian drought and subsequent mass starvation with heartbreaking scenes of skeletal children, dust-blown farms, and morgues filling with the dead. The Church of England reminded their parishioners that Ethiopia was a Christian nation, and something had to be done.

This plea was picked up by Bob Geldof, the lead singer of the Irish rock band Boomtown Rats. Geldof wasn't a major pop star, but he was charismatic and extremely persuasive as he started phoning the really big rock stars and telling them his idea in profanity-loaded detail. The project was called Band Aid. Geldof wanted the biggest names in England to participate in an anthemic Christmas single and film that could potentially raise millions of pounds for Ethiopian famine relief. Bob Geldof wrote the lyrics—"Do They Know It's Christmas?"—set to music by Midge Ure of the band Ultravox. All the famous musicians would squeeze into a studio and belt out "Do They Know It's Christmas?" in a good old display of British initiative and holiday cheer.

The first call Bob Geldof made was to the lead singer of the biggest band in England. "Hullo, Charlie? Have you seen this fookin' shite on the telly about fookin' Ethiopia? We fookin' gotta do something!" Simon Le Bon committed Duran Duran without talking to anyone else in the band. With that, Geldof and his wife, Paula Yates, started working the phones. U2 signed on, then Spandau Ballet and dishy girl group Bananarama. George Michael said yes, as did Phil Collins, Boy George, Sting, Paul Young, and Paul Weller. Jody Watley was a late addition, persuaded by Paula Yates to add some female color (along with Kool and the Gang) to the diversity-challenged group of Band Aid's pop stars. In mid-November, the song's basic track was recorded at Midge Ure's home studio, with Andy Taylor on guitar, John Taylor on bass, Phil Collins on drums, and Ure on keys and synths. The video of all forty participating stars singing "Do They Know It's Christmas?" was scheduled for production on November 25 at the Notting Hill studio of producer Trevor Horn, who'd had a UK #1 with "Relax" by Frankie Goes to Hollywood.

Meanwhile, Duran Duran was furiously promoting *Arena* in Europe. On November 24, they taped "The Reflex" and "The Wild Boys" for a German television program called *Thommys Pop Show*. That night, they went to a club with Billy Idol, Spandau, and the Thompson Twins and got so drunk that Andy had to be carried to their hotel. They woke up the next day with brutal hangovers and almost failed to make the flight back to London to tape "Do They Know It's Christmas?" The taping was finished the following day, prominently featuring Duran Duran (except for Andy, who didn't much care for Geldof).

Band Aid's record was released on December 3. It immediately went to #1 in England and remained at the top of the chart for the rest of the year. It sold about three million copies and reportedly earned about $20 million for Ethiopian famine relief through 1985. Band Aid also inspired the two new music charities USA for Africa and Live Aid, which would earn even more money for global food aid in the coming year.

But trouble was brewing for Duran Duran. In the days leading to Christmas, as the *Arena* album hit the Top 10 in the UK and United States, John was seen squiring sultry Jody Watley around London clubs. Janine was out of the picture; gossips said she was fed up with John's dope intake. John then had an emotional breakdown at his parents' home on Christmas Day: he tore up four postal sacks of fan mail in a manic explosion before his horrified parents and then, as soon as he could, boarded the supersonic Concorde for New York so he could conspire with Andy, as far away from Duran Duran as possible.

John checked into the Carlyle Hotel on Madison Avenue, where David Bowie and British royalty and diplomats often stayed. He was surprised to see Simon there as well. To see off 1984, they jumped onstage with Frankie Goes to Hollywood and sang "Relax" for *MTV's New Year's Eve Rock 'n' Roll Ball.*

John and Simon wouldn't see each other again for nearly six months. Duran Duran was nearly finished.

But John and Andy now pressed forward with their outlaw project they were calling the Power Station. According to Andy, "This was born out of our frustration at not playing the way we wanted in Duran Duran. It gave us renewed focus, and for that I was grateful." It was also an antidote to the tedious ordeal of making *Seven and the Ragged Tiger.* The early idea was for Andy and John to work with Tony Thompson, former Chic drummer, recently with David Bowie. They'd talked about this with Thompson when he came through Sydney on Bowie's Let's Dance Tour. They worshipped Tony Thompson. They wanted to be a rock band, not a pop group. They wanted to be Led Zeppelin Junior. Tony was considered the best rock drummer of the era, and indeed he would play with Led Zeppelin at the Live Aid concert that summer in place of the late John Bonham. "Tony was a big happy guy," Andy said later. "Nothing in the music industry had taken a toll on him like it had on John and me. He was just a big, powerful, superfit drummer with a great spirit. I thought, I can work with this guy."

The initial concept had them working with different singers on different tracks: Jagger, Idol, Ferry, maybe even Bowie. They wanted Nile Rodgers to produce, but Nile wasn't about to dump Madonna for a Duran Duran spin-off. Tony Thompson strongly suggested Bernard Edwards instead. The former Chic bassist had moved into production like his colleague Nile and was more than familiar with the Power Station's wood-paneled studios. Hadn't Edwards's work with Chic inspired the teenage Nigel Taylor to take up the bass guitar in the first place? Bernard was humble, funny, avuncular—the opposite of party animal Nile Rodgers. It seemed like a perfect fit.

Andy was direct with Bernard about their vision. "We explained to Bernard that we wanted to retain certain values of Duran Duran, but it was time to change the rhythm and be more creative, with a harder guitar edge." This meant less or no synths and more blistering hard rock.

The two Taylors had earlier recorded demos of two songs in Paris: "Some Like It Hot" and "Murderess." They invited their old friend Robert Palmer, who had written lyrics for "Some Like It Hot," to the Power Station's top-floor Studio 3 to sing on that and a third song, "Communication." When Robert heard they'd also recorded "Get It On (Bang a Gong)," he mentioned he'd been a T-Rex fan and asked for a chance to sing on the track. Inspired by Tony Thompson's swinging, stomping drum wallop, Palmer delivered an impassioned reading that in turn inspired Bernard to suggest that Robert sing the whole album. John and Andy readily agreed. They'd known Robert for years, and he would bring his veteran professionalism to their new band. They felt he was someone they could both trust and look up to. While he was in the vocal booth—in a tailored gray flannel suit and tie—the studio filled up with stars from other studios, wanting to hear Robert Palmer sing. It didn't hurt that long rails of chopped rock cocaine were laid out on a table. There were Mick Jagger and Jeff Beck, who was playing lead guitar on *She's the Boss*, Jagger's first solo album, plus producers Nile Rodgers and Arthur Baker. Mick was bopping up and down to Tony Thompson's atomic rock. Everyone applauded the surprised singer when he finished the track and stepped out of the booth. "Fuckin' hell," he said, "a full house!"

Tony Thompson fondly remembered Robert's first appearance: "Robert came in, sang 'Some Like It Hot,' and then asked us what else we had. Then he did 'Get It On,' and we said, 'To heck with Jagger. This is it!' It's kind of a Chic funk foundation, with a Duran Duran rock 'n' roll top, and [an] R&B feel—courtesy of Palmer."

Then Jagger tried to steal Tony for his own sessions.

John and Andy moved into the Carlyle Hotel in January 1985. They would stay there for six months while they recorded as the Power Station and would spend around $500,000 (millions in today's currency) on hotel suites, room service, and champagne. They weren't terribly concerned about the expense because after hearing the "Some Like It Hot" demo, EMI/Capitol signed the Power Station to an exclusive recording contract with a large cash advance after figuring out the label wasn't going to get any new Duran Duran product to sell, at least for the foreseeable future.

Andy took some of his money and paid off the mortgage on his father's semidetached house in Cullercoats. He also bought him a seven-series BMW with a personalized license plate.

John loved the Power Station itself. The studio had a freight elevator that could carry limousines to whatever floor they were working on. "Plus," John wrote, "I'd never seen more drugs in my life. The access to cocaine was unlimited. . . . There was nowhere I would rather be than in the safety and security of the studio, poised between shelter and control, totally coked out of my brain."

After recording with John and Andy, Robert Palmer went back to the Bahamas, where he wrote and recorded his vocals. Andy also played blazing lead guitar on Palmer's new songs "Addicted to Love" and "Riptide," which would be featured on Palmer's upcoming new album ("Addicted" would be his biggest hit record). Meanwhile, the Power Station's horn section was borrowed from *Saturday Night Live*'s house band, led by Lenny Pickett on sax.

Duran Duran met up in Paris later in January, and there was a tense conference since the band was obviously drifting apart. John and Andy explained the Power Station setup to the others, announcing a long tour of America that summer. They both now disliked snobbish, effete Nick Rhodes so much they could barely look at him; Andy didn't like Simon either. Simon was unbothered, saying he was planning on going sailing anyway with the Berrows. Nick said little, but it was already understood that he and Simon were going to make a get-even album of their own. Roger just listened, saying nothing. Later he told *Melody Maker*, "I'm just a warrior anyway. I just want to make everyone happy."

Duran Duran honored a commitment to appear at the San Remo Festival in Italy on February 10, where they played "The Wild Boys" and "The Reflex" before an adoring crowd. Simon limped onto the Teatro della Vittoria stage and hobbled his way through the songs, having injured himself during winter sea trials of his new sailboat, *Drum*. This was a seventy-seven-foot ocean racing yacht with an experimental new keel, bought by Simon with Paul and Michael Berrow with the intention of sailing around the world in the prestigious

Whitbread Cup race. *Drum* cost so much to buy that they deferred the steep insurance payments, which ran about £30,000 annually. Andy complained that the Berrows were fucking stupid to risk Simon's life on hazardous blue-water sailing races while the band was still working.

In February, Robert Palmer exchanged Bahamian zephyrs for Manhattan's icy winds off the Hudson River. On February 16, the Power Station appeared on NBC's *Saturday Night Live* and played "Some Like It Hot" and "Get It On (Bang a Gong)" with the show's horns; the producers asked volcanic Tony Thompson to play a bit softer since he'd blown a speaker during the rehearsals. They also shot two sexy, semianimated videos, with Andy's hair teased up like he was in a Sunset Strip hair metal band. "Some Like It Hot" debuted on MTV on February 22, introduced by John and Andy. "Some Like It Hot" was released as a single late that month and was a Top 20 record in both the United States and England. (Spin-off bands rarely sold as well as this.) A month later, *The Power Station* album was released worldwide. Its eight tracks included the two singles, five so-so songs including rock-noir "Murderous" (faux AC/DC) and "Communication" (big beat, obsessive). This was all the material the band had, and it wasn't enough music for a proper album, so Bernard Edwards had them cut an R&B cover of the Isley Brothers' "Harvest for the World," which Robert Palmer didn't sing on.

At the same time, Simon was writing the lyrics for "A View to a Kill" on guitar at Paul Berrow's apartment in Paris. He estimated it took him about half an hour, because it was based on a lyric he was already working on called "That Fatal Kiss." Much later, Nick would recall, "We said, 'At least it wasn't called *Octopussy*,' so we wrote the song."

Ian Fleming's short story "From a View to a Kill" was first published in 1960 as one of the 007 tales from the collection *For Your Eyes Only*. The plot, which involved James Bond killing a Russian spy, was completely dropped from the script for the latest Bond movie, starring Roger Moore. The new Bond villain was called Max Zorin, a megalomaniacal business tycoon plotting to destroy California's Silicon Valley so he could monopolize the manufacture of microchips and achieve world domination. The part of Zorin was originally written with David Bowie in mind, but Bowie backed out when he saw the script. Sting was then approached and also declined. The Zorin part was finally cast with American actor Christopher Walken, a song-and-dance man with a sinister flair. Zorin's henchwoman was played with feline menace by Grace Jones.

Duran Duran's job was somehow to work with veteran movie composer John Barry, who had already written and recycled themes and cue music for the Bond film's soundtrack. Now they had to fold in the music for "A View to a Kill" with Barry's orchestral score. Plus, it had to be good enough to anchor the movie and also had to be a hit single. Producer Cubby Broccoli didn't think there was much risk in this, since "The Reflex" was a worldwide #1 record when he first made the deal. Nile Rodgers was asked to produce but had a prior commitment, so Bernard Edwards stepped in and flew to London to pull "A View to a Kill" together.

This proved to be challenging.

The first attempt at getting music on tape took place late the previous November on the day when the new Beaujolais wine arrived from France. Duran Duran met John Barry in the pub around the corner from John Taylor's Knightsbridge house in Ennismore Mews. Barry brought along a young New York musician, Jonathan Elias, whose claim to fame was that he'd composed the charging MTV theme, played every time the channel's Moon Man appeared with his MTV flag. John Barry was a funny old Yorkshire musician type in his early fifties. He'd apparently had one or two drinks before he arrived and was speaking in a rather posh accent. He'd scored dozens of films since 1960, including ten James Bond movies. In the smoky pub on a rainy afternoon, Mr. Barry made it quite clear he wasn't used to working with pop stars wearing eye shadow. As they drank a few bottles of the 1984 Beaujolais Nouveau, John Taylor noticed Barry glaring at Nick, who *was* maybe wearing a bit too much blush, and knew they were in for a wild ride.

They moved on to the top floor of John's house, which looked like a rock star's version of 007's bachelor pad. It was a long, well-lit white room with a white grand piano, a tribute to John Lennon. There was a huge Sony television console, and the walls were adorned with kinky photographs of models in lingerie, some bearing whips. With Barry at the piano, a crystal tumbler of whiskey in hand, they managed somehow to arrange at least the first verse of the song, but the vibrations began to get a bit strained.

As John later reflected, "Barry hated most of us, and most of us hated him. It was a real show of fucking big egos." Nick and Barry weren't going to be friends. They found it hard just being together. They were both control freaks and wanted things done their way. John tried to serve as an intermediary, conferring with Jonathan Elias, conveying ideas between composer and rock star. John was desperate not to lose this once-in-a-lifetime connection with the James Bond energy. He *had* to make this work. But at around five o'clock, Barry disappeared, only to show up again, a few hours later, in John's kitchen, seemingly tired and emotional. He was poured into a taxi and driven back to his hotel. This went on for days. The nearby pub did a good trade. John would receive phone calls from a growling Barry, very late at night, demanding that John "sort out this bloody bullshit."

It wasn't only John Barry, though. The band was tense; it was hard to get them in the studio at the same time. Everything was a little drama. Simon acted like he owned "A View to a Kill" and was in what the others called his "self-important phase." Andy could barely stand being around him now. Duran Duran had been through so much during the last five years that they were through with each other.

Andy said that "John came up with a wisp of a tune for the opening part of the song. Simon worked with John Barry, and they came up with 'Meeting you, with a view to a kill.' Roger and I developed a hybrid drum/electro sound, and Simon added the chorus. . . . Nick seemed to be resentful of the whole project because it was organized by John Taylor."

Nick did seem petulant. Barry would ask him to try something, and Nick would retort, "I am fucking *not* doing that." Barry kept reminding Nick that this was Barry's gig and, insufferably, kept addressing him as "young man."

Andy later noted, "Nick hated cocaine. Absolutely. So he wasn't appreciative of [John's] and my behavior. [He'd say,] 'It doesn't matter if you have a great song—you've done it in a way I don't like.'"

$\sim$

Fortunately, Bernard Edwards managed to produce the track, blending Duran Duran's theme with Barry's score. Simon credited Barry with taking some of the band's input and finding the exactly right chords to make it sing. They recorded "A View to a Kill" with a sixty-piece orchestra at Maison Rouge Studios in West London, which once again was besieged by fans when they learned the band was inside. Nick added ingenious sound effects: hissing hydraulic doors, shocking sonic shards, shattered metal, "that fatal sound of broken dreams." Some fans still consider Simon's vocal—"that fatal kiss is all we need"—the best he ever recorded in his entire career. John Berry's corny instrumental version of "A View to a Kill" (for the single's B-side) featured a wistful flute solo credited to Susan Milan.

The tapes were then sent to New York, where Bernard and engineer Jason Corsaro mixed them down at the Power Station. John Barry went home to Long Island. He rang up Cubby Broccoli and told the producer *never* to do this to him again. The message seemingly stuck; Barry would score only one more Bond film for Broccoli's Eon Productions.

But John Taylor was relieved. He'd pulled it off. "I could not have been happier with the end result. I thought ['A View to a Kill'] was our best record so far, on every level."

At the end of the day, Andy would credit optimistic, positive Simon for trying to bring the band's competing factions together to make this great new record a success. But, as Andy recollected, "this was a power struggle that deep down we should have all known could only end in tears for Duran Duran."

ARCADIA VS. THE POWER STATION

Boy bands rarely stay together, and one factor that pulls them apart is their romantic lives. They grow up, meet girlfriends, get married, have children, and don't hang out together anymore. It's only natural.

By 1985, Nick and Julie Anne were settled into their Chelsea house, spending a fortune on art and decor for their new home. Andy's wife, Tracey, was suffering from serious postpartum psychological problems, and he was more interested in looking after her than he was in being in Duran Duran. Beautiful Giovanna Taylor was very worried about Roger's recovery from physical and mental exhaustion and wanted him out of the band. Very sensibly, she asked, did they really need so much money? This left swinging London bachelors John and Simon, but both would soon be claimed, their wandering days done and dusted.

John was at Billy Idol's birthday party at Limelight, the deconsecrated church that had been converted into one of Manhattan's hottest nightclubs, the night he met Danish model Renée Simonsen. Actually, he offended her at the club—he didn't know who she was when she approached him—and she called him an asshole. On the way back to his apartment, his companions explained that the girl he had snubbed just happened to be on the cover of that month's *Vogue*. She also happened to be on the jacket of the album leaning against his stereo—Roxy Music's *The Atlantic Years 1973–1980*. It was his favorite record; he'd been looking at Renée's face for a couple of years. Mortified, John tracked down her phone number, humbly apologized, and asked her out. They clicked immediately, which seemed to calm down hard-charging John a little. They liked to walk through Central Park holding hands, with John happy he could be out with a girlfriend and not be mobbed like in England. When his parents arrived in New York to see his new apartment (and his new parrot), they were happy to find John in a state of domestic bliss with Renée, a big contrast to the meltdown he'd suffered at their home over Christmas. She was charming and intelligent, and they were relieved that their son the rock star seemed to be in good hands.

By March 1985, Nick and Simon were back in Paris working on their own recording project, an album to be called *So Red the Rose*, produced with Alex Sadkin, whose sonic perfectionism aligned well with Nick's obsessive compulsion in the studio. The band would be called Arcadia, after the idealized landscape of classical romance. Nick wanted this music to be more emotional and serene than the bombastic thud of the Power Station. Nick wanted delicacy and light as opposed to weaponized crunch. Still, they needed a drummer and managed to enlist Roger, partly based on the promise that Arcadia wouldn't tour.

In Nick's memory, "Arcadia was a great time for Simon and me because we managed to escape from the craziness. We escaped to Paris, which sort of became our second home. We could walk in the street without minders. No one cared enough to bother us." But after he was swarmed by British tourists while eating breakfast at the Café de Flore, Simon dyed his hair black, after which he was mostly left alone.

Meanwhile, Simon was enjoying the charms of the French capital with Yasmin Parvaneh, the now twenty-year-old model he had unsuccessfully tried to seduce a year earlier. Yazzie was born in Oxford in 1964 to an English mother and an Iranian father. She had been modeling for about three years and had been on the cover of *Elle*. She was bright, funny, and fierce, and Simon told Nick he was falling in love with her. Simon: "We'd gone out together for two weeks, and then we lost touch. Why? She wouldn't fuck me. I couldn't figure for the life of me why not." But now she moved into Simon's rented apartment on the Rue de Rivoli. Speaking later, Simon said that Yasmin had a beautiful flame burning inside her. "She's a very pure girl."

Simon's feelings were returned this time. "The fires of passion began to burn in a very big way for me," Yasmin said a year later. "Paris is a great place to be in love."

⁓

In April 1985, all five members of Duran Duran flew to Paris to film the video for their new single, "A View to a Kill." If anyone thought things couldn't get worse for this band, it was making this clip that finished them. The Power Station didn't speak to Arcadia, and Arcadia didn't speak to the Power Station. Roger had a foot in both camps. Paul and Michael Berrow were on the outs with Andy and John, who let it be known he was looking at new management in New York.

The most exciting scenes in the new Bond movie featured the Eiffel Tower, which overlooked the City of Light and its winding river Seine. Roger Moore (Bond) chases Grace Jones (May Day) up the tower's iron stairs, blasting away with his Walther PPK, until they reach the top and May Day eludes him by parachuting to the streets below. For the video, EMI and Paramount Pictures agreed that Duran Duran would be portrayed as spies, interspersed with actual scenes from the film. Russell Mulcahy said it was "naff," and he didn't want to do it.

Instead, they called in Kevin Godley and Lol Creme, who had made the "Girls on Film" video back in what seemed another lifetime. One of the tower's highest levels was rented at extremely high cost (a reported £20,000) and closed to tourists for a long day's video shoot. Set amid the usual postures of Cold War conspiracy and hot pursuit, the band was cast as various 007 tropes: Simon was a secret agent getting instructions (via his Walkman) from Roger, playing a master controller; Andy was a blind assassin; Nick was an asset posing as a fashion photographer; John was James Bond's daring grandson—or something like it. The video reached a climax when Simon pushed a button on his Walkman and blew up a helicopter.

The production was excruciating. Duran Duran hated every minute of that video shoot. Simon said later, "The thing about videos is they're awfully long days. At midday, a big glass of whiskey or a fat line of coke seems like a great idea. But come eight p.m., when you've been on set for hours, it's fucking awful. You can see in that video which Duran Duran members were getting too high. They're usually covered up with sunglasses." (This was a jab at Andy.)

According to John, "The videos had gotten too big. After *Thriller* they had to be like little movies. Early on Duran Duran had shot on video and worked very cheaply. After Michael Jackson, they started shooting on film and everything became much more expensive.

"When we did the 'View to a Kill' video, I don't think there's any shot of the band, all of us together. You couldn't get us in the same space at the same time. You know—I wish I could say, 'We *loved* being famous,' and we had *even more fun* together than when we started.' But, it wasn't like that. . . . We were now too big to get in one frame."

The on-set photographer was Cindy Palmano; she needed a band shot late in the day. No one wanted to do it even though she begged them to comply, promising it would only take five minutes.

John recalled, "We'd done this a lot, everywhere the sun shines. But today felt different. It was as if we couldn't be friends anymore." The five minutes felt more like five years. The band photograph was never used.

Poor Roger, in a somewhat fragile physical state, watched all this—rows, dope, even some tears—unfold with disappointment. He told a reporter that whenever his mother called him, she wanted to know if the band was finished. Speaking with *The Face* magazine, he said it was his understanding that Duran Duran would reunite in September. He was definitely wistful for the lost camaraderie of their early days as a band: "We'd get ten pounds a week, we didn't have apartments, but we were very happy. Now we're all millionaires. We've got everything we've ever wanted, but sometimes we don't seem as happy as we were." There would be a semitriumphant last gasp in that coming summer of 1985, but Duran Duran was over, at least for the time being.

In May 1985, the Power Station was in New York planning a major summer tour. John and Andy were excited to be in a touring band with Robert Palmer and astounding Tony Thompson. Arcadia was still in Paris, working on their album at the improbably named Studio de la Grande Armée, living much of the time on an entire floor of suites at the Hôtel Plaza Athénée (then the most luxurious hotel in Paris). Long before it was even mixed in New York, Arcadia's album was slated to be one of the most expensive recordings ever made. "A View to a Kill" was released as a single in North America and within days became Duran Duran's second US #1 on the *Billboard* chart. On May 16, *Top of the Pops* broadcast Duran Duran miming "A View to a Kill." While in London, they also taped a live performance of the song for a gala TV tribute to the aging American comedian Bob Hope. Meanwhile, the Power Station's "Some Like It Hot" was a Top 10 record in America, and they announced their summer tour on New York's crucial Z-100 radio station on May 17.

Early in June, an immensely proud John escorted Renée Simonsen on the red carpet as Duran Duran attended the world premiere of *A View to a Kill* at the Odeon Leicester Square. As John remembered, "The Prince and Princess of Wales were present, and we lined up in our tuxedos to greet them again. None of us were going to miss that." But then the new Bond movie got scathing reviews, like almost all of Roger Moore's oeuvre. Several critics proclaimed it the worst Bond yet, but as usual it was a big financial success.

This was when Simon got the first call from Bob Geldof. The manic Irish rocker was planning yet another fookin' charity concert for the fookin' starving Ethiopians: one huge stadium show in England, another stadium show in America, both on the same day and featuring most of the important musicians in the Western pop pantheon. He mentioned—top secret, don't breathe a word—that Led Zeppelin would reunite in America. Bob Dylan had agreed to appear with Stones Keith and Woody. Geldof—future Knight of the Realm—was asking Duran Duran to headline the American concert, scheduled for Philadelphia on July 15. Geldof told Simon that Duran Duran was the only current English band with decent sales in America. "So if you come on board," he said, "it means America will come on board."

Simon told him that Duran Duran would be there.

⁓

Another reason Live Aid had to happen was that Bob Geldof had no intention of letting his Band Aid project be topped by USA for Africa. This was the brainchild of veteran New York singer/activist Harry Belafonte, friend of Martin Luther King, who thought "Do They Know It's Christmas?" was amateurish and insular. What Belafonte wanted to hear was an inclusive anthem the whole world could sing in aid of African relief. He called producer Quincy Jones, who enlisted Michael Jackson and Lionel Richie to write a song called "We Are the World" to raise funds for a new aid group called USA for Africa. Suddenly, a planetarium of American music stars wanted to sing on the recording with Michael Jackson, then the biggest star in the world. Quincy rounded up Ray Charles, Diana Ross, Stevie Wonder, Bob Dylan, Bruce Springsteen, Cyndi Lauper, country music "outlaws" Willie Nelson and Waylon Jennings, and many lesser luminaries. The video of the recording of "We Are the World" made its debut on MTV, and the single—which *Rolling Stone* opined sounded like a Pepsi jingle—sold in the millions, reaching #1 in the United States and Britain. USA for Africa raised much more money than Band Aid, with a better song and bigger stars. But back in London, Bob Geldof had an even bigger idea.

⁓

In New York, the Power Station was preparing for a forty-date summer tour of North America when Robert Palmer called John to say he wasn't coming. In fact, he was quitting the band. Palmer was finishing his new album *Riptide* (with Bernard Edwards), and Island Records boss Chris Blackwell convinced him it would be a huge mistake to go on a long tour with the Power Station when he should be promoting what looked to be the biggest-selling album of his career. And with that, Palmer was out of the Power Station—at the last possible minute.

Now they needed a singer. Andy suggested Paul Young, a big star in England—but he was unavailable. Who was available turned out to be Michael Des Barres, their English friend from Chequered Past. Michael flew to New York, sang "Bang a Gong" in a rehearsal studio, was approved by Tony Thompson, and began fronting the Power Station at the Hartford Civic Center in Connecticut on June 30, followed by a showcase at the now-crumbling Ritz in Manhattan the following night. (Part of the ceiling collapsed the night after that, and Tony Thompson's bass drum wallops were blamed.) The Power Station summer tour had been saved from humiliation and ignominy. John's Taylor's girlfriend, Renée, took some time away from a hectic Manhattan modeling career and her coke-fueled boyfriend to fly to Israel and work on a kibbutz all summer.

⁓

In early July 1985, Bob Geldof and Midge Ure were frantically trying to pull the international double Live Aid concerts together by July 13. No one had ever staged an event of this scale before. Broadcasting the two concerts involved building the biggest and most complicated international satellite television links ever attempted in order to reach a global audience of two billion viewers. The seventy-two thousand seats at Wembley Stadium sold out in a day; likewise, the ninety-two thousand seats in Philadelphia's JFK Stadium were sold almost immediately. In England, Geldof invited Prince Charles and the Princess of Wales to preside over a concert starring David Bowie, Elton John, the Who, Dire Straits, Sade, Paul Young, and many more. Live Aid at Wembley would climax with Paul McCartney at the piano. Geldof had hoped for a Beatle reunion, but there would never be one. Roger Waters also refused to re-form Pink Floyd.

The American Live Aid concert was produced by San Francisco impresario Bill Graham. Bob Dylan agreed to appear early on, so most of the Rolling Stones said yes. So did Madonna, Tom Petty, the Beach Boys, Santana, the Pretenders, the Four Tops, Patti Labelle, and Run-DMC, among many others. Simon had signed Duran Duran up as well, a massive draw since "A View to a Kill" was the current #1 single in America. Despite being two weeks into a national tour, the Power Station also got on the Live Aid bill. Their record "Some Like It Hot" had hit the Top 10, and Tony Thompson was also playing with Led Zeppelin.

On July 9, the Power Station was playing in Hollywood, Florida, when they were visited backstage by Don Johnson, the hottest TV star in America, known for his role as detective Sonny Crockett on *Miami Vice*. Don was a former boyfriend of Michael Des Barres's wife (the beautiful and legendary groupie Miss Pamela), and he came to wish Michael well. They quickly discovered they were all headed to Live Aid in Philadelphia in a few days. Charming, affable, Arkansas-born Don agreed to introduce the Power Station for their coveted two-song Live Aid slot. Two days later, after rocking the Florida State Fair in Tampa with hammering Tony Thompson, the band (and Don Johnson) boarded their plane and flew to Philadelphia, where John and Andy would meet up with Duran Duran so they could rehearse their allotted four songs for Live Aid.

The Four Seasons Hotel was lousy with superstars. Mick! Tina Turner! Neil Young! Jack Nicholson, king of Hollywood, titular host of the American event, held court in the bar. Carlos Santana was shouting in Spanish at someone in the lobby. This being a dinosaur event, some of the bands booked into Live Aid—including Duran Duran—hadn't played together lately. The Beach Boys hated each other. Mick and Keith weren't speaking. Crosby, Stills, Nash & Young all loathed each other. Led Zeppelin was now three elderly rockers, leaning heavily on Tony Thompson. Bob Dylan was then irrelevant. The Live Aid promoters were desperately counting on younger MTV bands like Duran Duran, Simple Minds, and the Thompson Twins to guide a new generation toward mainstream rock philanthropy.

~~~~~

Duran Duran descended into Philadelphia from Florida (John and Andy), France (Nick and Roger), and the deck of the sailing yacht *Drum* (Simon, the Berrows). Andy said Duran Duran's initial meeting was deadly, if looks could kill. John was so thin from his cocaine regimen that he looked skeletal, especially when holding his bass guitar. Andy and John were touring and playing nearly every night, so the rhythm section at least was right and tight. Nick had been working on the Arcadia project in Paris and arrived ready to play, long hair dyed blue-black. Roger—exhausted and psychologically frail—told Andy that he was only hanging on by his fingernails; he also told Tony Thompson that he wished Tony were playing with Duran Duran instead of him. Simon was tanned and handsome, if a bit overweight. His yacht *Drum* had just won a big circuit race around England and Scotland, almost setting a new record for the fastest time. Simon told *MTV News*'s Kurt Loder that he was excited to be playing the biggest gig in the world, and for a worthy cause.

The rehearsal was crucial because there would be no sound check at the stadium, and Duran Duran had never performed "A View to a Kill" live before. Andy Hamilton was on hand to play saxophone, along with Raphael DeJesus and a second percussionist (who would switch to drums if Roger fell ill). Andy Taylor recalled the rehearsal as a disaster. They hadn't played together for months, and they only had one day to get four songs together. The rehearsal space was crowded with "bloody rubberneckers," as Roger called them—people who wanted to be near the band with the #1 record in America. Andy finally refused to play until the room had been cleared of everyone but the band and crew. "Nick and I barely exchanged a single word, save sorting out the set list, which suited us both fine," he recalled later. "Roger looked like death warmed up, almost as if he wasn't there; you could see the strain of our spirit-sapping lifestyle etched across his face."

The only time the band was together in one place was when they posed for the program photograph. Hair and makeup at the hotel: John's teased-up shag mullet required weapons-grade hairspray. He and Andy wore Power Station black. Simon sported short hair and a red jacket over an Australian glyph. Nick was in New Romantic purple. Roger rocked a blue wife-beater tank top.

Duran Duran was now ready to rock Live Aid in Philadelphia.

On the morning of July 13, as Joan Baez opened the American Live Aid concert singing "Amazing Grace," the temperature in JFK Stadium was heading toward ninety degrees. Duran Duran watched the live feed of the London concert in their hotel suites via MTV. They saw U2 play an epic, passionate set and then Queen's heroic act, with Freddie Mercury hitting a high falsetto that would be dubbed "the note heard round the world." David Bowie's five-song set was also a major deal, the coolest music Live Aid would produce. They watched, aghast, as Prince Charles boogied to Dire Straits.

Considering their recent history of hostility and bickering, Andy was relieved that the bus ride to JFK Stadium was so quiet. In fact, he later said it felt like Duran Duran was going to its own funeral. "Things continued to get darker on the ride to the stadium. We were hailed in the press as the Fab Five, the most successful British band since the Beatles, but instead of celebrating any of this, we just got on the bus and sat in silence."

The only people talking were Tony Thompson and Danny Goldberg, who managed Michael Des Barres. Danny had worked for Led Zeppelin in the seventies and had run Stevie Nicks's record label in the eighties. Now he was a nascent LA talent manager, one who saw Andy, soon to be separated from Duran Duran, as a hot property in the city's scalding hair metal scene that was breeding bands like Motley Crüe, Poison, and Guns N' Roses.

Live Aid backstage was controlled wonder and mayhem—Hollywood meets the rock stars. Jack Nicholson was handing out joints. Madonna (short red hair, two Latino dancers, hot band) went out to an inhuman roar. Andy later said he'd never seen a stadium that full before. Eric Clapton was warming up in a corner. David Crosby was turning blue in another. Tina Turner was stretching to prepare to dance with Mick Jagger. Keith Richards and Ronnie Wood arrived in a limo to play with

Bob Dylan; both were so drunk that they fell out of the car when the doors were opened. Woody was laughing so hard he had to be helped up to the stage. It was brutally hot; steam was rising off the crowd, which had swollen when the turnstiles had been overwhelmed and ticketless fans ran in. As heat casualties began flooding aid stations, staff began spraying the estimated 120,000 fans with the stadium's fire hoses to cool them down between acts.

Jack Nicholson, Bette Midler, Don Johnson, and comedian Chevy Chase were introducing the acts. It was announced that two billion people were watching Live Aid via satellite. Simon later said he thought this had to be the peak of Duran Duran: playing their #1 record for two billion people around the world, for charity. How, he wondered, could it ever get any bigger than this?

Introduced by Don Johnson, the Power Station went on stage at six forty-five in the early summer evening, following a solo set by Neil Young. When Tony Thompson started "Murderess," the building began to shake. "Get It On" drew a similar throbbing response. It was the hardest rock, but it also had an extra swing—dance-floor style—that was almost unique for its time. Then Andy broke a guitar string and his amp malfunctioned; they recovered after a delay, but the Power Station failed to recapture the rapture of their big moment.

The Thompson Twins ("Hold Me Now") were next, supported by Madonna and Nile Rodgers. Led Zeppelin went on with Tony Thompson at 8:10, embarrassing themselves with a sloppy three-song set. Crosby, Stills, Nash & Young followed, and then it was Duran Duran's turn.

At eight forty-five, Chevy Chase stepped up to the microphone and shouted, "Are you ready? Here they are—*Duran Duran!*" Roger hit the drum beat of "A View to a Kill," and everyone got up. Andy had been drinking chilled white wine since the morning. There were too many people in front of him to make out individual faces. Duran Duran was more used to indoor arenas than American football fields, but Andy was pleased the epic aspects of the gig didn't seem to bother the band—until something caught his eye. "Then as things were coming together, I noticed Simon's voice is getting a tad croaky. He looks great, but it's been a while, and I can tell he's straining to hit his notes." Andy hoped Simon wasn't thinking of hitting that high note on *need* on the final "that fatal kiss is all we need." Then he recalled that thinking on stage was never a good idea.

"Then . . . *shit!*" Simon's voice cracked. The song's final, vocally broken *need* sailed north of Philadelphia and morphed into an electronic impulse. Noted by the two billion viewers, Simon later called it the worst moment of his career. If Freddie Mercury's banshee scream in London was the note heard round the world, Simon's vocal gaffe in America was soon described as "the bum note heard round the world."

But the audience didn't care and gave Duran Duran a standing ovation as Roger rumbled the number to a staggered halt. Stage patter had never been Simon's forte: "Hello—good evening, Philadelphia, and to the whole world that is watching. Tonight we are here to celebrate something [meaning charity concerts] that has worked so far. So . . . this is a song called 'Union of the Snake'!"

As John recalled, "I thought playing with Duran Duran was fun. I had forgotten how much. More fun than the Power Station."

They followed this with "Save a Prayer," then Simon came back to the microphone to announce "The Reflex." "If you've got any energy left . . . we'd like to see you dancing! . . . This one . . . is about a little friend of mine." (In the sacred annals of rock, this might have been the only instance of a rock star describing his penis as "little" for an audience of two billion.) JFK Stadium seemed to lift off its foundations, eliciting the craziest response from the audience that day. As they left the stage, the noise was deafening, and even people backstage were applauding Duran Duran.

"Not bad after Led Zeppelin," Andy thought to himself.

But despite the fact that they'd pulled off the set, there was only gloom in the Duran Duran camp. Other bands coming offstage were hugging each other and congratulating themselves as if they'd won the Super Bowl or an English Cup final. "It was like we were completely foreign to each other," Andy recalled, "and it was the last time we played together for almost twenty years."

PART 8

Live Aid proved to be important to all the musicians who appeared at the two concerts, not least Duran Duran. Record sales exploded for participating bands, and old reputations were enhanced. U2 moved up into the pop premiership, while Queen was suddenly seen as the best rock band in the world. The event was also immensely lucrative; the initial figures indicated that they'd raised $40–$50 million and the same number of pounds of food aid for Africa, and this figure was said to double and even triple as 1985 went on.

Just as U2's star arose in the East, Duran Duran's star began to sink in the West. In America, Duran Duran's three-year run of hits could not compete with the energies of the big stars of 1984—Madonna, Prince, Van Halen, Bruce Springsteen. In England, the spangled British pop stars began to lose ground to new groups, mostly northern, mostly depressed. The Smiths and Pet Shop Boys began to make excessive romantic demands of pop music, as if trying to solve the world's problems in three-minute bursts of insight and joy. Songs like the Pet Shop Boys' "West End Girls" (#1 in England, #2 in the United States) were celebrated as music for thinkers and feelers as opposed to fans of yachts and models. The new pop presentation became nonpresentation. When the Pet Shop Boys appeared on *Top of the Pops* in 1985, Chris Lowe was plinking single notes on his synth keyboard while Neil Tennant only grudgingly moved one knee to the beat. Tennant told *The Face*, "We always set out to make something not-cheerful into something that has mass popularity." The group then began dominating the UK charts with four #1 singles.

After "A View to a Kill," Duran Duran has never had another #1 record. Their imperial phase of chart domination was over.

⌒

After Live Aid, the band scattered once more.

John, Andy, and Tony Thompson flew south to keep the Power Station's tour on the road. The night after Live Aid, they played the Municipal Auditorium in Nashville. The audience expected Spandau Ballet to open, as advertised, so they threw bottles at the replacement band and drove them from the stage. The Power Station then played through August, with OMD opening most of the later shows. Almost inevitably, tensions developed between John and Andy, with after-show parties being held in two different hotel suites. Later in the month, John somehow sustained a badly gashed forehead in his San Francisco hotel. On July 31, he performed at the PNE Coliseum in Vancouver with a heavy bandage around his head.

Nick flew back to Paris on Concorde and began layering guest artists onto Arcadia tracks that he, Alex Sadkin, and Roger had already begun. These included Sting, jazz star Herbie Hancock, Pink Floyd guitarist David Gilmour, Bowie guitarist Carlos Alomar, drummer Steve Jordon, and Roxy Music's Andy Mackay.

Simon Le Bon went to sea.

On July 21, the sailing yacht *Drum* competed in the Seahorse Maxi Series race, setting sail from Cowes on the Isle of Wight. Simon and his brother Jonathan were among the crew, and their boat finished fifth but managed to win the race on points. This encouraged them to enter *Drum* in the upcoming Fastnet race in August and then announce that they planned to race her in one of the sport's most prestigious competitions, the Whitbread Round the World Race, later that year.

No one else in Duran Duran thought this was a great idea. Everyone remembered or was reminded of the notorious Fastnet Challenge Cup race in 1979 when rough seas sank five boats and capsized another fifteen, and nineteen people drowned, including fifteen crew and four rescuers. Duran Duran was still a functioning band and a multimillion-pound corporation. They were still planning on reconvening in September to discuss their future plans. If anything happened to Simon, it was doubtful Duran Duran could continue.

What's more, Simon owned the $1.4 million *Drum* along with the Berrows. Surely there was some conflict of interest going on. Managers were supposed to look after clients, not put them in mortal danger. Nick later said, "No one wanted Simon to do the boat thing. We thought it was an unnecessary risk, and of course look how it turned out. It's not very rock and roll, is it?" Andy was furious enough to tell his wife he was leaving the band as soon as he could get away from his contractual obligations and that they were moving to Southern California to start a new life.

Simon and Yasmin had decided to marry, and she accompanied him to Cowes. *Drum*'s experienced American captain, Skip Novak, led reporters curious about "the Duran Duran boat" on tours and explained some of the yacht's unique features. He claimed *Drum*, at seventy-seven feet, was the largest molded-hull sailing yacht ever built. Its new keel's design was a closely held secret, being somewhat experimental. Simon mostly stayed out of sight except to pose for a few press photos.

Drum set sail on August 11 for a trial run at sea with a twenty-four-man crew. The race was about six hundred miles. The goal was to sail along the south coast of England, go around Fastnet Rock off the southwestern tip of Ireland, and then sail back again, this time with the wind at their backs. *Drum* was about three miles off the coast of Cornwall when a force-nine squall started slamming the boat. Simon had finished his four-hour watch and was relieved to finally be able to get some rest. He had just climbed into his berth when the boat began to pitch sickeningly as the helmsman lost the tiller. The boat went around sideways against the current, then capsized as the new keel broke away. *Drum* didn't sink, but it lay on its side and began to drift. Simon and five other crew were trapped in an air pocket amid a tangle of gear, rope, and cables. The others went into the water or hung on to the hull.

As Simon later recalled the harrowing experience, "I was thrown out of my bunk. There were a couple of loud bangs, then the boat went over. I couldn't believe it! This thing is going to go over. Then some heavy sails fell on top of us. Suddenly I saw this patch of blue and I thought, 'God, the boat's upside down.' We were completely disoriented."

Fortunately, the Royal Navy and Coast Guard were nearby, monitoring the race after the disasters of 1979. Simon and the others tried to maintain their equipoise, certain that someone would come to their rescue. But the atmosphere in their air pocket became thick with diesel fumes and battery acid. Simon thought his parents would be angry if anything happened to his brother Jonathan. Meanwhile, those listening to the Coast Guard radio transmissions began calling London newspapers and radio stations to report Simon Le Bon possibly lost at sea. An anonymous person telephoned Simon's father and told him the news.

But the navy's response was immediate and heroic. Within an hour of the accident, a diver found the air pocket, and Simon and the rest were able to swim to safety. Everyone aboard *Drum* survived. They were taken, soaked and exhausted, to a hotel in Falmouth to recover. Uninsured *Drum* was salvaged and towed into port to see if she could be repaired. In London, Birmingham, Liverpool, Newcastle, and Glasgow, editors ripped up their front pages and the headlines blared the news for all.

Yasmin, on the other hand, wasn't told any of this until everyone was sure Simon was alive and well. Upon learning the news, she caught the ferry across the Solent and was driven six hours to Falmouth, where the crew of *Drum* had an emotional reunion with their tearful wives and girlfriends. The hotel bar stayed open until dawn to accommodate the party.

The next day, Simon invited the naval officer who rescued him to dinner at the hotel. (The man was later awarded the George Medal for bravery.) The (shocked) Power Stationers heard about the accident as they were about to go onstage in a suburban amphitheater near Chicago on August 12. Andy told John that the four most beautiful words in the English language were "I told you so."

It cost an estimated $400,000 to refit uninsured *Drum*; this time, the Berrows insured her. She sailed from Portsmouth at the end of September on the first leg of the Whitbread race, but Simon Le Bon was not on board.

Simon was not aboard *Drum* because he was in New York with Nick and Alex Sadkin, getting ready to release Arcadia's album. However, Simon did return to *Drum* for the last leg of the Whitbread race later on. Asked about Simon's seamanship, Captain Novak was quoted saying that the rock star was a reliable hand when it came to cleaning the toilets.

On September 28, the Power Station played at the Brendan Byrne Arena in New Jersey, across the river from Manhattan. While Andy was throwing out shards of guitar metal during the encore, a little man appeared from the wings with a broom and started sweeping the stage. WTF? John went over to intercept the man. Why were the roadies laughing? The sweeper turned out to be Nick, who proceeded to play air broom with Andy. The kids up front loved this and began yelling for Simon and Roger too (who weren't in the house).

Nick was actually working hard in New York to finish Arcadia's album and their new videos. Their label, Parlophone, wanted Arcadia on the road to promote the album's November release, but Roger was in no condition to go on the road. Arcadia would do interviews and appearances, but there would be no tour.

At the time, Nick and Julie Anne were living in a suite at the Ritz-Carlton Hotel on Central Park South. He spent his time away from the studio buying art books at Rizzoli Bookstore on West Fifty-Seventh Street, near the hotel. Many evenings were spent dining at the Odeon restaurant downtown with Andy Warhol and occasionally Jean-Michel Basquiat. Warhol was trying to advise Nick on acquiring art in New York. After Nick purchased a piece by Keith Haring, Warhol strongly suggested buying a piece by his friend Basquiat, the East Village graffiti art star, but Nick wasn't interested. "Nick Rhodes buys art," Warhol told his audio diary in October, "but he doesn't listen to anybody, and I told him that it's stupid not to, that it's just like buying stocks. But he said, 'I just buy what I like.'"

While Nick was spending long nights in the studio, Simon was making the rounds of talk shows and magazines. Late-night TV hosts like David Letterman and *GQ* interviewers were more interested in Simon's nautical disaster than in Arcadia's new album. Simon admitted that he was asleep when the ship went over and was so traumatized he couldn't sleep for weeks afterward.

The Power Station was on TV as well when the group appeared on NBC's *Miami Vice*, playing—what else?—a rock band blasting "Get It On" in a nightclub before a chair-throwing brawl breaks out.

The first Arcadia video was shot in October, directed by Roger Christian, the Oscar-winning set director who'd worked on the first *Star Wars* movie and later *Alien*. "Election Day," the first single from *So Red the Rose*, featured the usual prancing models and unusual mythic beasts. Nick and Simon were in black, formal pre-Goth attire and dark dyed hair; Roger was noticeably absent from the video and subsequent press materials. After shooting another video ("The Promise") by Marcelo Anciano (featuring a fun house that looked like a Basquiat nightmare), Nick and Simon boarded the supersonic Concorde to Paris, then went on to Munich to begin European promotion for Arcadia—which everyone was annoyingly referring to as a Duran Duran side project.

The foundations supporting the House of Duran Duran (a.k.a. "Durania") began to crack in October 1985. Andy and John wanted to fire the Berrows and get out of Tritec Music. The Berrows, on the other hand, were trying to renegotiate with everyone and were fighting for control. Stressed-out Roger told an interviewer that he never wanted to tour again. All the while, EMI was reminding everyone Duran Duran was contracted for another album. Expensive flocks of lawyers and solicitors were beginning to fly around the ailing body of Duran Duran like vampire bats at sunset.

It was in this atmosphere of mixed-up confusion that the Power Station broke up at the end of the month, still owing EMI one more album. Hardly anyone had enjoyed the band's summer tour—except for the young Duran Duran fans, who kept screaming every time the video screens zoomed in on John. The general feeling was that the whole tour was horrible. The third single, "Communication," failed to sell. And the drug use continued to escalate backstage. Even hard-partying Andy was alarmed at John's cocaine habit. Paul Humphreys (from OMD) said he'd seen a lot of coke on various tours but nothing like what went on backstage with the Power Station. At the end, even the road crew was calling them "the Powder Station."

After the band broke up, Andy Taylor moved his young family to California as promised. He didn't officially announce his departure from the band because his new manager, Danny Goldberg, reminded him that he was still committed to appearing on Duran Duran's next album. Meanwhile, Danny began trying to build a lucrative solo career for Andy, the latest flash English lead guitarist to wash ashore in the Los Angeles basin.

EMI and Capitol Records released Arcadia's *So Red the Rose* in November 1985. Even Simon admitted that it was the most pretentious record—ever. Others said *So Red the Rose* was the best record Duran Duran never made, with some gems embedded among the nine tracks. "Election Day" was a Roxy Music revival; so was "The Promise," with Simon channeling Bryan Ferry's suave crooning style. "Goodbye Is Forever" was New Romantic, while "Rose Arcana" and "Lady Ice" were doomy meditations that conjured a morning of magicians. The first single, "Election Day," was a Top 10 record in both the UK and the United States, but the next one ("Goodbye Is Forever") only got to #33 on *Billboard* and didn't even chart in England. Paul Berrow later said the album's demos had been terrific, but all the energy had been drained out of the music during Nick's obsessive remixing in New York.

Arcadia did receive some initial buzz. MTV devoted an hour to Arcadia upon the album's release. Nick and Simon even had a set built in the studio, a pop-up room painted white. During the interviews, Keith Haring produced some of his trademark stick figures of dogs, babies, and running men on the walls. Simon's mother, Ann, also figured in the program. After the launch, Parlophone kept releasing Arcadia singles well into 1986, and more videos were made, but without a tour, media exposure, or solid reviews in the United States, the Arcadia project was generally deemed an honorable mistake.

Roger Taylor's departure from Duran Duran was announced in December. The twenty-five-year-old drummer pleaded exhaustion and symptoms of acute anxiety from five years of life in the band, and he said he was leaving the music world entirely. "He didn't like being in the public eye," Nick explained, "and he'd become very disillusioned with the whole thing. He really only liked playing his drums and being with Giovanna. It was very difficult for us to deal with. He never cared about the rest of the stuff; in fact, he really disliked all of it."

Simon later recalled that Roger was in a sad state. "I don't think Roger ever had a nervous breakdown, but you could see something coming on. He was developing agoraphobia and a fear of confronting people and being confronted by them. [His leaving] caused a big hole in our hearts."

Not to mention a big hole in the band. Roger and Giovanna bought a remote farm in Gloucestershire, not far from Prince Charles's estate. Roger recalled, "I had quite a bit of land, a few chickens, and some horses. We had children and lived the life of landed gentry for the next few years. A bit *Spinal Tap*, I know. Everyone thought I'd gone crazy, but I had to relearn how to live my life, away from the band."

Though the band missed him dearly, Roger's departure was amicable. He had alienated no one and stayed friends with the band; he was assured he could come back to Duran Duran anytime.

In Manhattan, meanwhile, Boy George shared the twenty-seventh floor of their Upper West Side apartment building with John and his girlfriend, Renée. Culture Club was on hiatus, so its singer was hosting around-the-clock parties for fellow London exiles in New York, plus the heroin dealers who supplied them. John and Renée were now popular guests at music and fashion industry parties, often joined by Nile Rodgers. Andy Warhol recorded John handing out joints at various affairs. Boy George later wrote that he sometimes found Renée crying in their mutual hallway after a row with John, probably over his ferocious appetite for cocaine. Renée might have also resented John's blatant obsession with her colleague Christy Turlington, the sixteen-year-old future supermodel whom *Vogue* suggested was the most beautiful girl in the world. Still, by Christmas Eve, John's publicist announced that John and Renée were engaged. They would never marry each other.

All of Duran Duran except John had come home to England for Christmas in the winter of 1985. On December 27, Simon married Yasmin in a (seemingly rushed) civil registrar ceremony in Oxford. In attendance were the couple's families plus Nick, Andy, Roger, and their ladies. The low-key reception was held at the Bear Hotel, a thirteenth-century former coaching inn, in the Oxfordshire town of Woodstock. Simon and Yazzie are still married to each other as of this writing.

"Arcadia and the Power Station were commercial suicide," Nick said later. "But we've always been good at that."

In January 1986, Duran Duran owed their record company another album, but the two side projects had pretty much drained the creativity of the three (and a half) remaining members of the band. Duran Duran's fourth studio album would prove hard to produce.

Nick and Simon were now in wintry London with their pregnant wives. Simon bought a small house in Battersea, south of the Thames, to live in while their new home in Chelsea was refurbished. John was six thousand miles away, in sunny Los Angeles, trying to convince Andy (who had relocated his family to nearby Malibu) to help Duran Duran make a record. True to his word, Danny Goldberg had launched Andy's new solo career with a $2 million advance from MCA Records. In a suburban neighborhood near LAX, Andy discovered former Sex Pistol guitar hero (and recent immigrant) Steve Jones living in relative poverty with Michael Des Barres and his wife, Miss Pamela, who was hard at work on her memoir (which later became a bestseller). Millionaire rock star Andy gave Steve Jones $50,000 (in cash) to get settled in LA and purchase some guitars, the idea being that Andy and Steve would make a record and tour together.

John also got a deal to work on the soundtrack to *9 1/2 Weeks*, a steamy romance movie that was sure to be a box office success. Michael Des Barres had a song called "I Do What I Do," which John adapted along with new colleague Jonathan Elias, who had worked on "A View to a Kill." This song was released as John's first solo single later in February. Andy also went Hollywood. His song "Take It

Easy" was used in the film *American Anthem*, and "When the Rain Comes Down" appeared on the *Miami Vice 2* album.

In the meantime, Simon had left Yasmin in England and gone off to join *Drum* on its quest for the Whitbread Cup. When Yazzie miscarried a few weeks later, she could only reach Simon via a radio telephone link somewhere in the Pacific. When he arrived home, Simon and Nick began the daunting task of somehow cobbling a new Duran Duran album together, with no drummer, no guitarist, and a bassist who had major drug issues and seemed to be losing interest in being in a band.

Nick, John, and Simon hired Nile Rodgers to coproduce the group's next album. John was aiming for a Prince-inflected funk sound for the new music ("glam boys becoming bad boys"), but Nick wasn't so sure about a change of course, and Simon was adamant that Duran Duran should not fake the funk. They hired top American studio drummer Steve Ferrone for the *Notorious* album and tour. (John Taylor was obsessed with the movies of Alfred Hitchcock, and *Notorious* was his favorite.) Andy Taylor was supposed to join the band as they moved between four or five London recording studios, including Abbey Road. But Andy completely ghosted Duran Duran. He didn't show up for the sessions, and no one could even get him on the phone.

The members of Duran Duran were now basically managing themselves, but they did have some help along the way. Mike Warlow kept up with the merchandise projects and the tour books. They also hired efficient former EMI staffer Jane Potter to run their new production office in Wandsworth, South London. It was Jane who reminded Andy that he was contractually obligated to play on the next Duran Duran record and that there could be legal issues for him if he refused to appear. Danny Goldberg advised Andy that he needed to play on some of the tracks, and then he could announce his departure from the group.

Duran Duran badly needed a reliable and professional rock guitarist to play on the album and the next tour, so there was some irony in that it was Andy's solo career that propelled his brash, aggressive, Brooklyn-born replacement into the band.

Dale and Terry Bozzio had been fronting Missing Persons, one of the better bands in LA, since 1980. Missing Persons also consisted of bassist Patrick O'Hearn and guitarist Warren Cuccurullo, whom the Bozzios had met while working in Frank Zappa's band. They made catchy, radio-friendly power pop songs like "Destination Unknown" and were big on MTV; singer Dale Bozzio's sexy stage outfits were popular with the fans. Like Duran Duran, Missing Persons was also signed to Capitol Records, and the two bands had met at various industry functions over the years.

But Missing Persons ground to a halt after Dale and Terry split up, and then Dale went home to Boston and retired. Meanwhile, Andy, looking for musicians for his new band alongside Steve Jones, started jamming with Terry and Patrick, leaving Warren Cuccurullo on his own. But with that came a new opportunity, Warren reasoned; if Andy had quit Duran Duran, that band needed a guitarist. So Warren made a demo tape and sent it to Duran Duran via EMI in Manchester Square. Along with the cassette was a note that said, "I'm Warren from Missing Persons, and I'm your new guitarist."

This was a cheeky, and puzzling, move. Nevertheless, EMI listened carefully to Warren's arsenal of riffs, runs, licks, and vamps. The guy could really play the electric guitar. Someone casually opined that Warren was actually a better musician than Andy Taylor.

As 1986 drifted into summer, Nick, Simon, and John worked on new ideas with Steve Ferrone. Andy was still nowhere to be found, despite various diplomatically worded legal threats. John constantly argued over rhythms and mixes and even threatened to quit. It took Nick begging John to get himself together and stay in Duran Duran, at least through the next album and tour. It wasn't all for nothing; the new album did showcase some good new songs—"Notorious" about money and control, "Skin Trade" about sex and strange behavior— and Steve Ferrone, a Black drummer, was an energizing addition to the group. But the members of Duran Duran were often distracted by fraught business meetings with attorneys and accountants, and Nile often had to push hard to get the band into the studio.

The lack of a guitarist was causing major problems. Nile Rodgers had been playing guitar on Duran Duran's new tracks, such as

"Notorious," and Andy had eventually dubbed some chords onto "American Science" and "A Matter of Feeling." But the band still needed a guitar player to complete the album and then spend much of 1987 on tour. In September, Warren Cuccurullo was formally invited to audition for Andy's job. He turned out to be an intense, short, body-builder type, with dark hair, strong Mediterranean features, and a thick Brooklyn accent. He had a quirky sense of humor and was crazy about girls. Nick was a bit afraid of him, but they hired Warren on salary, and he moved into the house in Battersea that Simon and Yasmin had vacated. Warren Cuccurullo stayed in Duran Duran for the next fifteen years.

The summer brought with it other memorable moments. Andy Warhol visited London for a gallery show of recent work in Mayfair, and Nick and heavily pregnant Julie Anne attended a dinner party for him at Mr. Chow's, along with Mick Jagger and Jerry Hall. Warhol asked Nick if he knew the sex of the baby, and Nick told him they were expecting a sculpture. Their daughter, Tatjana Lee Orchid, was born in August. Later that month, Simon also served as best man when Bob Geldof married Paula Yates.

Previously in New York, John had developed a crush on now seventeen-year-old model Christy Turlington and wanted her on the jacket of the *Notorious* album. Still a minor, she arrived in England accompanied by her mother; she was then photographed for the album jacket and also appeared in the video directed by Peter Kagan and choreographed by Paula Abdul. Simon didn't make it to the album's photo shoot and had to be photoshopped in later.

Duran Duran was now a trio—Nick, Simon, and John—with a hired drummer and guitarist. They moved production to New York that autumn and released the "Notorious" single in October. The *New York Times* critic welcomed the band's new direction, which leaned toward bass funk and brass. "Notorious" was a Top 10 record in England and got to #2 on the *Billboard* chart in America. MTV jumped on the video's dark and sexy dance moves and gave them an hour-long special. They filmed dozens of promos for Japanese television. The *Notorious* album came out late in November, in time for the holiday rush. The record sold respectably, making #12 in America but a disappointing #16 in England. A sleeve note stated that *Notorious* had been "engineered and mixed in the Summer of Love 1986."

In early November, Andy Warhol fretted to his diary that he knew that Nick had been in New York for weeks but hadn't called, and it seemed that he was keeping his distance. But then, after the album release, Nick did call. On December 12, he and Julie Anne had dinner with Andy and Keith Haring before heading out to Nell's, the hip new nightclub on West Fourteenth Street. The following month, Warhol met Nick and Simon for dinner at Il Cantinori and picked up the $240 check. It was the last time Nick would ever see his friend Andy Warhol, who died in February 1987 while recovering from an operation connected to the attempted assassination he suffered in 1968.

⌒

Duran Duran, a horn trio, and two singers began tour rehearsals at the Brooklyn Navy Yard in December. New lead guitarist Warren Cuccurullo, a graduate of Brooklyn's Canarsie High School, was on his native ground and quickly began to assert himself as the band's new pair of balls, replacing Duran Duran's original testicles, Andy Taylor. But it wasn't until the band headed out on tour in March, across Japan and later Europe, that they learned about Warren's eccentric road habits. Warren was thirty, older than his bandmates in Duran Duran. He liked to adorn his hotel room with colored lights and posters of scantily clad young women, and then he barely ever left the building. There was a party in his room almost every night after the show; Warren often received his (mostly female) guests in pajamas, seminude, or in drag (Frank Zappa called him "Sofia Warren" because he often appeared onstage in a dress). To Nick's refined taste, this was vulgar. Duran Duran set lists now included songs from the Power Station and Arcadia albums. Duran Duran played in Japan in March, and then Europe, Ireland, and Scandinavia in April.

But Warren wasn't the only one debuting a new wardrobe ensemble. The previous summer, Simon had been hanging out in the south of France with INXS singer Michael Hutchence, who informed Simon that no self-respecting lead singer in a rock band ever wore underwear onstage. Simon took this to heart and went commando on tour—until he tore his trousers at a concert in Rotterdam. "I had done a star jump. Another rock singer told me I shouldn't wear underpants, so when I landed, my trousers opened at the seam and everything went sort of flying toward the audience."

Later that May, Duran Duran played Wembley's arena for three nights and then went on to perform in bullrings in Spain and soccer stadiums in Italy, where they were rapturously received by heaving crowds, like they were old gods of the Roman Pantheon.

$\sim$

Back in California, Andy released *Thunder*, his solo album featuring Steve Jones, in June. This was a fairly tuneless, thrash-and-burn, Hollywood metal record that peaked at #39 in the United States and #22 in the UK, and it was noticeably absent from the radio. Andy and Jones went out on the road, opening for bigger acts, but Andy kept getting fired from various tours, like the Psychedelic Furs (playing too long; annoying the unions) and Heart (not showing up at all for a show in Atlanta).

While Andy's solo career began its death spiral, Duran Duran stayed on the road that summer of 1987, supported by UK synth-pop band Erasure. They were playing on the West Coast when they heard that producer Alex Sadkin had been killed in a Miami car crash. They then joined the Canadian (and final) leg of David Bowie's Glass Spider Tour as coheadliners in Toronto, Montreal, and cities in between. In late August, Duran Duran and Nile Rodgers supported Lou Reed at a charity concert at the Beacon Theatre in Manhattan, providing backing for the Velvets' "Sweet Jane" and Lou's "Walk on the Wild Side." Finally, after five months of almost constant touring, Duran Duran returned home and rested for the rest of 1987.

Though it had only been a few years since their meteoric rise, much had changed back home. The local council in Birmingham took the land under the Rum Runner by eminent domain, the old warehouse was torn down, and today the space where Duran Duran came of age is occupied by the health spa of the Birmingham Hyatt Hotel. It was also around then that Simon learned that his old friend David Miles had overdosed on heroin. This was a devastating blow, but one that would lead to one of Simon's best lyrics just a few years down the road.

In early 1988, Duran Duran played concerts for the first time in Brazil: Rio (at last!) de Janeiro and São Paolo. They also hired Peter Rudge, who had worked with the Rolling Stones, to help manage the band. They needed to write and record another album for EMI and Capitol Records.

There was a new style of music sweeping England in 1988 called house music or acid house, defined roughly as banging dance beats underneath vintage psychedelic or spacey grooves. The epicenter of acid house wasn't London but Manchester in northwest England, particularly the Haçienda nightclub. Bands like Stone Roses played at illegal raves in fallow fields and parking lots before thousands of kids high on MDMA/ecstasy and dressed in baggy jeans, hoodies, bucket hats, and smiley-face shirts. If Duran Duran wanted to stay in business, they would have to penetrate rave culture and the thrills of ecstasy-fueled urban nightlife.

Duran Duran began recording in Paris in April. They called themselves the Krush Brothers and sent out demos that wouldn't be prejudged as just more Duran Duran. They also started mining songs by other bands for ideas. The track "Big Thing" sounded like INXS. "I Don't Want Your Love" owed a bit to Chic and rave rhythms. Prince could have sued Duran Duran over "Skin Trade." One heard twists of Fleetwood Mac in "Too Late Marlene." "Drug" sounded like a dream date with George Michael or *Bad*-era Michael Jackson. "Do You Believe in Shame?" sounded like the Lizard King fronting U2. "All She Wants Is" featured screaming sirens, sex orgasms, the

LinnDrum, and drones. Other tracks echoed Simple Minds, "Moon-light Mile," and Led Zeppelin's dinosaur stompology.

The new album was called *Big Thing*. They began that spring, making the videos for three singles. Gone were the sailboats and the unstructured pastel suits; in was the contempo-Goth aesthetic, with dark clothes and new hair. The clip for "I Don't Want Your Love" featured shouting old lawyers and a young couple dancing and fight-ing. The "All She Wants Is" video portrayed hot models on an LSD voyage in the land of Magritte. "Do You Believe in Shame?" showed John, Simon, and Nick on the move in Manhattan.

The first single off *Big Thing* was released in September 1988. "I Don't Want Your Love" reached #4 in America but only got to #14 in England. MTV was now no longer the lifeline between the band and their young fans. Under new management and with all the orig-inal VJs gone, MTV was changing—and quickly. So while Duran Duran's videos still got played, there was nothing like the heavy rota-tion of the early years. Steve Ferrone wanted to move on and recom-mended New York drummer Sterling Campbell, then twenty-four years old, to replace him. "All She Wants Is" came out next and was a Top 10 single in England but only made #22 in America. Once MTV's darlings, Duran Duran was finding it hard to compete with the big hair metal bands—Poison, Ratt, Motley Crüe—oozing out of West Hollywood and dominating MTV along with ascendant Guns N' Roses.

Big Thing came out in October. The new songs were published by Duran Duran's new company, Skin Trade Music Ltd., as the musi-cians struggled to get free of Tritec and the Berrows. Production credits went to the band, Jonathan Elias, and programmer Daniel Abraham, and they dedicated the new album to recently deceased friends: Alex Sadkin, Andy Warhol, and David Miles. To promote their record, the band embarked on the nine-city Caravan Club Tour across America, playing mostly theaters and big clubs like First Ave-nue, Prince's home venue in Minneapolis, and Roseland Ballroom in New York. This pushed *Big Thing* to #24 in America, but sales in England were better, and the record eventually reached #15. When Duran Duran returned home that November, Nick told friends that New York didn't feel right to him now that Andy Warhol was gone.

That winter, the Big Live Thing Tour played a series of European venues. But John's drug issues continuously got in the way, with some less-than-magic gigs adding to low sales in some markets. Other concerts were downsized or canceled. In the middle of this, with John unwell, the band spent a few days in Venice, which was in flood and seemed to be doomed in a romantic sort of fashion. Duran Duran also appeared incognito as the Krush Brothers on occasional off nights, playing substantially different sets and almost none of Duran Duran's big hits, trying to change industry perceptions of Duran Duran as a boy band.

Duran Duran ended the year at home, playing the Birmingham NEC on Christmas Eve. The sold-out concert started early, at seven thirty, so their fans could get home before the trains shut down for the holiday.

The band continued the Big Live Thing Tour in the early months of 1989, playing their new-look, funkier styles in American arenas. They toured Japan in February and were received by screaming fans like saviors from the West. They also performed in the Far East, trying their luck in places they hadn't played before, like Taiwan and Manila. Then it was back to the United States, where they did good business in smaller venues—theaters, halls, and dance clubs.

Meanwhile, Renée Simonsen wanted to have a child with John, but he was having a hard time looking after himself, let alone a baby. She was popular with the band, who were sad when John announced that he and his beautiful girlfriend had broken up.

The last *Big Thing* single, "Do You Believe in Shame?" was released in April 1989. Duran lip-synched the record once again on *Top of the Pops* and launched their Electric Theater Tour of the British Isles. Drummer Sterling Campbell and Warren Cuccurullo were fitting in well onstage, and they were made members of the band that month.

In May, the group began to work on a new album called *Liberty* at their Wandsworth demo studio, later moving to Olympic Studios in Barnes, south of the Thames. By that time, they were mostly producing themselves, along with programmer John Jones and Chris Kimsey, who had worked with the Rolling Stones. From June through August, Duran Duran appeared at several European music festivals: a bullring in Cadiz, Spain; a beach fest on the North Sea in Belgium; Smukfest in Skanderborg, Denmark. In Italy, they were again besieged by delirious mobs of fans, ecstatic that Duran Duran was really in their midst.

There were personal joys for the bandmates as well as professional ones. On August 28, after suffering through two miscarriages, Yasmin gave birth to Amber Rose Le Bon, the first of her three daughters.

Duran Duran was back at Olympic Studios by late September 1989, working on new tracks for *Liberty*, under pressure to get the album out by the following year. John was balancing a Peruvian cocaine intake with chillums full of hashish oil. The others wondered if they would have to replace John. Simon thought this unthinkable but admitted the situation was strange. It also made it hard to work. "That's when we kind of lost our concentration," he said later. "I don't even remember making *Liberty*. That was when I fell apart."

When it was realized there would be no new Duran Duran album for the holidays, the record company demanded to release an album titled *Duran Duran's Greatest Hits*. Nick didn't like hits albums and fought against it, to no avail. But he refused to work on what came to be titled *Decade*. Other hands went to work choosing tracks, making a twelve-inch Duran Duran mash-up record for the dance floor, and producing a similar mix-up video to promote the entire project.

Decade was released on November 15, 1989. The band chose the fourteen tracks, sequenced in chronological order by producer Daniel Abraham. He brought the songs up to date with mostly brighter singles mixes, digitally tweaked edits, and dance versions such as Nile Rodgers's remix of "The Reflex." (Contemporary fan club material indicates disappointment that "New Moon on Monday" and "My Own Way"—both UK hit records—were left out.) Producer John Jones was tasked with cutting up bits of all these songs into the 3:55 mash-up titled "Burning the Ground" and "Decadence," released on different sides of a twelve-inch vinyl record only released to radio—and left off the album; this remix leaned heavily on Simon's "Notorious" vocal, with its subtext of someone's been foolin' around. The artwork for "Burning the Ground" and *Decade* were by fashion designer Stephen Sprouse, chosen by Nick because Stephen was a friend of Andy Warhol, who had admired the designer's flashy, Day-Glo graffiti style. (Keith Haring had been Nick's original choice, but Haring was now too ill with AIDS.) The album jacket and CDs may have looked like crudely drawn cartoons with space shuttles, but many longtime fans regard *Decade* as one of their favorite albums. This left Adrian Martin to assemble and direct the "Burning the Ground" video, an intense, lurid ride through eighties videography, from yachts and models to 007 in Paris to distressed sailboats to darker visions of aging and competition. It remains the best record of Duran Duran visuals in under four minutes.

Decade only rose to #67 on the *Billboard* chart in America.

It was the nineties now, not exactly Duran Duran's prime time. Their competition was now not only younger bands but whole waves of new styles. If the eighties was "the decade that taste forgot," the nineties was the decade that looked back to the UK's cultural past. This was especially true for the Britpop bands, who borrowed sounds from the sixties and seventies for inspiration and whose record producers often succumbed to creative temptations offered by the newer digital samplers. Oasis blatantly stole from the Beatles. (It was almost embarrassing.) The Verve famously sampled the Rolling Stones and paid a horrible price when they were sued.

Change was coming to the political arena as well. In 1990, Margaret Thatcher's premiership ended when her Tory party revolted. She had been the longest-serving British prime minister in the twentieth century. Reviled and beloved, she had owned the eighties as much as Ronald Reagan, Duran Duran, and *Miami Vice*. When the Iron Lady stepped down, an era had definitely come to an end.

In America, the competition for radio play was dominated by the grunge movement: heroin-infused bands from Seattle (Nirvana, Pearl Jam, Soundgarden) re-creating the blazing, flannel-shirted authenticity of primal rock bands like Neal Young and Crazy Horse. MTV now mostly played hip-hop and rap, so was lost to Duran Duran for the time being. American airplay for *Big Thing* had been minimal, as the new-look Duran Duran didn't fit into either the alternative or dance-pop formats that dominated radio.

As the nineties wore on, England would be rebranded Cool Britannia. There were new faces in the headlines and splashed across big screens: Naomi, Kate, Cindy, David Beckham, Tony Blair, Hugh Grant, and Elizabeth Hurley. Damien Hirst put farm animals in embalming fluid and took over British art. The Spice Girls became one of the biggest acts in the world. David Bowie, now the pope of pop, retreated into industria and throbbing drum and bass. Almost none of the New Romantic bands that came up with Duran Duran in 1982 would survive the nineties.

But Duran Duran managed to keep going by chameleonic adaptation: making records that resembled whatever was cool at the moment. In the coming decade, they would churn out more albums—some of them brilliant, some less so. They would even lose John for a while. Nick would keep collecting art, would become abstracted from the band, would even lose his mansion to his bank. Simon would disappear for extended periods and was dry for lyrics when he came around. These were years when Duran Duran was held together by Warren Cuccurullo, whose edgy, experimental guitars ignited mediocre Duran Duran songs into pyrotechnic sonic auroras.

But Nick and Simon were determined: Duran Duran was not going to die. Not yet. Nick recalled, "We were broke at the end of the eighties, just like everyone else. What disturbed me greatly was that at midnight on New Year's Eve, people thought that the door was going to slam on the vault and shut people like me behind it."

Duran Duran spent most of 1990 finishing up their sixth studio album, *Liberty*. The title was meant to convey their independence from old management structures and locked-in styles. They were a rock band now, making a rock record with a veteran rock producer at Olympic, where the Stones had made some of the greatest rock records ever. In interviews, Simon made it clear that they were ready to do anything to keep going. "We're not afraid of being sold a bit," he said. "We're not afraid of being called prostitutes."

Most of the tracks were finished by March. In April, they made the videos for the two singles—"Violence of Summer" and "Serious"—in

Paris. Back in Wandsworth, someone burgled their office; they took the computers but left the gold and platinum records on the walls. So they sold the building to Mick Jagger and moved to Fulham, West London.

"Violence of Summer" was released in August, along with *Liberty*. The eleven tracks were a mixture of spacey textures, cyber-funk, and metallic sex chants in various modes. The radio groove "Serious" could have been on Fleetwood Mac's recent *Tango in the Night*. "First Impression" could have been on the *Flashdance* soundtrack. "Venice Drowning" was a sensuous catechism about a seemingly doomed ancient city. (Simon's vocal was one of his better Doors tributes.) "Downtown" combined Zeppelin-flavored "Dancing Days" with some antique T-Rex sizzle.

By September, however, "Violence of Summer" was only at #67 in America. *Liberty*, which received indifferent reviews in the United States and little airplay, stalled at #46. "The album is idiotic," wrote *Trouser Press* in America, "with lyrics that set new standards for pretentions gone out of bounds." Doubts again began to disturb the minds of the Capitol staff at Hollywood and Vine. But in England, *Liberty* eventually became a Top 10 record, reaching #8. Inspired by this success, EMI rushed out the "Serious" single in October; but this was the hour of Oasis, Blur, Pulp, and the other Britpop groups, and "Serious" only got to #46.

Duran Duran didn't tour behind *Liberty*, which hurt sales. However, Simon, Nick, and John spent the rest of the year doing promotion for the album, including a long journey over to Australia and New Zealand. Most of Duran Duran were thirty years old now, or pushing thirty, or over thirty, and their maturity was starting to show in the way they talked about the band, both its history and future.

Many questions were asked about the split in the band and the two side projects. In response, Nick explained, "We were in grave danger with Duran Duran of getting into a rut. Arcadia and the Power Station pulled us out and made us find a new direction."

Simon added, "We did those projects for our own reasons, and it's a bloody good thing that we did it. As a writer there were times when I sit at home and can't think of the next word. If that goes on for weeks, it's very depressing. It's scary. We got out of Duran for a bit:

change of scenery, change of people. It made us come back to Duran with a new strength."

Without Andy and Roger, the feel of the band had changed. According to John, Andy left because "he didn't love the band enough. There were a lot of insecurities that had gone on with him. I know he felt that he didn't get enough attention. Now what he's doing gives him the right to stage center. He's in control now, working with people who put him at number one, not one of five."

As for Roger, Nick explained that "basically, he opted out. He just decided he didn't want to be in a band anymore. He wanted a different kind of life."

John agreed: "He loved to play his drums, but in a band, time is taken up with different considerations—photo sessions, interviews, or just running the band. Roger had no interest in any of that and just got less interested as time went on."

"At the end of the day, what we have is three band members who are most comfortable with the music—and the image," Nick concluded when talking about where the band was headed next.

To this, John added, "And we're not as cautious as we used to be, of each other. Before, we would question everything. 'Is that the right thing to say?' 'Do I want Nick to hear that?' It's much more open between us now. There's not much point in holding things back." Maturity, both personal and professional, had done a lot to heal bonds between the band's three remaining original members.

As Simon put it, "We can accept each other's differences now and not try to live up to certain images that we made of ourselves."

Looking back on their massive rise to popularity, the band members also mused about the impact their fame had on their development as a cohesive unit. As John reflected, "Fame is a bit of a freeze period in a way. You almost stop growing in some ways. Because you're pampered, and there's a certain way you're treated. Some ways you grow quicker, but in other things you just freeze and stop growing. We were all, like, *eighteen*—for four years—until we wised up. Perhaps it's not conscious, but people do try to keep you like that."

Now, on the other hand, things had changed. According to Nick, "It's great, that the three of us are now supporting each other in the studio. This is because, sometimes, I can get *obsessively* stuck—on one little thing, and now, of course, there are two other people there to help you sort it out." (No Duran Duran obsessive reading Nick's quote believed a word of it.)

John agreed: "In the past, it was our own insecurities that caused us to say things like, 'Don't tell me what to play,' and 'I know my instrument.' We just wanted to make a great record, and now, rather than five egos, now it's more like a cooperative."

"There's more teamwork now," Nick clarified. "It used to be that Andy would put two guitar tracks down and I'd think, 'Well, he's got two tracks on this, I'll have to put three down.' It wasn't quite that ridiculous, but there was that sort of concept, about filling up the space."

John also said a lot changed when Duran Duran recorded Notorious, which turned out to be a big success. "That album was more heartfelt, more emotive. We loved working with Nile Rodgers again. You cannot say enough about what Nile Rodgers means to us. . . . Now it actually sounded like—a group playing a song! It didn't sound like just a mix of sounds."

Simon added, "The songwriting process feels like magic again, the three of us. I'll find some lyrics that feel right with the music that the two of them are doing. Writing music is almost something that's like an extension of your tactile senses. It's just floating in the air, and you have to touch it. It's like a magic path that the light catches in a certain way, and you can only see at certain times. You have to be there at the right time and be able to put yourself in the position where you can find . . . the words! And you—me!—don't necessarily have to be . . . technical . . . to find it."

Above all else, John was relieved Duran Duran was still a band. "I keep using the word 'organic' about us now. . . . I don't really like that, as a word, but it's also a nicer way—it's less 'synthetic,' basically. . . . I think we've all improved, musically. We're kind of like the Blob, you know? Somebody took a chunk out, and we've had to improve to cover it up."

"That's right," Simon confirmed. "The membrane has been stretched, and it's even more exciting because of that."

Despite the positive energy between members of the band professionally, personally things were about to get rocky. In December, John was driving—erratically—from Knightsbridge to Chelsea with Simon in the car when he was pulled over by the traffic police on the Old Brompton Road. John was found to be intoxicated and was taken into custody. The magistrate fined him £250, and John lost his license for a year. And there were other bad omens—if you knew where to look for them. Duran Duran wouldn't release another record until 1993, but then it would turn out to be worth the wait.

Duran Duran was at its lowest point in early 1991. Despite its perch in the UK Top 10, the international commercial failure of *Liberty* brought new scrutiny from the record company; it had cost a fortune and had been "a bitch to make," according to Simon. Sterling Campbell quit the band and went back to New York. Morale was also low because most of them had cash-flow problems after not touring. Simon was so broke that his credit cards were often declined. John sold his house in Paris. Nick was £2.5 million in debt to his bank but bought a new Picasso painting anyway. His marriage to Julie Anne was breaking down, and the divorce was going to cost him dearly. Simon remembered, "Duran Duran had kind of fallen down the back of the sofa there, and we needed to get back on the mantelpiece." There wasn't much forward movement for the band until early in the year when Warren Cuccurullo stepped up and assumed control.

First, Warren installed a recording studio in the front room of the house in Battersea that he'd bought from Simon. This was Privacy Studio, and after some persuasion, Nick came over from South Kensington and agreed to work with him on new music there, away from the sterility and plastic plants of the typical studio. Warren turned out to be a font of new ideas. He wanted to write with the band. He wanted them to go acoustic for the next cycle. MTV had snubbed the *Liberty* videos, he argued, in part because the cable channel was having success with *MTV Unplugged*, in which musicians performed on almost exclusively acoustic instruments. Warren also wanted to get around the creative problems by doing an album of covers of their favorite songs, and it didn't take much convincing to get Simon to sing the Doors' "The Crystal Ship."

If the Duran Duran veterans were tired and discouraged, Warren was like a heart transplant. "I was the hungriest," he said later. "I wanted success. I wanted to go beyond where I'd gone. I'm not saying the others weren't motivated, but I didn't have any family to distract me. All I had was my music, and I am quite an extreme boy."

So that winter, Duran Duran started playing together at Warren's house. Privacy Studio was sometimes less than private after the local kids spotted Duran Duran going in and out. But the band continued, and after a couple of weeks, spirits were raised when Simon brought in the lyrics to "Ordinary World." The lyrics were prompted by the guilt Simon felt when David Miles, his "very, very, very best friend," accidentally overdosed. Simon felt that if he had called David that night, he might not have gone to see his heroin connection instead. "Where is my friend when I need you most? Gone away." The song suggests that seeking solace in everyday life is the way to a certain kind of salvation. When paired with a fugitive guitar line that Warren had in mind, it was clear "Ordinary World" could be a major moment for the band.

Nick later said, "'Ordinary World' seemed to come out of nowhere" as the four of them were riffing on acoustic guitars. (The working title of the next album was *Four on the Floor*.) Warren had been playing a faster, pretty melody that they slowed down, and something happened. Nick remembered, "It came from air, from space. We were just playing, and it came out and somehow all those bits that make up the song came together in one instant. All I can say is that the song goddess looked upon us kindly that day." "Ordinary World" would premiere in April, when Duran Duran appeared at the charitable Jerusalem for Reconciliation Concert at the Royal Albert Hall, with John Jones on piano and a drum machine.

After much consideration, EMI agreed to an advance for a new Duran Duran album, but under strict conditions. The last two records had cost too much and sold too little to justify the band's previous work habits. John reported that "the label said, 'This time we're only going to give you this much money, and then you're going to come back and play us what you've written, and if we like it, we'll give you some more. And this is going to be good for you!' So it was the first record we ever made that was tightly A&R'ed."

Single again, John met the notorious Amanda de Cadenet at a London party in April. Amanda was a teenage celebrity TV presenter with a bad-girl reputation, having first gained fame when she fled her posh boarding school and ran off with a much older man. She was a darling of the British tabloids, voluptuous and intelligent, and John took to her immediately, so much so that he whisked her off to the Caribbean in June (where she got pregnant). They called each other "Noodle" and "Noodlehead," each vowing to give up drugs. When Amanda was six months pregnant, the two got married in a hurry at the Chelsea Registry office on Christmas Eve with only his parents and a few friends present. *Hello* magazine sent a photographer. After the new year, Amanda went back to the Caribbean with some friends to spend her last trimester away from the English winter. Somewhat bemused by his new wife's abrupt departure, John returned to London and continued to work on the new album, now called *Duran Duran*, better known to fans as *The Wedding Album*.

Early in 1992, Capitol Records offered Duran Duran a million-dollar advance to reform the original band for several album-tour cycles. This was really tempting to the guys with the cash-flow issues (Nick, Simon, and John), but the others less so. Andy was busy producing records for himself, Rod Stewart, and other bands; he had also bought London's famous Trident Studios and a nightclub in Birmingham. Roger told them he wasn't physically and mentally ready to come back, as he and Giovanna raised their children in England's countryside.

Meanwhile the new album was coming together. "Ordinary World" would be the surefire first hit single, with the Sade-like rhythm of "Come Undone" following as the second single. Warren's idea of a cover album resulted in a sultry version of the Velvet Underground's "Femme Fatale," with Simon channeling both Mick Jagger and Jim Morrison in his vocals. Warren also had a connection to bossa nova singer Milton Nascimento through his Brazilian girlfriend, resulting in the collaboration "Breath After Breath." There were topical songs in the mix too, like "Sin of the City," referring to the infamous Happy Land nightclub arson fire in New York, which had killed eighty-nine people in 1990.

Amid the new music, the bandmates were also steeped in personal drama of their own. Nick was officially divorcing Julie Anne, who revealed (to *Hello*) that she was stifled and lonely because Nick lived and breathed only the band. Amanda de Cadenet returned to London and gave birth to John's daughter, Atlanta Noo, at the end of March. She then told John she wanted them to move to Los Angeles to get away from the British press and further her career in Hollywood.

Topping it all off, in July, Simon was involved in a widely reported motorcycle accident in Wales, which left his groin area bruised and abraded. "I went over the handlebars," Simon said, "and my balls swelled up like grapefruits and split."

When a reporter later asked about Simon's genitals, Yasmin replied that his balls were OK. She added, "If any of their girl fans get too close and too friendly, I would grab him by the balls and stand there, holding them, going, 'These—*they're mine!*'"

⌒

In September, John and Amanda moved to a rented house on Lookout Mountain Road in Laurel Canyon, above West Hollywood. Amanda got an agent and started going to auditions and parties while John stayed home with the baby and the nanny. John and Andy talked about restarting the Power Station, but nothing came of it.

The following month, someone at Capitol Records leaked "Ordinary World" to a couple of radio stations in Florida. Music was almost all digital now, and the song "went viral" and began to take on a life of its own as Capitol was now forced to rush release the single to keep up with demand. MTV desperately wanted the "Ordinary World" video, directed by Nick Egan, which showed the band at a wedding in the lush grounds of the Huntington Library in Pasadena. (The video for "Come Undone," directed by Julien Temple, depicted "Sofia Warren" in full drag and artfully smeared lipstick.)

All the members of Duran Duran were in Los Angeles by the end of the year, where Nick would meet his new girlfriend, Madeleine

Farley, at a Christmas party. Professionally, things were looking up as well for the veteran band. They played holiday shows for LA rock powerhouse KROQ—"K-Rock." "Ordinary World" was everywhere, and Duran Duran was back with a hit record—Top 10 in England and #3 in America.

In January 1993, Duran Duran returned to New York as they prepared to release *The Wedding Album* and stay on tour for the whole year. They were all over the radio and television, promotion in motion. Reviews were ecstatic for "Ordinary World." It was called an opera, a saga, a cathedral of sound. The cadenzas that Nick and John Jones had created were compared to composers William Walton and Vaughn Williams. The song, *Rolling Stone* said, "opened up vistas· of wishful passion and hope." Simon called it "a renaissance for this band," and Sting even confessed to John that he wished *he'd* written it.

After cutting a blistering demo of "White Lines" with the composers Grandmaster Flash and Melle Mel, Duran Duran reconfigured itself as a softer stage act for big rooms. Warren wrote clever new arrangements that John and Warren played on acoustic guitars without losing the swing and excitement of a hits concert. Simon toned it down—just a little. They hired drummer Fergus Gerrand and soul singer Lamya Al-Mugheiry (from Soul II Soul) to provide expert backup and countermelodies. This ensemble played four "Acoustic Evenings with Duran Duran" at the Academy Theater on Broadway in February.

Released on February 23, *Duran Duran* marked a new era for the band and a rebirth of sorts. It was called *The Wedding Album* because the compact disc booklet featured the wedding photographs of the band's parents. This was Nick's idea, an ironic one since his divorce was getting very messy. The album went off like a cannon, reaching #4 in the UK and #7 in the United States. It was their best-selling album since *Seven and the Ragged Tiger* in 1984.

John later credited Warren for this: "Bringing Warren in, and just giving him full rein to his talents is what *The Wedding Album* was really all about. Rather than trying to control it, just acknowledging what Warren had to offer is what made that album work."

The Dilate Your Mind Tour began in March, playing all over Europe, with many shows in Spain. These were electro-acoustic concerts, which included a mix of their greatest hits (for fans who'd never heard them in concert before) as well as covers and newer material. The set list often included the Doors' "The Crystal Ship" and Iggy Pop's (hilarious, bitter) "Success." They played La Cigale in Paris and Birmingham Symphony Hall as the "Come Undone" single was released; internationally, it was a Top 10 record but only reached #13 in the UK. Fans, many of whom had never heard the song before, loved hearing it live.

And the tour didn't stop in Europe; rather, it was just getting warmed up. Duran Duran played in the United Arab Emirates in April and then became the first big band to play in South Africa (albeit, protected by armed guards) after anti-apartheid sanctions were lifted, giving ten concerts in Cape Town, Johannesburg, and others. From there, they crossed the South Atlantic and played in Argentina and other emerging South American markets for big rock bands.

They hadn't lost their fervent fans either. On May 15, they were playing a few songs and signing CDs at Tower Records on Sunset Boulevard in West Hollywood when things got out of hand. The event had been widely promoted on KROQ, and there were so many fans on the Sunset Strip that the line stretched uphill, all the way to the Roxy nightclub. Sheriff's deputies were called out when traffic stalled, some bottles were thrown at the cops, and the band had to be spirited out the loading dock. After that, it was back to the Continent, mostly Spain and Germany, then across arenas and a few bullrings in Mexico, and then over to the West Coast and Las Vegas by August. The summer capped off with a huge outdoor festival in Germany on August 28, where Duran Duran played alongside musicians like Tina Turner, OMD, and the Artist Formerly Known as Prince.

But Simon's voice began to fade in September. He could barely hit the high notes in "A View to a Kill," and the song was dropped from the set list. In Rotterdam, he lost his voice during "Hungry Like the Wolf," and tenacious, beautiful Lamya admirably sang the rest of the show. The doctor said Simon's sore vocal cords had to be rested, and three weeks of crucial European shows were canceled.

They tried again in October. This time, the Cranberries opened for them, and their fans loved it when adorable Dolores O'Riordan sang "Linger," a radio favorite. Five shows in, Simon tore a vocal cord; the promoters agreed to postpone—not cancel—the tour. Dolores O'Riordan embarked on a torrid affair with studly Duran Duran tour manager Don Burton and married him a few months later.

After another month of rest, Simon had recovered enough for the band to appear at Sony Music Studios in New York to tape a segment of *MTV Unplugged*. They played a forty-five-minute hard-rocking "acoustic" show as a nine-piece orchestra, with drums, percussion, John Jones on piano, a string section, and some new songs. Warren's new arrangements turned "Girls on Film," "Planet Earth," and "Rio" inside out for a more contemporary and happening feel. The response was great, and ratings were impressive. After some concerts (and hectic postshow runners) in Japan (Tokyo, Osaka, Nagoya), they finished touring with the Cranberries in December. On New Year's Eve, Duran Duran headlined the bursting-to-the-rafters Great Western Forum (the "Fabulous Forum") in Los Angeles, with old comrade Adam Ant and the surviving members of the Village People, to welcome in 1994.

Just as Warren had seen that Duran Duran had to play acoustic guitars to get on *MTV Unplugged*, now he understood that Duran had to enter the hip-hop universe because the young suburban kids in America who bought CDs were buying mostly hard-core rap records—gangsta rap, murder music—not Duran Duran albums. When the Dilate Your Mind Tour continued into 1994, Grandmaster Flash and the Furious Five were sometimes on the bill, and production on their incandescent cover of "White Lines" continued apace.

In January, the band was back in the northeastern United States, playing theaters and clubs, like Aerosmith-owned Mama Kin in Boston and two nights at the glamorous Radio City Music Hall in Manhattan's Rockefeller Center (a Bowie favorite). Next up, there were sold-out shows back in England at the Wembley Arena and more across Europe. After two concerts in Tel Aviv's Cinerama club, Duran Duran decided finally to take a rest and make their covers album. Flush with cash from the EMI advance, Nick hired John Jones to rent a villa on the Riviera and build a studio for Duran Duran to record the album in.

In late winter, Antibes, a hazy-sunshine oasis overlooking the placid Mediterranean Sea, still resembles a painting by Paul Signac or some other pointillistic impressionist. Scott and Zelda Fitzgerald famously lived there in the Roaring Twenties and befriended Picasso, who stayed for a year and painted. In the off-season, fishing vessels dominate the harbor instead of summer's yachts and models. The bistros and brasseries are free of tourists. Good wine, cocaine, and hashish were readily available.

In this atmosphere, with other tax-exiled English rock stars littering the hills above the town, which Somerset Maugham called "a sunny place for shady people," Duran Duran made their seventh studio album, using gear trucked down from London and installed by John Jones. They built "White Lines" into a vortex of turntables and guitars, with Steve Ferrone on drums. Lamya was on hand to sing, while Melle Mel lent the magisterial authority of hip-hop royalty, just enough to make it feel current. Duran Duran changed "911 Is a Joke" from a Public Enemy track to more of a Beck Hansen feel. Bob Dylan's "Lay Lady Lay" became a samba. Warren got Missing Person Terry Bozzio to play on "Success," which they'd been performing live. Simon channeled Jim Morrison (in an American accent), while treating "The Crystal Ship" as a faithful recitation of classical material. Led Zeppelin's "Thank You" got the same respect and would provide the album title. Tony Thompson (who thought he was working on the Power Station's second album) came in and launched Sly Stone's "I Wanna Take U Higher" into orbit around the world. Roger even came back briefly and joined them in Antibes to play on a reggae version of "Watching the Detectives."

Recording completed, Duran Duran went back on tour in April, this time to Hong Kong, Singapore, Jakarta, and Bangkok. It was after a sold-out concert at the Bangkok International Convention Center that Duran Duran learned that Nirvana's Kurt Cobain had shot himself. This came as quite a shock; Nirvana was sort of the anti–Duran Duran, but Kurt had said he'd been a fan when he was younger. John was the most deeply affected by this death: "When Kurt Cobain died, he made me feel like I was a real sellout. I wasn't really living my life. I wasn't really doing what I wanted to be doing, and it kind of kicked my ass."

Least affected was Warren Cuccurullo, who kept on with his lingerie-clad postconcert nightclub parties in redecorated hotel suites full of lovely Asian women: "I went all over the world with Duran Duran and never got out of the hotels. Didn't see a thing I didn't have to. I did see a lot of girls and had a lot of fun."

The band stayed in France through the summer of 1994. Simon had bonded with INXS singer Michael Hutchence, who was living near Antibes and who seemed to be having a torrid secret affair with sexy Paula Yates, Sir Bob Geldof's wife and mother of his children. (Simon might have thought, "Is there something I should know?") Simon and Michael knew each other from Duran Duran's Australian days and had now become nearly inseparable friends; they were sometimes joined by U2's Bono, who was also spending the Illyrian summer nearby. Much hilarity ensued. The trio called their enchanted circle the Lead Singers Club. Nick recalled, "Trying to pry Simon away from Michael Hutchence and get him in the studio was something of a trial."

Then the new album got delayed. Boston-based producer Anthony Resta, who specialized in recording with vintage, tube-y audio equipment, was still remixing the tracks in London in late September. The delayed delivery of the new album was a particular disaster for Nick, mired in debt for what the papers called his lavish lifestyle. His mansion in South Kensington was repossessed by Coutts Bank, an ancient institution whose patience had run out.

In December, John went on the band's AOL forum and officially informed fans that Duran Duran's new album was on hold while the mixes of "Lay Lady Lay" were sorted out. It would be five more months until *Thank You* saw the light of day in 1995.

John Taylor didn't look like himself when they were shooting videos for the two new singles, "White Lines" and "Perfect Day," in early 1995. This may have been because John's life was coming apart. He was unhappy in the band and with his career; he desperately wanted to try something new. At the same time, his marriage was deteriorating as Amanda relentlessly pursued a career that wasn't taking off, spending time with her new best friend, Hole front woman and Cobain widow Courtney Love (with whom she attended the 1995 Academy Awards). There were also Hollywood whispers about Amanda and actor Keanu Reeves, with whom she was later publicly aligned.

John's drug habit had also come back with a vengeance; various attempts at sobriety hadn't taken. In spite of this, John and Andy had tried to reboot the Power Station in 1994, making demo recordings (with Robert Palmer back in the fold) and shopping for a new record deal. Just as they were about to sign with Polydor Records, John decided he couldn't do it anymore. He quit the Power Station project, told Amanda he wasn't coming home, and checked himself into a rehab. In John's own words, "I'd got to the point where I was miserable. I didn't like anyone, and I was paranoid. I hated who I'd become, and it became a question of actually surviving. It's depressing when cocaine doesn't work like it used to. I needed to be born again, for want of a better expression."

Though he tried to get his life back on track, John's drug use also made him an inconsistent—and unreliable—member of the band. Duran Duran had a big gig in Italy, at the San Remo Music Festival, on February 25, with Melle Mel on hand to rap on the big crowd-pleaser "White Lines." Everything almost came to a standstill when John didn't show up. This had never happened before to Duran Duran. Once again, Lamya saved them by taking over on bass guitar. John did arrive in Las Vegas on March 10 to help open the Hard Rock Hotel with a short set lit up by a hard rock "Rebel Rebel," recorded for the covers project but left off the final album.

In March, Simon was interrogated, in bed, by Paula Yates for one of her famous "on the bed" interviews for the popular UK show *The Big Breakfast*. (He noticed she wasn't wearing underwear.) A few days later he was back in New York, performing with the band on MTV's *Most Wanted* program to promote their new album, *Thank You*, released late in the month. The album was well reviewed in England and reached a respectable #12 in April, but it didn't have as much luck in the United States; it appeared at #19 for one week only and promptly vanished from the *Billboard* chart. Likewise, their new single, "Perfect Day," got on the radio in England and peaked at #28, but it failed to make the *Billboard* Hot 100 in America. *Rolling Stone* complained that Duran Duran made angry "911 Is a Joke" sound like a whiny complaint by weedy singer Beck. The *Observer* said it was the "worst cover version—ever." *Q* magazine called *Thank You* "the worst album of all time." It wasn't all bad reviews, though; Lou Reed gratifyingly described "Perfect Day" as "the best cover ever completed of one of my songs."

Despite bad reviews, the band continued to flog their new record. They mimed "Perfect Day" on *Top of the Pops* in London and played it live on *The Late Show with David Letterman* in New York. In May, after shows in France and Scandinavia, Duran Duran embarked on the Radio Station Festival Tour with drummer Steve Alexander, playing station-sponsored gigs in mostly outdoor sheds. John was miserable and shaky on the road now, and he seemed to be having chronic equipment problems. He stalked off the stage in Detroit, then again in Chicago, leaving Nick to wander backstage trying to find him while Simon talked to the fans. The misery came to a new low on June 24 in California, when most of the audience fled the Irvine Meadows Amphitheater as Duran Duran took the stage. Hurt and embarrassed, the band played a shortened set and walked off. There was no encore.

The band's downward spiral continued through the summer. By July, the blistering "White Lines" single had stalled at #17 in England and was basically ignored in America. The band was told that no alternative-format radio station would play a song with a rapper in it. Some found this surprising because "White Lines" was the hardest rock Duran Duran had ever recorded and even managed to capture some of the manic and lurid downtown craziness of Jean-Michel Basquiat's Afro-hoodoo paintings (so admired by Andy Warhol; Basquiat had overdosed on heroin in 1988). For their performance on *Top of the Pops*, they introduced singer Tessa Niles, who became the female voice of Duran Duran for the next few years, replacing the amazing Lamya.

Now, having failed to cross over into the hip-hop arena or be taken seriously by rappers and their fans (which had indeed happened for Aerosmith and Run-DMC ten years earlier), Duran Duran limped back to London. Undeterred, Warren booked them into an inexpensive studio and tried to get new material underway for the next album. Simon, on the other hand, was totally blocked and couldn't come up with lyrics. Sometimes they couldn't find him, and Yazzie said even she wasn't always sure where Simon was. John, now thirty-five, appeared to be in agony with marital, pharmaceutical, and professional problems beyond his ability to cope. The others were relieved when John decided, in August, to go home to Los Angeles to try to pull himself together. With John gone and Simon unproductive, Nick and Warren were left to their own devices. They used already booked studio time to begin work on an experimental, avant-garde side project of Nick's that later became known as TV Mania.

Back in LA, John found himself at loose ends. He and Andy had officially parted company over the Power Station fallout. One night, John went to hang out at the Viper Room, the infamous Sunset Strip nightclub in which actor Johnny Depp had a financial interest. (The club was also a drug den. Movie star River Phoenix had overdosed on cocaine and heroin in the club in October 1993 and died on the sidewalk outside before help arrived.) It was at the Viper Room that John discovered he was not the only rock star at loose ends in LA, and he soon started collaborating onstage with his longtime peers. He was invited to jam with the house band: Duff McKagan and drummer Matt Sorum from Guns N' Roses, Steve Jones on lead guitar, and various singers from English bands like Billy Idol and Ian Astbury. Some nights Guns' Izzy Stradlin and Slash joined the band. When John was onstage, Duff played rhythm guitar. They called this group the Neurotic Boy Outsiders, and their favorite cover to play was "Janie Jones" by the Clash. Slash—centaur of rock—was especially taken with John. "Fuckin' John Taylor," he said, "was *the* quintessential fuckin' pop star—and he only played bass so he wasn't too complicated." Perhaps Slash couldn't help comparing tall, elegant John with Slash's nemesis—runty, beady-eyed delinquent Axl Rose.

Soon the Viper Room's jam band became a real group that got signed to Madonna's label, Maverick Records, as the Neurotic Outsiders. They released an album in 1996 and played in North America and Europe through most of that year. John also worked on songs for movies and music of his own. At a party in Beverly Hills, he met Gela Nash, founder of apparel brand Juicy Couture and divorced mother of two. Gela was a glamorous artist and businesswoman who didn't drink or smoke, and she was far removed from the music scene at the time; the only band she had ever heard of was Genesis. John told friends she reminded him of Renée a little. He and Gela would marry in 1999.

⁓

Meanwhile, the band's remaining members were occupied with various side projects. Warren was working on various tributes to Frank Zappa, who had died in 1993. Andy was still invested in the Power Station project; after John left, Bernard Edwards rerecorded John's bass parts on all the tracks. Nick was recording tracks back in England, living with his new girlfriend, Madeleine Farley, in a smaller, book-stuffed house in Chelsea. She was ten years younger, a bit of a free spirit. Nick enjoyed taking her to Harvey Nichols and expensive London boutiques, buying her clothes, making her over from a jeans-wearing country girl into a pop star's arm candy. "He taught me how to wear makeup and how to dress," she said of that time. "He totally transformed me. Nick's the closest link between gay men and straight women." She later joked that Nick was definitely the woman in their relationship.

In April, Simon flew to Tokyo for a Chic-themed charity concert with Nile Rodgers and Bernard Edwards. Bernard looked uncomfortable and seemed to struggle through the concert; later that evening, he died from advanced pneumonia in his hotel room at the age of only forty-one. He and Nile had been inspirations to Duran Duran when they were just kids and, later on, became valued and trusted collaborators and friends. Simon recalled the flight back to England as the saddest experience he'd been through since David Miles died.

Simon's creative period further stalled after he had dental surgery that October. The dentist gave him the anesthetic midazolam, which in turn gave Simon lurid visions of other worlds, in other galaxies. His writer's block elongated into an era of mystical lassitude. When he came out of these mental status changes, he told his wife that he'd been to "Medazzaland" and back again.

In December, Simon ran into Andy Taylor in Tokyo. They talked about getting the original band together for a lucrative tour. But this wouldn't happen—just yet.

Back in London, late in the year, Sir Bob Geldof, trying to contain himself, called Simon and told him that his wife, Paula Yates, was pregnant with Michael Hutchence's child and was leaving him and their daughters for the Australian rock star. Geldof knew that Simon and Michael had become very close in France that summer. Did Simon know about Paula and Michael? Hadn't he been the best man at their wedding? All Simon could say was that he hadn't known about the affair. Six months later, Paula Yates gave birth to a baby girl.

Around this time, Simon went to the LA Fitness gym in South Kensington to work out. When he came through the door, someone whistled at him. It was newly divorced Diana Spencer, spinning with friends in the back of the gym. Simon laughed and waved, and Diana waved back. "She wolf-whistled me like a brickie [laborer]," Simon said later.

PART 9

In January 1997, John Taylor finally quit Duran Duran after playing a solo gig at a Duran Duran fan convention in Los Angeles. With old friend Gerry Laffy on guitar, he formed a band called Terroristen and began to play out in Southern California.

Back in London, Duran Duran was now a trio: Nick, Simon, and Warren. They owed EMI/Capitol another album and kept working in Warren's house, transforming some of the brittle, avant-garde TV Mania concepts into workable songs for the band. Simon's writer's block was so intense that even Nick started working on lyrics, some of which dealt with his hurt feelings about John leaving the band. After forays into *Unplugged* and hip-hop, Nick wanted to aim squarely back at the dance floor. "Electric Barbarella" came out of this, as did the cut-up "Medazzaland," redolent of Simon's state of mind during and after treatment with midazolam, which seems to have helped him through a psychic portal to write new lyrics. They thought a song called "Out of My Mind" had the best chance of being the new album's first single. These and other tracks were sent to be remixed by Anthony Resta. While the band filmed the ghostly period video for "Out of My Mind" in Prague with director Dean Karr, John Taylor's bass parts were removed from all the tracks but four: "Medazzaland," "Big Bang Generation," "So Long Suicide," and the Beatles-like "Midnight Sun."

With new tracks well underway, Duran Duran was back in America in April, mostly doing radio interviews and in-store appearances. Their record sales may have declined, but when KROQ told listeners that Duran Duran would be at Tower Records in Hollywood, fans still blocked Sunset Boulevard until the cops shut down the event. While it hadn't broken out upon its release in England back in March, the break-up ballad "Out of My Mind" was used in a remake of *The Saint* and reached #21 on May 24.

Also in the spring, the band filmed the video for "Electric Barbarella," directed by Ellen von Unwerth (the German model-turned-photographer who had made the lurid, downtown-noir "Femme Fatale" video). The scenario involved Duran Duran purchasing a sex doll and then bringing her to life with unhappy (but hilarious) results.

The Londoners tried to keep up with what their former comrades were up to in America. John Taylor was acting in a movie, making an album, and promoting himself through new media, including internet chat rooms via America Online, Prodigy, and Sonic Net. Andy Taylor and Robert Palmer took the rebooted Power Station on tour that September, playing for respectable-sized crowds at smaller venues.

In August 1997, Diana Spencer was killed in a car crash in Paris.

The new Duran Duran album, *Medazzaland*, was released in the United States on October 14, 1997. The music was harsh, saw-toothed rock and roll aimed at the twenty-first century and sounded loud, intense, and immediate. But fans found the songs confusing. Critics were unusually cruel. Even Yasmin Le Bon, when she'd heard the bright, top-heavy final mixes, asked her husband, "Where's the fucking bass, Simon?" Insiders knew that "Michael You've Got a Lot to Answer For" and "So Long Suicide" were about Michael Hutchence and the Paula Yates affair. The band threw itself into furious rounds of sincere promotion to save the album, appearing on *The Tonight Show with Jay Leno* and doing dozens of radio call-ins, patiently answering fan questions, explaining why Barbarella was such a foundational myth for Duran Duran. Asked about John's departure, Simon answered, "I really miss him. I wish he hadn't got into the personal mess he got himself into."

Nick said, "We were sad to see him go, but at the same time we've never been afraid of change. To be honest, he wasn't around much after 1992, so we kind of got used to him not being there."

The "Electric Barbarella" video was banned in Canada.

In November, Duran Duran began a two-month American road trip, the Ultra Chrome Latex and Steel Tour, at the Mohegan Sun Casino in Uncasville, Connecticut. Warren's friend Wes Wehmiller was now on bass, with Steve Alexander again on drums. Playing in clubs, theaters, and casinos, they mixed songs from *Medazzaland* with most of the hits (and TV Mania's "Mirror Mirror"). "We're working harder now than we ever have," Simon told a radio host in New Jersey. When they reached New York City on November 19, they signed CDs at the Virgin Megastore in Times Square, appeared on MTV at their new studios across Broadway, and then played a full show that night at the Roseland Ballroom—all in a single day. The aggressive touring was not, however, without its consequences. Nick became ill with a virus, and some shows had to be canceled or postponed. His girlfriend, Madeleine Farley, reportedly made videotapes of all the concerts they were able to play.

The losses continued well into the fall. Two days after Nick fell ill, Michael Hutchence killed himself in his Sydney hotel room, death by hanging. The next night, Simon was seen crying onstage during "Ordinary World" at a concert at a high school auditorium in Lakewood, Ohio. Shortly afterward, Simon came down with strep throat and was put on intravenous penicillin for the rest of the tour as they played Disney World in Florida and venues in New Orleans and Puerto Rico, the last without their stage set and lighting rigs. The tour ended at the Universal Amphitheater on December 9.

And still, there was more bad news to come. Competing with electronica dance groups like the Chemical Brothers and the Prodigy, *Medazzaland* had only reached #58 in America. Capitol had been pushing for the grungy anthem "Who Do You Think You Are?" as another single. When the tour ended, and the album stalled, they changed their minds. EMI pushed back the UK release of *Medazzaland* and "Electric Barbarella." As they flew home, Simon and Nick were unsure if Duran Duran was still in the record business. In January 1998, rumors reached Privacy Studios—where Warren had them back at work—that Duran Duran had been fired by EMI. In April, it was publicly confirmed that after seventeen years, Duran Duran was no longer on EMI/Capitol's artist roster. It was also reported that the band only owned one of their albums—the ill-fated *Medazzaland*. Around then, Duran Duran also parted company with its managers, Left Bank Management.

John Taylor was on the road with his band Terroristen in America in May, playing the national House of Blues circuit, until the gigs started getting really small. Only a dozen people showed up on a weeknight at the Moto Lounge in Jacksonville, Florida. There was about that many the next night at the Button in Hallandale. Despite this, John felt, "at least I was playing music with my own band, calling the shots, however wrong they might have been, doing what I really wanted to do, for the first time in years."

In November, EMI released *Greatest*, a nineteen-track upgrade of *Decade*, with a DVD implanted with hidden digital "eggs" that revealed occluded images and interviews. *Greatest* proved to be the biggest-selling Duran Duran album ever, reaching platinum status in most markets within a few weeks. MTV's "adult" cable channel VH-1 signed up the band for its popular *Behind the Music* series and conducted interviews with almost all of its members, past and present (except Roger), in December.

Fueled by the uptick in public interest, Duran Duran and their booking agent jumped on this literal bandwagon and, with drummer Joe Travers, embarked on the Latest and Greatest Tour of English arenas in the run-up to Christmas, cashing in on the "greatest hits" before sold-out houses. After twenty years, Duran Duran's fans still were happy to party down and dance on a cold English winter's night. At Wembley, on December 21, they were reunited with old friend sax man Andy Hamilton for a riotous "Rio." On New Year's Eve, to top off a tumultuous year, they flew to Scotland and played the hits for thousands, piled high in stands in the forecourt at Edinburgh Castle, as incandescent fireworks burst over their heads.

Even without a record deal, Duran Duran habitually returned to work on new songs. The early months of 1999 were spent in Warren's studio, developing an album to be called *Pop Trash Movie*. As EMI released a two-CD set of remixes called *Strange Behaviour*, Duran Duran began talking to Hollywood Records, the recording arm of the Walt Disney corporate empire. At Hollywood Records' studio in Burbank, Nick and Simon played new Duran Duran tracks for the A&R staff, including "Lady Xanax" and "Last Day on Earth." With Hollywood on the line but still not the hook, the band moved into familiar Maison Rouge Studios, with Nick writing lyrics when Simon's muse didn't come through or the singer just didn't show up. Nick: "Simon maintained a punishing social schedule. I'd be in the studio until midnight, and he'd show up at the opening of a toilet seat."

By June 1999, negotiations with Hollywood Records had concluded and Duran Duran was back in Burbank to sign a three-album contract, including the inevitable reunion album when the original band got back together. Extending the momentum, earning much-needed cash, the band then set off on their Let It Flow Tour through American pavilions, music centers, casinos, and Houses of Blues, ending in early September.

Now Duran Duran's personal and professional lives were changing. After Nick and Madeleine Farley broke up, he stayed single for a while. Then one rainy evening in London, when he went to hail a taxi to take him to photographer Mario Testino's book launch, a tall blonde model wanted the same cab. It turned out she was going to the same party as Nick. She didn't know who Nick was, so she was shocked when they arrived at the gallery and a dozen paparazzi opened fire with their flashguns.

Meredith Ostrom, a kindhearted and friendly girl from New Jersey, was much younger than Nick and much taller, which he liked. She soon moved in with Nick and his cat, and for the next decade Meredith and Nick were key players in the city's arts-and-fashion social scene, even rising up to #28 on *Tatler* magazine's list of "100 Most Invited."

Later in November, in New York, Simon Le Bon joined John Taylor's band at Joe's Pub downtown to celebrate Juicy Couture's new store on Madison Avenue. John told Simon he could see returning to Duran Duran under the right conditions. It wasn't a promise, but it was a start. Meanwhile, hoping to finish the year off with a bang, Duran Duran launched the Overnight Sensation Tour with two concerts in Dublin, followed by a big gig at Earl's Court, a San Diego radio station's "Jingle Ball '99," a theater in Phoenix, and a New Year's Eve concert at a private mansion outside Atlanta, Georgia.

The twelve songs on Duran Duran's tenth studio album, *Pop Trash*, sampled multiple styles: electronica, industrial, hard rock, synth pop, Britpop, and soul ballads. The producer's credit went to TV Mania, which meant Nick and Warren. Hollywood Records hated most of distinguished British engineer Ken Scott's mixes, and the tracks were turned over to LA engineer Chris Lord-Alge, who had worked with Stevie Nicks. The first (and only) single released was the doleful ballad "Someone Else Not Me," with a digitally animated video of the band produced by internet designers Fullerene. Standout tracks included "Pop Trash Movie" (with lyrics by Nick); "Mars Meets Venus"; and hard-rocking "Last Day on Earth," which sounded like INXS with Doors lyrics. (This song had been submitted to the producers of the James Bond film *Tomorrow Never Dies*, but it was rejected. Given new lyrics, it came out on *Pop Trash* instead.)

Pop Trash was officially released to the public on June 19, 2000. It was marked by firsts and lasts; it was the first Duran Duran album with no input from John, and it would be the last to feature Warren. Disney executives had strongly advised against calling the album *Pop Trash*, saying it would be commercial suicide. But the band held firm, so Hollywood Records decided not to promote the record. Despite another *Tonight Show* appearance and a segment on the VH-1 series *Storytellers*, the label's lack of faith meant the album failed to break into the American charts and only reached #58 in England. Still, the band was mobbed at a signing at Virgin Records in Manhattan's Union Square on June 17, and tickets for the summer-long Pop Trash Tour were selling well. Duran Duran played all over North America in the summer of 2000. During a stopover near Pittsburgh, Nick and Simon visited the new Andy Warhol Museum in honor of their late friend. In September, Simon was sad to learn that Paula Yates had died at home from a heroin overdose.

The tour wound down with a six-night residence at the House of Blues in West Hollywood. During this time, Nick and Simon went to John Taylor's house to talk about getting the original band together for a massive reunion, album, and tour. There would be new management, they promised, along with a new label to work with, because they hated the guys from Hollywood Records (the feeling appeared to be mutual). They also called up Andy and Roger, who both tentatively agreed. Nick and Simon then broached the idea of keeping Warren and going out with two guitarists, but Andy put his foot down and said no fucking way, mate.

Now that the twenty-first century had arrived, Nick Rhodes had the idea that Duran Duran should align itself with the fashion industry. From the beginning, the band had been associated with luxury items—yachts and models—and there was no reason that a mature version of Duran Duran couldn't appeal to the mature clientele of designers, watchmakers, perfume merchants, and the rest of the booming luxury industry. Nick started attending fashion shows in London, learning the territory, becoming familiar to the fashionistas. Besides, it was a good way to meet models, especially tall ones. Nick was thirty-eight and unmarried.

It was at a fashion show in Knightsbridge that Nick ran into Stephen Duffy, late of Duran Duran and still very much in music. In 1995, he had teamed with singer Robbie Williams and cowrote and produced Williams's *Intensive Care* album, which went to #1 around the world and quickly sold seven million albums. Stephen mentioned that he'd recently found a cassette of a 1979 Duran Duran show while he was still in the band, and it sounded great. When Nick heard the tape, he had the idea of rerecording the songs using only analog studio gear available in 1979 (with the ProTools app for backup). By October, as Nick and Simon were beginning to work on lyrics for a new Duran Duran album, Nick and Stephen also began working on replicating Duran Duran's original sound. They called this projected group the Devils.

But the Pop Trash Tour was far from over. In December, the tour continued in Great Britain, beginning in Aberdeen, Scotland,

and moving through two shows at the Manchester Apollo and on through Wales, Nottingham, and the Birmingham NEC. The *Guardian* newspaper reviewed Duran Duran's Overnight Sensation show at massive Earl's Court arena in London: "[Simon] Le Bon is taking the markedly ungentle Mick Jagger route into that good night, high kicking in tight trousers, scrambling atop amps to strike attitudes in defiance against age, his fall from fashion, and the erosion of his band."

On New Year's Eve, Duran Duran was at Disney World in Orlando, Florida, where they played two shows (8:00 p.m. and 10:00 p.m.) for their now-hated Disney paymasters, with Nile Rodgers and Chic taking the stage between the band's sets.

HOLLYWOOD GOODBYE

Duran Duran began 2001 by getting fired. Hollywood Records executives told colleagues they had been screwed by Duran Duran, who, they asserted, had submitted substandard, uncommercial music and had been difficult to deal with since there didn't seem to be much in the way of management. Disney's lawyers informed Duran Duran that their contract was terminated with immediate effect, for cause. Kicking Duran Duran while they were way low down, Hollywood Records also deleted *Pop Trash* from their catalogue, making it almost impossible for fans to buy their latest CD.

Ditched by Disney, Duran Duran would now be without a record label for the next three years. At the same time, it was an era-ending period for the recording industry itself, decimated as it was by piratical internet sites like Napster, which let fans access popular music for free. After almost a century, the excited dash to the record store for new music would be replaced by the anodyne downloading of a computer file. Duran Duran now was part of a once-mighty recording industry desperately struggling to survive. Nick and Simon knew that after fifteen years, the only way to come back was to reunite the Fab Five, the original Duran Duran. Other than that, they might as well call it a day.

Andy Taylor was busy moving his family from Malibu to the Balearic island of Ibiza, rave capital of the Mediterranean, when he got a call from John Taylor about re-forming their original lineup. Andy recalled they all had a meeting at a lawyer's office in London. The last time he'd seen him, John Taylor was dead-eyed and skeletal from drugs. The last time Andy had seen Nick Rhodes, Nick and Andy had argued bitterly. But this time, the meeting went well. John pointed out that they were all forty years old, or almost (or just beyond), and if a reunion didn't happen now, it would probably never happen. Both Andy and Nick thought that touring might not be the best way to go about a reunion, but the increasingly lucrative offers coming in from America were hard to resist. By this point, cash flow was an issue for everyone. As Andy recalled, "Nick and Simon were insisting that Roger and I should be on a smaller percentage share of earnings than the other members of the band. They argued that they'd kept things going while we were away, and so they were entitled to a greater cut." Andy and Roger agreed on the condition that if the reunion were successful, the takings would be split five ways again—"like in the eighties." The best part for Andy was the change in John. "He had a new light in his eyes, and he was clearheaded. He had sobered up. I sensed he was carrying a few battle scars, but it was good to see him looking so well."

The reunion was on. But it would be months before the news was shared widely, as previous commitments were fulfilled by Duran Duran's latest lineup.

In January 2001, a Taylor-less Duran Duran was back in America, playing a concert in Miami and two in Clearwater, Florida, where Simon's mother, Ann, was living. Things were starting to look up. A concert at the Beacon Theatre on Manhattan's Broadway sold out in one day, and another was added. In February, Duran Duran was behind the former Iron Curtain for the first time, appearing in Moscow and then at gigs in the Ukraine, Estonia, and Croatia before unusually rabid crowds. At the same time, they were working on new songs, including an aspiring, hopeful song called "Sunrise."

In March, it was back to the United States for the Up Close and Personal Tour. This did respectable business at the Astrodome in Houston before hitting the House of Blues circuit, plus Native American casinos in New England and the Golden Horseshoe, on a riverboat moored in the Mississippi.

Meanwhile, the three Taylors were jamming at a quiet location in Wales to prepare for the reunion. They hadn't played together since 1986, but John and Andy had kept working on their solo careers and sounded fresh together. Long-retired Roger, however, was another matter and worked hard to bring the band's rhythm section up to speed.

Despite some sincere attempts at secrecy, word about the long-awaited reunion began to leak. Internet chat rooms made privacy almost obsolete, as superfans outdid themselves in posting information, no matter how obscure or wrong (or right). Warren Cuccurullo learned he was out and felt betrayed. Then in May, Simon mentioned the reunion to a university journalist, and the news went viral. On May 6, Duran Duran officially announced the reunion of the original band. Warren Cuccurullo would stay in through a Japanese tour in June. Then the Fab Five would make a new album and tour in 2002.

At least, that was the plan.

After gigs in Tokyo and Osaka, Warren put his London house on the market and returned to Los Angeles, where he set about re-forming Missing Persons. He had held Duran Duran together for more than a decade, but whether or not he felt slighted, he never complained publicly about how that gig had ended for him.

After Nick and Simon were interviewed for the *Twenty Years of MTV* special in New York, the new/old band reunited in San Tropez, back on the languid summer French Riviera, and started working on a new album of songs for whatever record label could be convinced to take on the original gangsters of Duran Duran.

In July 2002, Nick and Stephen Duffy (a.k.a. the Devils) released *Dark Circles* on their own Tape Modern label in England. Hypnotic songs like "Memory Palaces," "Aztec Moon," and "World Exclusive" gave fans a taste of the throbbing, mechanistic (and tasty) dance-floor music of Duran Duran in 1979. By November, Simon and Roger could barely squeeze into the Harvey Nichols store in Knightsbridge with a thousand fans to support their bandmates and witness the Devils' only UK gig—ever. The Devils played their final show in Cologne, Germany, in February 2003. After that, it was time to get the band back together.

The year 2003 marked Duran Duran's twenty-fifth year. Fan websites glowed with pleasure when a long-overdue press release announced the Fab Five's first international tour in eighteen years. Promoters around the world started booking the band; in Tokyo, the Budokan martial arts arena sold out in thirty minutes, breaking a record set by the Beatles almost forty years earlier. Capitalizing off the growing enthusiasm, EMI released the *Singles Box Set 1981–1985*, a deluxe thirteen-CD compilation of Duran's original 45-rpm records, backed with unreleased remixes, twelve-inch night versions, and live performances. It was a connoisseur-friendly package and the first time many of the tracks had appeared in CD form. The set sold so well that a companion set, *The Singles 1986–1995*, came out the following year.

Duran Duran was now managed by Wendy Laister, a cousin of Nick's. She was a veteran music publicist who had worked with Aerosmith and then started her own management company, Magus Entertainment, with Aerosmith as her first client. Wendy's job was to get Duran Duran a record deal—and make it fast. In the years since the band had separated, many of its members had begun running out of money. Simon Le Bon later claimed he spent £300,000 in the three years it took to make the reunion happen.

In June 2003, Duran Duran was photographed for British *Vogue*, the original lineup's first photo call in years. Then it was around the globe to Los Angeles, where they announced dates for the Reunion Tour on KROQ and played a nostalgic set at the Roxy on the Sunset Strip, the first venue they'd ever played on the West Coast.

The Reunion Tour began in July with six shows in Japan. At the Tokyo Grand Hyatt Hotel in Roppongi Hills, they ran into Robert Palmer, who was also playing in town. Andy and Robert spent a drunken weekend laughing and crying about the Power Station's wild ride—a weekend that Andy would soon find himself grateful for. A few weeks later, Robert died of a heart attack in his Paris hotel room. Later that year, Tony Thompson would also die of kidney cancer, thus sealing the fate of the Power Station.

After shows in California and Las Vegas, Duran Duran landed at Webster Hall in Manhattan in late August. This was the old Ritz, the first place they'd played in New York City, now newly renovated. The after-party guest list included Debbie Harry, Christy Turlington, and seemingly almost every working model in New York. Nick told a *New York Post* reporter that he was shocked that all his artist friends—Andy Warhol, Basquiat, Keith Haring—were now dead.

The tour continued in California with concerts in the Santa Barbara Bowl and San Francisco's Golden Gate Park. The band then headed back home and ran through English arenas with much attendant sound and fury, these being the Fab Five's first UK shows since 1984. London's *Evening Standard* reported that there were two hundred thousand online requests for a gig at the Forum in Kentish Town, which has only two thousand seats. In December, Duran Duran were "special guests" on a Robbie Williams tour of Australia and New Zealand, which meant they opened for the wildly popular crooner in giant rugby grounds that had sold out in an hour. They also played some solo shows in Down Under band strongholds like Sydney, between stadium concerts.

The tour finally ended in Singapore on December 16, but the band hardly stopped to take a break; instead, they were ready to make a brand-new record and do it all again. Meanwhile, Wendy Laister was talking to EMI and Virgin in England and Epic Records in New York, where Magus Entertainment was primarily based. One of these would be Duran Duran's next label.

Rejuvenated after a successful 2003, the early weeks of 2004 found Duran Duran in Texas, where they played at the Super Bowl's pre-game "Tailgate Party," which was seen by millions of football fans. Once they returned to London, they headed right back into the studio with American producers Don Gilmore and Dallas Austen on album tracks while Simon seemed to be doing better with the lyrics. On February 17, Justin Timberlake presented the band with a lifetime achievement award at the Brits, the UK music industry's version of the Grammys.

Roger and Giovanna Taylor separated and would eventually divorce.

The British leg of the Reunion Tour featured seventeen concerts across April, supported by synth-pop duo Goldfrapp and later the Scissor Sisters, who opened Duran Duran's two sold-out Wembley Arena shows. During "A View to a Kill" at Wembley, the video screen showed a scratchy amateurish film of a young girl in a red dress. Then she was down to sheer panties, stockings, and a garter belt. She was then seen in the shower with a knife, cutting herself, first near her thumb, then by an eyebrow. Her face was never shown, but she had long dark hair. She touched the knife to her tongue. As "A View to a Kill" came to an end, the screen showed bloody water swirling down the drain.

Asked about the film by a reporter covering the concert, Wendy Laister said the girl in the film was Elizabeth Hurley, in 1983 an aspiring actress who was friends with Nick. "She'd come over for a bit of fun," Nick had said, having captured the scene with his JVC camera.

The blood was fake, of course. (Nobody who saw the film actually believed the blood was fake.)

Over the course of that spring, Duran Duran played to a quarter million fans and broke house records all over the United Kingdom's four nations. Concerts began with "Sunrise" and ran through the band's jukebox hits, with interludes of "Come Undone," "I Don't Want Your Love," and "What Happens Tomorrow." Press accounts noted that the audiences were mostly middle-aged mothers and their teenage daughters, plus the normal contingent of gay fans. A concert highlight was when Simon asked the audience to "show us some color," and everyone lit up their cell phones.

A&R executives were invited to hear some of the songs the band was working on for their new album, now titled *Astronaut*. EMI passed again, but Epic Records, part of the Sony Music Entertainment conglomerate, decided to take a chance on a resurgent Duran Duran, and a four-album deal was announced in June. To start things off, they made music videos for "Sunrise," the first single, and "What Happens Tomorrow." "Sunrise" was all bright desert verité, while some fans consider "What Happens Tomorrow," with its teen lovers seeing the band in star constellations, to be one of the best ever Duran Duran videos.

"Sunrise" was released as a single on September 27 and headed all the way up to #1 on *Billboard* magazine's download chart. The full album, *Astronaut*, came out worldwide on October 11. American network TV welcomed back the Fab Five with open arms. West Forty-Fourth Street in New York was closed so Duran Duran could play three songs in the street for the ABC network's *Good Morning America*. Telegenic as ever, they also appeared on *The Tonight Show* and *The Ellen DeGeneres Show*. After the "What Happens Tomorrow" single was released in December, Duran Duran ended the year with shows in Southern California. Disneyland reportedly contacted the band's booking agent; their request for a New Year's Eve concert in Anaheim was turned down.

The Astronaut Tour began in 2005 at the Hammersmith Palais in West London on January 13. "What Happens Tomorrow" dropped in early February and reached #11 in England. The song—a meditation on fate, fear, and hope—sold slowly in America until the momentum of what was billed as Duran Duran's biggest-ever tour kept it midchart for weeks.

Duran Duran liked to play in New Orleans, where they began a sixteen-show American run at the UNO Lakefront Arena on July 13. They worked their Japanese strongholds of Osaka and Tokyo in August, a few days before the levees broke and New Orleans was flooded and almost destroyed by Hurricane Katrina. Eager to help New Orleans recover, they agreed to appear at Radio City Music Hall for a post-Katrina benefit concert in September.

In October, Duran Duran filmed a London concert using fourteen high-definition cameras, directed by Lawrence Jordon. This documented the Astronaut Tour set and would be released on DVD as *Duran Duran Live from London* in late 2005. The band finished the year in front of an insanely partisan Argentine crowd (flares, fireworks, smoke bombs, tear gas) in Puerto Madero, near Buenos Aires, on December 3. Then it was on to Norway, Belgium, and UK shows ending with two London dates in gigantic Earl's Court just before Christmas. "We've never worked so hard in our lives," Nick confided to *Tatler* magazine.

Magus Entertainment had a producer client in Northern California named Michael Patterson, so in January 2006, the band was in his studio composing songs for an album with the working title *Reportage*, resulting in a dozen or more tracks that would never be released. The band did play a shambolic gig at the Morongo Key Club in Cabazon, California, on January 15. The following month, they appeared at the Winter Olympic Games in Italy, and Nick and John released the album *After Dark*, a compilation of the music they programmed at the Rum Runner between 1978 and 1981.

By the spring of 2006, it was obvious that Andy was going to leave the band again. There were arguments over money, and he was unhappy with their management. He'd had what he described as a nervous breakdown a few months earlier, and his father had died. There were rows over lyrics, touring security, their "incoherent schedule," and the band's direction when some wanted to work in New York with producer Timbaland and others did not. Andy continued to work on the new tracks at Sphere Studios, but "there wasn't much melody to any of them. I'd been sitting there for days doing nothing apart from listening to John [who was trying to produce the sessions] go over the same old things every time the studio door opened." Meanwhile, Duran Duran played some well-paying corporate shows to try to cover soaring studio expenses.

Andy wasn't the only one who was frustrated with the band's lack of progress on a new album. "Two A&R guys from Sony came over to London in May to listen to our material," Andy would later explain. "[They said,] 'Do not mix and deliver the record yet, it's not finished. It will only be rejected, and you know you can do better with the right producer.' A&R people don't always speak in such direct terms, but these guys were very concerned."

There was now a lot of discussion about going to New York to work with Timbaland in September. But in August, Duran Duran played a concert for a German bank in Barcelona, and then at a Red Cross Gala in Monaco. This was Andy Taylor's last show with Duran Duran. He later claimed he had been unable to go to New York to work because his visa was out of date. After his daughter was in a car accident on Ibiza, Andy fired off an angry email saying he was quitting the band. In a more temperate mood, he later wrote, "I was unable to get a US working visa to attend the New York recording session because of administrative failures by the band's management. . . . I knew that after so much friction with other members of the band over lyrics and money, they might interpret the fact that I couldn't travel as a sign that I no longer wanted to be in the band, but I felt I had no choice."

Duran Duran flew to New York without Andy. These new sessions, John said, were "a nightmare" forced on the band by Epic, which wanted some heavier beats than the rock-sounding album the band was making. Nick Rhodes saw it more as an opportunity to work with one of the top producers in America. Nick later said he thought Timbaland was going to have a stroke when the heavyset hip-hop producer saw the guitars and the drums being loaded into Manhattan Center Studios. "Everything's in a box with those guys," Nick said.

In October, Andy's departure was made official, with London band leader and session guitarist Dominic Brown taking his place. Dom Brown had learned Duran Duran's music by riffing on the job before 150,000 fans at a racetrack near Warsaw, Poland, and then through a series of concerts in Eastern Europe: Slovakia, Serbia, Romania, Bulgaria. In November, Dom earned his wings as Duran Duran played nine American shows, including Voodoo Music in rebuilding New Orleans and at a private home in New York.

In 2007, Duran Duran had some album tracks they thought were ready to cut. They worked with hip-hop producer Danja (Nate Hills, a Timbaland associate) and Justin Timberlake on what would become the album's first single, "Falling Down." By June, the twelve tracks of Duran's twelfth studio album were complete. But nervous Epic execs in the Sony skyscraper on Madison Avenue worried that the new songs weren't that great. The three tracks associated with Timbaland—"Night Runner," "Skin Diver," and "Zoom In"— appeared the strongest. Finally, Epic Records scheduled *Duran Duran's Red Carpet Massacre* for release later in the year, hoping that the band's exhaustive touring would maintain interest and sales in a drastically declining market for audio signals on plastic.

The Red Carpet Massacre Tour began in October and ran for a month. Duran Duran even starred on Broadway in a seven-night residency at the Ethel Barrymore Theatre on West Forty-Seventh Street that drew positive reviews in the New York papers and praise for new guitarist Dom Brown. Epic then released the full album in mid-November, featuring photographs by Nick on the CD case. The tasteless video for "Falling Down" portrayed white-coated Simon Le Bon as the attending physician at a mental hospital for sedated teenage models, with the unintended result that no one played it. "Falling Down" was released to radio stations, but no one played it either. Epic didn't bother to release a single in America because fans had stopped buying them. *Red Carpet Massacre* debuted in the United States at #36, then fell to #116 the next week. At home in England, the album got to #44, slightly better than *Pop Trash*. Duran Duran finished the year at the venerable Lyceum Theatre in London.

To pay their bills, Duran Duran stayed on tour, playing the hits, for much of 2008. March and April found them in Australia, Indonesia (Jakarta's Balai Sidang Convention Center), Manila, and the Pop TV Arena in the Kowloon district of Hong Kong. After dates in Japan and South Korea, it was back to America in May. They played on Paradise Island in the Bahamas and then at the SummerStage festival in New York's Central Park on May 30. Around this time, their management reportedly became aware that Epic Records, disappointed by low sales, was going to cancel their deal with Duran Duran.

The band was in Paris on June 10 to play a fundraising show for six hundred VIP guests at the Louvre museum, the first band ever to play in the old royal palace by the Seine.

But not everyone had lost faith in the band. Now hot young producer Mark Ronson (responsible for best-selling records by Amy Winehouse and Lily Allen as well as his own #2 album with three Top 10 singles) was keen to work with Duran Duran. The thirtyish Ronson was also a style beacon, soon to be voted best-dressed man in England. Most importantly, he loved Duran Duran, and Nick was hoping he would produce their next album—if there was one. (Nick later said they were actually desperate.)

That summer the band stayed in Europe, playing mostly outdoor festivals. The Naples concert was canceled when the band arrived but the equipment didn't due to the truck breaking down. Then enraged Neapolitan fans rioted outside the arena; the hotel had to put on extra security, and Duran Duran was advised to get out of town at first light. They finished the tour on July 26 on Malta, the sun-blasted Mediterranean island. It was the first time they played there.

After some time off, the Red Carpet Massacre Tour took off for South American national soccer stadiums beginning with a press conference in Lima, Peru, on November 1. Immense, crowd-heaving shows in huge national soccer stadiums followed in Chile (accompanied by tear gas), Colombia (where gunfire was heard from the stage), and Panama. The crowds were massive, undoubtedly some of the biggest—if not *the* biggest—of their whole career. By the time Duran Duran got to Brazil, Simon was dedicating songs to the newly elected American president, Barack Obama. Then Nick Rhodes got really sick, with a reported ear infection, and several shows had to be scrapped. Duran Duran went back to America in December to end the year playing in the Northeast and Canada.

Duran Duran and Mark Ronson then spent two years making their thirteenth studio album amid various challenges and personal upheavals. Nick and his girlfriend, Meredith, split up. Roger decided he wanted to be a DJ more than a drummer. Simon needed help with the lyrics and just wanted to sail. John told the *Sun* newspaper that it had been a relief to see the back of Andy Taylor. There were also disagreements over Mark Ronson's aggressively retro approach to their music, as he advocated a shameless return to the original yachts-and-models paradigm, plus a crisper, edgier sound. He even brought in a hotter (and younger) drummer, Nick Hodgson of the Kaiser Chiefs, to jam with the band at Sphere Studios to try to light a fire under Duran Duran.

In June 2009, Duran Duran played an outdoor show in St. Petersburg, Russia, in a blinding spring snowstorm. They flew across the Pacific Ocean and toured the West Coast in July. At the Fillmore West on July 15, Simon dedicated "Do You Believe in Shame?" to Michael Jackson, who had died at home in Los Angeles a few weeks earlier.

In 2010, Duran Duran was back in the studio, still with no record deal, and running low on cash. Spring found them back in Las Vegas and also playing lucrative corporate gigs for employees delirious that the real Duran Duran actually showed up at their convention/retreat/

company party. Duran Duran decided to release *All You Need Is Now* on their own label, Tape Modern, to be distributed by the independent S-Curve Records. Nick Egan was commissioned to make videos for two new songs: "All You Need Is Now" was filmed in black and white on a soundstage and in color at West London's uber-spooky Brompton Cemetery. "Pressure Off" featured Nile Rodgers riffing on guitar and hyperkinetic singer Janelle Monáe flying through the air. In early December, "All You Need Is Now" was issued as a download single via iTunes, followed by the album just before Christmas. *All You Need Is Now* proceeded to hit #1 on more than a dozen download charts around the world. The CD version, released a few months into 2011, featured five more songs than the digital version.

Duran Duran now spent a year promoting their music, the most recent via the internet and Amazon. The All You Need Is Now Tour started with a private fashion show in Milan's Teatro dal Verme in February and took them through a variety of venues and locales; by March, they found themselves playing the South by Southwest Festival in the parking lot of Stubb's Bar-B-Q in Austin, Texas. Around the same time, they also filmed an American concert helmed by cult director David Lynch. When this was released on DVD later in the year as *Duran Duran American Express Unstaged*, it was harshly criticized and deemed to be unwatchable.

When Simon was asked in an interview by the *Village Voice* how he felt about playing for smaller audiences, his response was telling: "The thing is, you've got shows you look forward to, and then you've got shows you know you're going to [have] to play. They're on the schedule, and you don't particularly look forward to them. But then you get to the venue that night, and you start getting the buzz. You hear the people coming in, and then the [PA] music comes on. You get your clothes on, and you get your face on, and you sort of pick up the excitement of it. And then the [opening band] Neon Trees go on stage, and they start playing their set, and they're pretty bloody good: that starts to make you feel competitive. And as you get closer to showtime, the excitement builds inside you. We all get our ear monitors in, and suddenly you turn the sound up and the aura's crackling in your ears. Then somebody hands you a microphone. . . . You're standing at the back of the stage . . . the band's out there playing, and suddenly . . . it's the most important thing in the world."

In spring 2011, Duran Duran was all over American media, with Simon, John, and Dom Brown playing acoustic sets on radio stations between gigantic gigs like the Coachella Valley Music and Arts Festival in Indio, California, in April. Sets included new songs like "All You Need Is Now," "The Man Who Stole a Leopard," "Girl Panic," and "A Diamond in the Mind." Then Nick became too ill to play, and dozens of shows had to be canceled through the crucial summer touring season. Nick issued a regretful statement to fans and promised he would be back soon. A tour documentary would later be released on DVD as *Duran Duran Live 2011*.

Nick recovered enough to appear in the long-form video for the single "Girl Panic" in June. This was the most ambitious video project the band had undertaken, featuring vintage supermodels of the eighties—Naomi, Cindy, Eva, Helena, and Yasmin—plus a dozen younger models acting as the film crew. The ladies pretended they were Duran Duran, and the band played interviewers asking them questions. The production, directed by Jonas Åkerlund, took over an entire floor of the Savoy Hotel. The models were filmed in decadent postures, wearing provocative lingerie in luxury suites. Nick was cast as a bellhop moving comatose girls on a luggage cart. Simon was a waiter delivering champagne to an orgy. The nearly ten-minute clip included glam outdoor scenes on the South Bank of the Thames and grainy security footage from the hotel. The credits cited the Swarovski crystal firm, which subsidized the film. A cheeky note appeared at the end with the disclaimer: "No supermodels were harmed during this production." Fan forums agreed that the older models looked even more beautiful than their younger selves and that Eva Herzigová had stolen the show.

After Nick recovered, the band spent the rest of the year playing shows postponed earlier, selling out Madison Square Garden on October 25. A December UK arena tour went off as scheduled. For the next three years, the band kept playing live: touring South America again, then Europe and the United States, usually available (at great cost) for private parties, Ivy League university reunions, and aristocratic British birthday celebrations. Dutifully, by 2014, they were back in the studio with Mark Ronson, working on their fourteenth album, *Paper Gods*.

And then a new record deal was finally on the table. With Nile Rodgers and Janelle Monáe featured on the funk-infused dance groove "Pressure Off," Duran Duran was signed to Warner Bros. Records in 2015. "Pressure Off" was released in June via Microsoft Xbox Music and later through Google Music, followed by the Paper Gods Tour that summer. On June 27, the band headlined a big outdoor festival at the Zuiderpark in The Hague. Playing to thirty thousand fans, Duran Duran delivered all the hits plus "Come Undone" and "Election Day," which Simon told the crowd was his favorite song to play live. "A lot of thinking goes into our sets," he explained. The reviews were good the next day, but one critic complained that there was no "The Reflex" and no encore.

At last, their efforts were starting to pay off. After several albums that came out to mediocre reviews and sales, *Paper Gods* was released in September and shot up to a Top 10 album in most markets, reaching #5 in England and #10 on the American *Billboard* chart after appearing on *The Tonight Show Starring Jimmy Fallon*. It was the band's first US Top 10 album since *The Wedding Album* in 1993. Reviewing *Paper Gods* favorably, the *New York Times* sagely noted, "It's not nostalgia if you never stopped."

The band's annual December tour of the British Isles featured a well-reviewed concert at London's O2 Arena on December 8, followed by an unusual gig on December 14. As winter's darkness closed in on the fallow fields, Duran Duran played a full set for about fifty people at the Ring O' Bells, a cozy country pub in the village of Compton Martin, near Bristol in North Somerset. (The pub was owned by a retired Parlophone executive who wanted to give his village a memorable Christmas treat.) Nick's friend Kylie Minogue joined the band onstage while the locals sipped their pints of lager, ale, and cider; devoured the tiny savory sausages on offer; and enthusiastically clapped along (on the counts of one and three).

David Bowie died of cancer in New York on January 10, 2016. This was a blow. Duran Duran used their website to eulogize him, the man who changed the world, affirming that without Bowie, there would be no Duran Duran. Then Prince, another main inspirer, died in Chanhassen, Minnesota, a suburb of Minneapolis, in April. Again, Duran Duran members poured out heartfelt tributes. This was an era when Duran Duran publicly mourned a lot of friends: early mentor Colin Thurston; Roger Moore, their very own James Bond (John: "A heck of a nice fella"); Lou Reed; engineer Jason Corsaro; Lamya (who sang on *The Wedding Album* and *Thank You*); Dolores O'Riordan; and Aretha Franklin. When Duran went back on the road in 2016, with Nile Rodgers and Chic, Simon often dedicated "Save a Prayer" to the sacred memory of Prince.

The band's parents started passing away as well.

In 2017, Duran Duran played concerts in Asia, South America, and the United States. The single "Last Night in the City" and the video (with singer Kiesza) came out in March, the most recent recording by the band as of this writing.

At this point, Duran Duran had been the high-end fashion industry's go-to guys for brand launches and PR events for at least ten years. For an undisclosed sum, Duran Duran would show up and help bring to market French perfumes, Swiss watches, German cars, British fashion, and American vodka. Over the years, they played "Rio" and "The Reflex" for Mercedes-Benz, Tiffany & Co., Burberry, L'Oréal, Moët Hennessy, and many others.

Then, in 2018, Duran Duran got into the fragrance business themselves, endorsing a line of perfumes blended by a company in Brooklyn. There were four different scents, each named for the band's songs. The company's descriptions were enthralling.

Hungry Like the Wolf: "Think leather and woods, under a powdery haze . . . notes of heather, atlas cedar, cade, sandalwood and patchouli that capture the energy of the original music video."

Come Undone: "Rebellious notes of saffron, coca leaf, geraniol, and tonka. It smells of body secretions, musk, hot breath."

Skin Divers: "Captures love in an aquatic landscape—think saltwater, citrus, . . . notes of seaweed, ylang ylang, vetiver and bergamot citrus."

You Kill Me with Silence: "Smokey Arctic wood . . . Nootka tree and wintergreen extract . . . moody, hostile notes of smoke, cistus, ice and incense . . . conjures up the feeling of being frozen out by a lover after a fight—like in the song."

Duran Duran's perfumes were sold in very limited editions, at first exclusively through Liberty of London. The venture was said to have been a great success, marketing-wise.

The early years of the next decade would signal the fortieth anniversaries of Duran Duran and the era of *Rio*. The band now began to plan for its fifth decade together. In the spring of 2019, Duran Duran inducted their heroes Roxy Music into America's Rock & Roll Hall of Fame. By September, they were back at work on a new album at Flood Studios in Willesden, North West London, with producers Giorgio Moroder, Mark Ronson, and the DJ Erol Alkan. For these sessions, Dom Brown was replaced by guitarist Graham Coxon, from ex-Britpop heroes Blur. Then plans were laid for a massive Duran Duran concert in London's Hyde Park in July 2020 to mark four decades since Duran played their first gig at the Rum Runner. By then, they'd sold a hundred million records and had twenty-one Top 20 records in the UK, and *Paper Gods* was their best-selling album in twenty-five years. With good momentum, a big fan base, and an ongoing recording deal with a major record company, the future looked promising.

Simon Le Bon was sixty-two in 2020. John Taylor was fifty-nine, as was Roger Taylor. Nick Rhodes was fifty-eight. Early in the year, Nick and John gave interviews promoting the Hyde Park concert set for July. With canary-yellow hair, a Savile Row blazer, and a punk T-shirt, Nick met reporters in the bar of Blakes Hotel, near the Chelsea home he shared with his girlfriend, Nefer Suvio. John spoke to the press in his London flat, which was described as looking like a gentleman's club with bad Victorian pictures. (John and Gela also own a fifteenth-century manor in Wiltshire with 007 connections.) Simon, still living in Barnes, South East London, with Yasmin and their daughters, was said to be working in the studio and unavailable. (Around this time, Yasmin and Amber, her eldest, were featured in glossy magazine ads for Boodles, the London jewelry house.) Roger was holed up in the country with his second wife, Gisella Bernales, and no longer gave interviews.

Nick said the new Duran Duran album was going to be "more handmade and guitary." He added that "John and Roger often will drive a track. [But] Simon gives all the songs our identity; it's his voice that tells you it's Duran Duran. My part has more to do with the sonic architecture."

John told the *Times* that the sessions could be difficult "because we have been down this road. We can finish each other's sentences, and I guess that we can do that musically as well. We're working with the same cast; it's like a soap opera." Asked about Andy Taylor, John said that they hadn't heard from him in a while. He was quoted, "Andy liked to tell people what they were doing wrong."

John said he'd been sober for twenty-six years and married for almost as long. But this made new music a challenge sometimes. "Take a song like 'Save a Prayer,' which is a great song about a one-night stand. It comes to a point where you can't write something like that. It isn't age appropriate, even if it's sexy. So how do you write if you're trying to keep a long-term relationship together? That's the challenge for any late-age pop star. How do you make it 'chic'?—to use one of Nick's favorite words."

Duran Duran had a big hit with their James Bond theme song. American teenager Billie Eilish had just scored with hers. "I was thrilled to hear Billie Eilish," Nick said. "I think it's by far the best Bond song since ours. I'm happy that she reached number one." ("A View to a Kill" had peaked at #2 in 1985.)

An interviewer pointed out that Nick was often mentioned in Andy Warhol's published diaries and that a Warhol retrospective had recently opened at the Tate Modern in London. Nick said he had treasured the friendship. "He invented the twentieth century," Nick averred. "Andy [Warhol] was making reality TV in the sixties. Can you imagine what he would have thought about the internet? It was all his dreams come true, but he would never have got any work done." Nick added that he stayed off social media. "It's not that I don't like it. I fear it. I'm going down a rabbit hole I may never get out of.

"Of course there've been big changes: marriages, divorces, kids, moving countries in John's case. But we've known each other for so long that when we're all together, there's no room for anyone to behave in a way which would be unacceptable. There's no room for divas. We have lasted longer than most marriages. Now, it's like being married to three people, but we each get to go home on our own every night."

Nick said he had chronic insomnia and was a strict vegetarian. He said he walked a lot to keep fit. John said, "I like to run. I do Pilates. I do yoga. I'm ninety percent vegan. I don't drink, take mind-altering chemicals, and I'm on and off sugar."

One month after these interviews, in April 2020, the COVID-19 virus reached England, and Prime Minister Boris Johnson locked the country down. Leaders in Scotland, Wales, and Ireland followed suit. The Hyde Park concert was postponed, and then everything closed down virtually overnight on a virally diminished planet. It wasn't hard to see that the rave was over, at least for a while. Well into 2021, Duran Duran stayed inside, close to their families, and looked forward to the moment when they could get back on the road again—making and sharing music with their fans. It wasn't a matter of if but when.

Nick Rhodes was certain of this. He added, "History will be very kind to us."

AUTHOR'S NOTES

If *fan* is short for *fanatic*, then I wasn't exactly a fan of Duran Duran before I interviewed the band in 2004, when the original Fab Five lineup reunited after eighteen years apart. But my respect level for the group shot up when I started going to their concerts on a sold-out English winter tour, and they reminded me what a great English rock band could sound like, playing live. Most impressive was the fervor, the fevered intimacy of their fans—both the original girls from 1982, now mothers, and their own teenage daughters on a fabulous night out with Duran Duran.

I was there because the band's manager wanted to capture the urgency of Duran Duran in reunion mode and tell their story in an autobiography. I met and interviewed the band members, mostly concerning their early lives and how Duran Duran came together. Backstage at Wembley Arena, I met their lovely wives, beautiful ex-wives, and (stunning, younger) girlfriends. I met and spoke with many of the band's colleagues, friends, and chronic hangers-on, plus the guy who played the saxophone in their live shows since the halcyon days of "Rio" and "The Reflex."

Duran Duran's autobiography was never published, and the band has yet to tell its own story. The interviews I recorded in 2004 are published here for the first time.

When I recently returned to these interviews, I conducted additional research relating to Duran Duran's later career, mostly with friends, former friends, musicians, and music professionals. Except where noted, many of my sources requested anonymity.

Several published books, including two by band members, were helpful in filling in details of Duran Duran's life and times.

John Taylor's *In the Pleasure Groove* (2012), written with Tom Sykes, is an autobiography necessarily concerned with John's life-and-death issues of addiction and recovery. Andy Taylor's *Wild Boy* (2008) is a heartfelt, grievance-informed account of why he quit Duran Duran—twice.

Duran Duran: Wild Boys (2005) is an unauthorized biography by British journalist Steve Malins containing interviews with important (but now deceased) contemporaries of the band.

Duran Duran Sing Blue Silver: Photographed around the World 1984 (1984), by Mike Warlow and Denis O'Regan, is a crucial visual document of the band's first world tour (from which they barely recovered).

Nile Rodgers's autobiography *Le Freak* (2011) has important insights by the producer of some of Duran's greatest hits.

I Want My MTV (2011), by Craig Marks and Rob Tannenbaum, details the interface with Duran Duran that helped the cable music channel dominate American pop culture in the 1980s.

The Andy Warhol Diaries (1989), edited by Pat Hackett, provides sometimes touching evidence of the pop artist's infatuation with Nick Rhodes and Duran Duran.

Who Dares Wins (2019), by Dominic Sandbrook, is critical to understanding the changing Britain of 1979–1982 that saw the emergence in popular culture of the New Romantic movement. Until someone publishes a proper book about the New Romantics, *Classic Pop Presents: The New Romantics* (2019) provides an informed, magazine-format look at an important artistic new wave that succeeded in bringing light and life to a young English generation emerging from the severe social unrest of the 1970s.

Foundational texts for this book also include *Barbarella* (1966), by Jean-Claude Forest, and *The Wild Boys* (1971), by William S. Burroughs.

Some quotations, interviews, and descriptive material are derived from the following sources: ABC (American Broadcasting Company), ABC (Australian Broadcasting Corporation), Amazon.com, BBC, *Billboard*, *Birmingham Evening Mail*, *Birmingham Post*, *Blender*, *Boston Globe*, *Brum Beat*, *Cashbox*, CBC, *Chicago Tribune*, CHUM, *Daily Mail*, *Daily Mirror*, *Details*, *Detroit News*, *Elle*, *Entertainment Weekly*, *Evening Standard* (London), the *Guardian*, *Guitar Player*, *Hartford Courant*, *Hollywood Reporter*, *Houston Chronicle*, *Independent*, *International Herald Tribune*, *Interview*, *Las Vegas Sun*, *Los Angeles Times*, *Melody Maker*, *Miami Herald*, Microsoft Music, *Mojo*, MTV, *Musician*, NBC, *New Musical Express*, *New York Post*, *New York Times*, *Newsday*, *Oui*, *Parade*, *People*, *Playboy*, *Q*, *Reading Eagle*, *Record Mirror*, *Record World*, *Rolling Stone*, *San Francisco Chronicle*, *Smash Hits*, *Sounds*, *Spin*, *The Face*, *Time*, *Time Out*, the *Times* (London), *Times Literary Supplement*, *Toronto Sun*, *Uncut*, *Us*, *USA Today*, *Vanity Fair*, *Variety*, VH-1, *Village Voice*, *Vogue*, *Washington Post*, and *Woman's Own*.

Special thanks to Ben Schafer, Carrie Napolitano, and Fred Francis of Hachette Books, as well as Carmen Nickisch, all of whom made it possible for these tales to be told.

David Vigliano is my protean literary agent, who spent the fateful year 2020 holding the fort on East Seventy-Third Street in Manhattan with his guard dogs, Pepper and Sonny. Thanks to him and star-quality associates Ruth Ondarza and Thomas Flannery Jr.

Thanks also to the following: Mike Warlow, Roger Steffens, Wendy Laister, Maria Evangelinellis, David Winner, Kayla Vitalbo from Getty Images, Nell Farrell-Tillotson, H. B. and Gertrude Arons, the Andy Warhol Foundation, Gosia Klecha at Nell Gwynn House, the Boston Athenaeum, the British Library at Kings Cross, Sister Ray and Reckless Records on Berwick Street in London, and Danny Goldberg (as ever).

Few authors can spend a couple of years writing a book without the support of their families. Thanks and love to India and John Goodridge; Lily Davis and Andreas Rink (plus Noah); Hana Charlotte Fischer; the Knüpfmachers; and especially Christopher Davis, whose methods are crucial in maintaining the Old Firm's editorial standards.

Oh! there is an organ playing in the street—a waltz, too! I must
leave off to listen. They are playing a waltz I have heard ten
thousand times at the balls in London, between 1812 and 1815.
Music is a strange thing.

—Lord Byron, *The Ravenna Journal,* February 2, 1821

INDEX